Ridiculously Inappropriate Magic

Books by Clayton Taylor Wood:

The Runic Series
Runic Awakening
Runic Revelation
Runic Vengeance
Runic Revolt

The Fate of Legends Series
Hunter of Legends
Seeker of Legends
Destroyer of Legends
Avenger of Legends

Magic of Havenwood Series
The Magic Collector
The Lost Gemini
The Magic Redeemer

The Magic of Magic Series
Inappropriate Magic
Ridiculously Inappropriate Magic
Ludicrously Inappropriate Magic

Ridiculously Inappropriate Magic

Book II of the Magic of Magic Series

Clayton Taylor Wood

Copyright ©2020 by Clayton Taylor Wood.

All rights reserved.

This book or any portion thereof may not be reproduced or used in any manner whatsoever without the express written permission of the publisher except for the use of brief quotations in a book review.

This is a work of fiction. Names, characters, businesses, places, events and incidents are either the products of the author's imagination or used in a fictitious manner. Any resemblance to actual persons, living or dead, or actual events is purely coincidental.

Published by Clayton T. Wood.

ISBN: 978-1-948497-13-8

Cover designed by James T. Egan, Bookfly Design, LLC

Printed in the United States of America.

Special thanks to Howie and Nancy, who have a kind of inappropriate magic all their own. And to the hidden magic within each of us, waiting patiently to be found.

DISCLAIMER:

This book contains (ridiculously) inappropriate depictions of (ridiculously) inappropriate people doing (ridiculously) inappropriate things. Including, but certainly not limited to, inappropriate language and veiled connotations of the naughty variety. Although not *quite* as veiled as the first book.

And of course, (ridiculously) inappropriate magic.

Table of Contents

Prologue 1
Chapter 1 6
Chapter 2 18
Chapter 3 30
Chapter 4 34
Chapter 5 41
Chapter 6 44
Chapter 7 54
Chapter 8 58
Chapter 9 66
Chapter 10 72
Chapter 11 75
Chapter 12 84
Chapter 13 89
Chapter 14 96
Chapter 15 105
Chapter 16 117
Chapter 17 122
Chapter 18 132
Chapter 19 135
Chapter 20 143
Chapter 21 149
Chapter 22 153

Chapter 23	160
Chapter 24	168
Chapter 25	172
Chapter 26	177
Chapter 27	180
Chapter 28	193
Chapter 29	198
Chapter 30	202
Chapter 31	209
Chapter 32	212
Chapter 33	220
Chapter 34	230
Chapter 35	237
Chapter 36	247
Chapter 37	258
Chapter 38	262
Chapter 39	270
Chapter 40	278
Chapter 41	281
Chapter 42	288
Chapter 43	297
Chapter 44	303
Chapter 45	311
Chapter 46	315
Epilogue	329

Ridiculously Inappropriate Magic

Prologue

When destiny knocked on Chauncy Little's door, his girlfriend Valtora decided she'd better answer it for him.

She was sitting at the kitchen table at the time, her chin in her left hand. A hand made entirely of diamond, naturally. She gazed lovingly at Chauncy as he made them breakfast, wearing the chef's apron she'd bought for him…and nothing else. It was how she demanded he make her breakfast, part of their morning routine. He was actually a pretty good cook, and while he never cooked for himself, he seemed to truly enjoy cooking for her.

"Such a *coot* widdle booty," she cooed as he turned up the heat on the stove, sizzling up some sausage along with some eggs. She'd sizzled his sausage – and poached his eggs – earlier that morning. Also per their morning routine.

Valtora smiled contentedly, looking about the small kitchen and dining room. *So* much prettier than when she'd first seen it six months ago. God it'd been awful. Honestly, she suspected Grandma Little had been colorblind…and that Chauncy had inherited that deficiency. Luckily, Valtora was an expert at making ugly things beautiful…and beautiful things more beautiful-er. That was her magic power, after all. And she used it on everything she could. Including herself, to *spectacular* effect. It was amazing what a woman's touch could do, really. As Chauncy had certainly enjoyed discovering.

Yep, after spending most of her life suffering in that godawful volcano with The Dark One, life had turned out pretty damn good.

She watched Chauncy cook for a little longer, then found her gaze falling to her left hand. Seeing its glittery diamond-facets made her grimace. It was a reminder, of course, of a teensy weensy little unfortunate fact that she'd kinda sorta hidden from Chauncy. A totally harmless fact, of course. And it didn't matter now, not one bit. So there was really no point in telling him.

Still…

Then came that fated knock on Chauncy's door. And, seeing as how Chauncy was cooking – and how his eggs and sausage were in full display – Valtora decided she'd better answer it for him.

"I'll get it," she reassured him. Chauncy skedaddled into the living room for a bit of cowering, and Valtora got up, making her way to the front door. She opened it…and saw a man standing on the doorstep.

A very peculiar man.

He was tall and slender, his back stooped with age. His face was lined with deep cracks and fissures, which was appropriate given the fact that he was clearly – and quite uncomfortably – old. With a long white beard that draped over his belly and chest, and long white hair peeking out from under a tall blue pointed hat, it was quite obvious that he was a wizard. The impressive wooden staff and fancy blue robes also gave it away.

"Oh," Valtora blurted out, her hand going to her mouth.

"Valtora," the old man greeted, glaring at her. Or maybe he was just looking at her…she couldn't be sure when it came to really old people.

"Impy!" she exclaimed, reaching out to hug him, then pulling her arms back in, then wringing her hands nervously. "Um…hi?"

For it was none other than Imperius Fanning, the great wizard of the Order of Mundus. Her mentor, her teacher. The man who'd guided her to her destiny a quarter-century ago…and who she hadn't seen since.

Still Imperius glared – or looked at – her.

"What a surprise," she continued, glancing furtively back into the kitchen. She spotted Chauncy peeking out from around the corner. Breakfast, to her dismay, was starting to burn on the stovetop. She stepped through the doorway, closing the door behind her. Then she crossed her arms over her chest, glaring back at the old man. "What are you *doing* here?" she hissed.

"I could ask you the same," Imperius replied. "But my gut tells me I already know the answer."

"I did everything you told me," she stated rather defensively. "And we beat Evermore and I saved magic. I mean honestly, what more could you want?"

"*Chauncy* saved magic," Imperius corrected.

"*We* saved magic," Valtora compromised. "The point is, after twenty-five years doing what *you* wanted, now I'm doing what *I* want."

"Oh, you've been doing what you want for quite a while now, haven't you?"

Valtora's eyes narrowed, and she switched to putting her hands on her hips. A practiced posture that screamed "pissed." Valtora prided herself in being awfully good at it…which was why she was a bit disappointed when Imperius didn't seem particularly impressed.

"What's that supposed to mean?" she demanded, narrowing her eyes further and clenching her teeth to add a good jawline-ripple. Neither of which had the desired effect.

"I told you to stay in Mount Thrall and ally with The Dark One for the time being," Imperius explained. "To use him for when his army would be needed."

"And that's what I did," she replied evenly, giving up on the posture. "My Amethyst Army was *spectacular*, by the way." She'd used her magic power of bedazzling to transform The Dark One's ugly little goblins into crystalline-armored beauties. Just the thought of them made her smile…until she realized Imperius was still glaring at her.

"Yes, well I didn't tell you to be enthralled by him and mount him!" Imperius snapped.

Valtora's eyes widened, her jaw dropping. Her cheeks flushed, and she crossed her arms over her chest.

"And how would *you* know what I've mounted?" she demanded.

"My gut told me," Imperius replied.

"Well keep your guts to yourself!" she snapped.

Imperius just stood there, raising one bushy eyebrow. She blushed deeper red, clenching her fists defiantly.

"I didn't exactly have options!" she complained. "A woman has needs!"

Imperius raised the other eyebrow to match the first.

"Look, it's none of your business who I mount," she snapped, regaining a bit of righteous indignation. "I'm a grown-ass woman, and you're not my daddy."

"Normally I would agree with you," Imperius replied. "But in this case it *does* matter."

"Why?"

"Indeed," Imperius stated. "Why *would* the great Imperius Fanning come to his old protégé's doorstep? Or any doorstep, for that matter?"

Valtora swallowed visibly, deflating a bit. She knew damn well what he was about to say, so she didn't say it for him. He was rather fond of saying it, and she didn't want to steal his thunder. And seeing as how he was a man, she knew she had to let him finish, or he'd be terribly frustrated.

"Our world is in grave danger," Imperius warned, his tone darkening dramatically. "The Dark One has resurrected, and is gathering his hordes. One day they will spread across the land like a great plague, and destroy everything you know and love!"

"Oh," she replied. And just stood there.

"Oh?" Imperius replied incredulously. "That's it?"

"That's it," she agreed.

He blinked.

"Golly, you know what? That sounds *super* bad," Valtora stated. "But I'm sure you and the rest of the ultra-powerful wizards at the Order of Mundus can handle it."

"Valt..."

"Good luck Impy! I believe in you!" she exclaimed.

And promptly slammed the door shut in his face.

Locking it. And deadbolting it.

There was a *thump* at the door, followed by a bit of cursing. Followed by another *thump*.

Then, to Valtora's profound relief, there was silence.

"Who was that?" Chauncy inquired, peeking around the corner again.

"Um...nobody," she answered. "Just another weirdo geezer trying to sell us crap we don't need."

"Oh," he replied, stepping into view. She smiled at the sight of eggs and sausage, then realized the ones on the stove were hopelessly burnt.

"Son of a...!" she blurted out, punching the wall to her left. With her diamond hand, unfortunately. It went right through the plaster, making a gaping hole there.

"Oh," Chauncy said, staring at the hole, then at her. It was the third hole that month.

"Oops," she replied. "Sorry."

"Hangry?"

"Little bit," she confirmed. Which was partially true. And at this moment, partial truths were unfortunately her specialty.

"It's okay," he reassured her. "I'll have another batch of sausage and eggs coming up shortly."

"Good," she replied.

She relaxed, pulling her hand free from the wall and walking up to kiss him. Then she looked down, arching an eyebrow and giving him a little smile.

"After you're done, I'm gonna have a batch of sausage and eggs coming up for *you*."

Thus, destiny having quite literally caught Chauncy with his pants down, it was once again deferred. And Chauncy was none the wiser, at least for the moment. Ignorance is bliss, but bliss, like any other emotion, only lasts for so long.

So at this point, dear reader, well…it goes without saying, really. It's terribly obvious where this is all going. But in the interest of consistency, we'll say it again:

And that, dear reader, was how the end of the world began.

Chapter 1

For the first time in Chauncy's adult life, life was exactly how he wanted it to be.

After Valtora enjoyed her sausage and eggs – and then his, for the second time that day – he donned his magical wizard's robe in preparation for work. His reward for braving the Cave of Wonder, it was white and sinfully silky on the inside, and loud, purple, and sparkly on the outside. It glittered even in darkness, but in the full light of the sun, it shone so fabulously bright that it was a sight that forced itself to be beheld. And while at first he'd rejected the thought of wearing it, now Chauncy actually looked forward to it. After all, for most of his life he'd been rather invisible, trudging from home to work and from work to home, comfortably at the sidelines of life. His wizardly robe forced him to the front and center, demanding the attention of all who beheld it.

He grabbed his Staff of Wind, a thick tree branch with just the right amount of twisty, then held the door open for Valtora. Who was busy glaring into a hand-mirror, her jawline rippling.

"Um…something wrong?" he asked. She turned her glare on him, and he took an involuntary step backward. After which she seemed rather pleased with herself.

"Coming," she said, bringing the mirror with her for some reason.

"Ladies first," he said with a little bow.

"My *hero*," she gushed, batting her eyes at him.

He grinned from ear-to-ear, following her out of the house and locking the door behind him. Down the front steps they went, then rightward down the sidewalk toward the city center. Hand-in-hand they strolled. Not walked…strolled. For with the sunshine warming their skin and the warm breeze ruffling their hair, there was nowhere else they wanted to be in that moment. Everything was perfectly perfect.

Or rather, it *usually* was.

For Chauncy couldn't help but notice that Valtora seemed a bit distracted. She was staring at her feet more than the scenery, and what's more, her hand was sweating. And if there was one thing that Valtora never did, it was sweat. Not after spending twenty-five years living on a live volcano.

"Are you alright?" he inquired.

"Hmm?"

"Are you alright?" he asked. She gave him a sweet smile, but one that looked suspiciously forced.

"I've been called more than alright," she quipped. "I mean, not by anyone in particular, just you know, a figure of speech." She gave a little laugh, which sounded awfully suspicious.

Chauncy frowned, becoming rather suspicious himself.

"What's wrong?" he pressed, slowing down, then stopping to face her.

"Nothing."

"Valtora..." he began.

"I'm *fine*," she insisted irritably. "God, can't a girl have an off day?"

His eyes widened.

"Is it...that time of month again?" he inquired. He never could keep track of her cycle. Her eyes narrowed murderously...and then relaxed. She gave him a relieved smile.

"You know what? That must be it," she agreed. "Gosh, I just *hate* it sometimes. All blood and clots and cramps and whatever. Girls are like, *so* gross."

Chauncy relaxed, smiling back at her and hooking his arm in hers once again. They resumed their stroll, and he felt the stress of their minor spat seep away. Onward they went, greeting people as they passed by, and eventually came to the city center. It consisted of a large circular courtyard bordered by a wide street lined with various shops. The courtyard featured a well-manicured lawn with benches and trees and wonderful flowers and such. And a statue of Archibald Merrick in the very center, the founder of Southwick...and a colossal prick. Or at least Chauncy assumed so. For in addition to founding the city, Archibald had also founded the Evermore Trading Company, a corporation that had hoarded nearly all of the magical artifacts in the world...and then nearly wiped all other magic off the face of the planet. Only through Chauncy's heroic efforts – along with the help of his friends – had Evermore been stopped before destroying magic in the last unspoiled kingdom in the world.

The magical kingdom of Pravus.

Southwick had been built up right against a two-hundred-foot tall gray stone wall less than a half-mile away. The silver Gates of Pravus, double-doors nearly as tall as the wall itself – gleamed bright silver in the sunlight. Up until a half a year ago, those doors had remained closed for over a millennia. Being a wizard, Chauncy could open them. Not that anyone in Southwick had to know that.

They crossed through the middle of the courtyard per their routine, and Valtora punched the statue of Archibald Merrick dutifully with her diamond fist. Unfortunately, it was the hand carrying her mirror, and the force of the blow shattered that mirror.

"God *damn* it!" she snapped. And promptly threw the mirror on the ground, stomping on it over and over. Chauncy watched this with an appropriate amount of alarm, taking a few steps back from her to avoid being next. She finished her tirade, then ran her glittering hand through her gorgeous hair, eyeing the demolished mirror with dismay.

"Well shoot," she complained. Then she glared at the statue, as if it were its fault.

"We have mirrors at the shop," Chauncy reminded her hastily, spotting a surprised looking boy walking with his mortified mother at the edge of the courtyard. Valtora spotted Chauncy spotting the boy, and cleared her throat, forcing a forced smile.

"Right," she muttered.

With that, she grabbed his hand, hauling him toward the shop. They reached the other end of the courtyard quickly, crossing the wide street to get to the shop.

A Little Magic was its name, the shop that Grandma Little had founded. Located on the first floor of a narrow, three-story-tall building facing the courtyard, below a dance studio and a lawyer's office. A prime location, Grandma used to boast. She'd swindled it from its owner Ginny Smithers decades ago, getting one of her doctor friends to diagnose poor Ginny with cancer. She'd promised to cure him with her "magic" potions if he gave her the shop, and lo and behold, his cancer vanished a few weeks later.

Chauncy shook his head, smiling ruefully. Grandma Little had been a master saleswoman. Why, the sheer volume of bullshit she'd sold over the years could've fertilized the entire country.

They made it to the front door, and Chauncy unlocked, it, ramming it open with his shoulder and allowing Valtora inside in his usual gentlemanly fashion. But instead of curtseying in *her* usual fashion, she stepped through mechanically. She even forgot to go to the closet to fetch Chauncy's broom for him.

Huh, he thought.

An uneasy feeling struck him then. The fact that he felt uneasy made him even more uneasy, for it was a feeling he hadn't experienced very much since saving the world. Saving the world had a tendency to confer a fair bit of confidence, after all. He felt its absence keenly.

Forced to retrieve his broom all by himself, Chauncy began the ritual of sweeping the inevitable dust-bunnies from the floor. A simply gorgeous floor, polished to a pleasant shine after Valtora had used her magic on it. The whole shop had been similarly bedazzled, making it the talk of the city. For no shop appeared as beautiful – no, as *magical* – as A Little Magic. And no shop in Southwick – nor Borrin, likely – had more magic items. *Real* magic, not the crap Grandma had sold. Every one of them created by Chauncy and made beautiful by Valtora.

He finished sweeping, returning the broom to its closet. Then he put his hands on his hips, gazing at the shelves of potions and lotions, and at the staves, wands, and rods hanging on the walls, with pride.

I did this, he told himself, puffing out his chest a bit. Then he glanced at Valtora, who was already seated behind the counter, staring off at nothing in particular. *We did this*, he corrected himself, feeling another burst of pride.

"Love you baby," he told Valtora. She flinched, as if the words had flown across the shop and slapped her.

"Huh?"

"I said I love you," he repeated, feeling rather irritated. Still he couldn't be mad at her. After all, it wasn't her fault that it was that time of the month. He would just have to go with the, er, flow.

"Oh," she mumbled.

He sighed, his chest deflating a bit. He went behind the counter, sitting on his seat beside her. There was an awkward silence between them, which – if you knew Valtora – *never* happened. The only thing awkward about Valtora were the looks other people gave her when she said terribly inappropriate things. Growing up with The Dark One, it turned out, gave one a dark sense of humor.

So they both sat there, Chauncy fidgeting nervously, and Valtora staring off at nothing, waiting for their first customer to arrive. Which didn't take long, of course.

Dong!

Chauncy perked up a bit, for that was the sound of the doorbell ringing. It used to go *ding* but now it went *dong*, because when it came to entrances – and exits, for that matter – *dongs* were what Valtora preferred.

An elderly man entered the shop. A terribly familiar old man, tall and thin, his back bent a bit with age. He peered at Chauncy over his thick glasses, waving one wrinkled hand.

"Good morning Mr. Schmidt," Chauncy greeted. "Welcome to A Little Magic!"

"Morning," Mr. Schmidt replied. And though his reply was directed at Chauncy, his gaze was focused on Valtora, as usual. It wasn't so much as a look or a stare as it was a leer, and a rather creepy one at that. Valtora strongly suspected that, while Mr. Schmidt was a law-abiding citizen, his mind's eye was guilty of an enormous variety of criminal acts. Most of them inflicted upon her. A suspicion that Chauncy shared, but tried desperately not to think too much about.

"What can I get for you today?" Chauncy inquired. Mr. Schmidt blinked, then looked at Chauncy, as if seeing him for the first time.

"Eh?"

"What can I get for you today?" Chauncy repeated.

"Lotion," he answered.

"The usual?" Chauncy inquired.

"Mmhmm," the creepy old man replied. Creepily.

Chauncy got up from behind the counter, making his way to the "Lotions & Potions" aisle. Mr. Schmidt took the opportunity to resume leering, and Chauncy browsed his wares, finding what he was looking for. He grabbed a shimmering silver bottle – bedazzled by Valtora, of course – and walked it back to Mr. Schmidt.

"There you are," he declared, handing it over. "Lucky for you we're having a 'Lotions & Potions' promotion today! It's only ten copper."

Mr. Schmidt fished in his pants pocket, which Chauncy fervently hoped was an attempt to get some coins. His hopes were not in vain, for the old man plunked ten copper coins into Chauncy's hand. Warm coins. *Moist* coins.

"Thank you Mr. Schmidt," he stated. The old man grunted.

"You're running low," he noted, eyeing the Lotions & Potions aisle. "You should keep 'em coming."

"I'll make more tonight," Chauncy promised. To Mr. Schmidt's obvious relief. Chauncy suppressed a sigh; making the lotion was awfully time-intensive, and it was Chauncy's least favorite job. There was no magic in it for him whatsoever, but people liked it, so he couldn't very well say no.

Mr. Schmidt turned about – after giving Valtora once last lingering leer – and exited the shop. Chauncy grimaced, depositing the hot, slippery little coins on the counter as quickly as he could, then wiping his hands on his pants. "Ugh," he muttered.

"Huh?" Valtora asked.

"Mr. Schmidt," Chauncy explained. "Always buys that lotion you make." It wasn't really magical, per se. The lotion was purely lotion, its only magical property the fact that Valtora had bedazzled it. And so it was glittery and smelled wonderful and was quite silky and such. A perfect gift for a girlfriend or a wife…not that Mr. Schmidt had either. "I really don't want to know what he does with it."

"I know what he does with it," Valtora replied. She engaged in a bit of offensive pantomime then, making Chauncy grimace.

"Stop, please," he pleaded, glancing out the window. His mind's eye had accumulated more than enough traumatizing images during his adventure with Harry and Nettie six months ago. He hardly needed any more.

"He probably imagines me saying that," Valtora pressed with a cruel grin.

"You can't say that," Chauncy protested.

"Why not?"

"It's inappropriate," he replied.

Dong!

Valtora giggled at the *dong*, although whether it was directed at the doorbell or the pantomime, Chauncy couldn't be sure. Either way, it was also inappropriate. But since it meant that she was acting more appropriately than she had been, Chauncy was rather relieved.

"Hello," Chauncy greeted as a woman stepped into the shop. She was short and a bit rotund, with wide hips that barely fit through the doorway. She was elderly, with curly white hair, and possessed of a chronic expression as if she'd bitten into a fresh grapefruit. Chauncy's eyes widened as he realized who it was, and he shot up from his stool.

"Mrs. Biggins!" he gasped, rushing around the counter to her side. "My goodness, I haven't seen you in ages!"

"Six weeks to heal my broken wrist," she complained, as complaining was her preferred method of communication. She pushed past him, hobbling right to the "Lotions & Potions" section. He and Valtora had hung a sign from the ceiling celebrating the promotion. "Fifty percent off?" Mrs. Biggins exclaimed, her facial muscles making a valiant attempt to show happiness. She grabbed two bottles of lotion – the same kind Mr. Schmidt had purchased – and went right for the counter. She plopped them before Valtora, then set about fumbling to open her pocketbook to pay. A process that, as it so often did with old people, took practically forever. It seemed that the elderly actually got *worse* the more they practiced things, for despite the fact that Mrs. Biggins had been paying for stuff her whole life, she seemed determined to spend the majority of her remaining time aboveground in the process of doing so.

Valtora watched as each copper coin *plonked* on the counter, her diamond-hand clenched in a fist. Chauncy recalled how she'd punched Marie Merrick in the head with that fist, killing the lady instantly. He walked behind the counter, sitting by her side and catching her eye.

"Don't do it," he mouthed silently.

Her fist relaxed. A bit.

After a few agonizing, soul-crushing minutes, Mrs. Biggins had placed forty coins on the counter. Chauncy let out a relieved sigh.

"I'd better count them again to be sure," Mrs. Biggins said.

"No!" Valtora blurted out, leaping to her feet. She slid all the coins into Chauncy's waiting hands just as quickly as she could.

"Oh," Mrs. Biggins said, quite taken aback at the speed at which this had occurred.

"I counted while you were getting them," Valtora reassured her, flashing a gorgeous smile. While she quickly placed the bottles of lotion in a bag for the woman. "Have a great day!" she added, waving goodbye eagerly. She even walked Mrs. Biggins to the door, all but shoving her out. But Mrs. Biggins stopped at the doorway, turning to Chauncy.

"My wrist still hurts," she complained, as if that were his fault.

"Terribly sorry," Chauncy offered.

"You should make something to heal me," she declared. "Being a wizard comes with responsibilities you know."

"Um…" Chauncy replied. He had Rooter, a stone golem with a plant atop its head that could heal wounds. But he'd left Rooter to keep the stone giant Rocky company by Rocky's bridge, back when they'd returned from Pravus. "I might be able to come up with something," he offered.

"Can you have it by tomorrow?"

"I'll try," he promised. And immediately regretted it. For if there was one thing magic hated, it was deadlines. But he couldn't very well say no to the woman.

"Hmph," she harrumphed. And eyed the Lotions & Potions aisle. "You're running low," she notified him.

"More coming in tomorrow," he reassured her. With that, the woman left. Valtora turned to Chauncy, giving him a look.

"Stop promising people shit," she grumbled.

"I can't help it," he replied. "I've got magic, and that means I should help if I can."

"Pfft."

"Being a wizard comes with responsibilities you know," he told her.

"Bull," she retorted. "You don't owe her a damn thing. You saved magic, remember?"

"True," he replied with a smile. "Thank you for not murdering her," he added.

"You'll take that back the next time she comes in," she grumbled.

"Probably," he agreed.

Valtora sat beside him once again, and they waited in silence. He glanced furtively at her.

"You alright?" he asked.

"Why wouldn't I be?" she retorted. He blinked. Valtora was typically tirelessly effervescent, in a dark and inappropriate kind of way. Combativeness was a trait she usually only showed before – and during – war.

"Just…wondering," he replied.

"Are you saying I'm not?" she snapped.

"Um…no."

"You wouldn't ask if you didn't think so," she pointed out. Quite accurately, to his dismay. He instantly regretted opening his big mouth. It didn't take long for him to realize there was no easy way out of this argument – not alive, anyway – so he decided on total, brutal honesty.

"I'm scared," he confessed. She frowned.

"Of what?"

"Of you," he clarified. She glared at him.

"Oh yeah?" she replied. "Why? Because I'm being a bitch?"

"Yes," he replied. Also honestly. Then he closed his eyes, waiting for the inevitable diamond-fist to his temple. A quick death, he hoped. Merciful.

"Sorry," she apologized. Chauncy cracked an eye open, daring to look at her.

"What?"

"Sorry," she repeated, grabbing his hand and squeezing it. She even gave him a smile. "I'm just…having a bad day, that's all. I love you baby."

"Aww," he replied, melting instantly. "I love you too, poopy-dooz," he added. It was her nickname for herself, oddly enough…and the nickname of a cat she used to own. A hellcat whose full name was ZoMonsterz, one of The Dark One's many minions.

"Kisses," he demanded, closing his eyes and puckering up…even as his sphincter below ceased to do so. He felt her lips crush against his, and relished the feeling. Then she gave him a bit of tongue, which was dangerous indeed. For Valtora's kisses had a habit of creating displays that Chauncy couldn't afford unless he stayed behind the counter…and to his dismay, he heard a *dong* at the door. He tore himself from Valtora's kiss, reflexively covering the *dong* under the counter.

"Oh," he blurted out.

"Welcome to A Little Magic," Valtora greeted effervescently.

Then, with each *dong* that greeted her that day, Valtora became a bit more like her normal self. She even held Chauncy's hand under the counter, and her touch put him completely at ease. Such that he soon forgot all about their unusual morning, enjoying the cheer of their well-worn routine.

At length, their day at the shop was near its end, and Valtora offered to go home first to help set up all the materials Chauncy would need to fix the hole she'd made in the wall. Chauncy took the opportunity to flip the sign on the door from "open" to "closed," and go behind the counter once again. There was a large painting of Grandma Little hanging against the wall, and he gazed up at it, smiling at it as it smiled back at him. Then he grabbed the frame, tilting the painting to reveal a wall-safe behind it. A secret safe that not even Valtora knew about, and for good reason. For within that secret safe was a safely kept secret. One he'd kept from her.

He twisted the dial on the safe, entering the proper combination: 9, 10, 34. His age when his mom had died, his age when his soul had died, and the age when it'd been reborn. Opening the safe, he found what he was looking for within.

A glittering diamond ring.

He pulled it out, staring at it. And he was struck with the sudden urge to put it in his pocket and run home to propose to the love of his life. To ask the ultimate question, and make Valtora his wife. But he hesitated for the usual reason: he hadn't imbued the ring with any magic. For as important as the ring was, it *had* to be magical. A mundane ring simply wouldn't do.

But what to imbue it with, Chauncy hadn't a clue. And magic wouldn't come when forced to. He had to wait for it, and he'd waited over a month already. And so he stared at it, waiting to feel something. Waiting for magic to come to him so he could give it away. But nothing happened.

"Oh well," he muttered, putting the ring back in the safe and closing it. He spun the dial, then righted the painting, feeling a bit glum that today wasn't the day. "One day," he promised himself, gazing up at the painting of Grandma Little. He smiled at the likeness. "You were a great grandmother to me, and I'll make you a great-grandmother one day, you'll see."

With this vow made, Chauncy left the shop behind. Off into the evening he went, making his way home to his love. Destiny had brought them together, and he trusted that it would seal the deal. If not today, then perhaps tomorrow, or whatever day it chose.

But destiny, of course, had other plans. And while it'd been quite patient the first time it'd been (rather rudely) put off by Grandma Little nearly a quarter century ago, it'd had quite enough of waiting, thank you very much. And if Chauncy had known what it had in store for him, he would have thought quite differently about Valtora's touch.

* * *

By the time Chauncy joined Valtora at home, it was nearly sunset. Chauncy got to work fixing the hole that Valtora had punched in the wall; after the first month living with her, he'd found it best to buy the materials for such repairs in bulk. And while his first time patching had been rather poor, now he considered himself quite the expert. In no time at all, the hole was patched and painted, so that no one would be the wiser.

"There," he declared, stretching his back and admiring his work.

"Well *done*, Chauncy," Valtora said, giving him a peck on the cheek. "You deserve a reward."

"Oh," he exclaimed quite excitedly.

"Dinner first," she chided.

One of Valtora's many gifts was her understanding of the male mind, which was not a particularly broad or deep subject. For it was mostly concerned with completing missions and releasing emissions, of which Valtora was intimately aware. As such, she knew precisely how to incentivize it…and Chauncy got to work preparing dinner with gusto.

"Pork and beans?" he inquired.

"Yes and yes," she replied.

Chauncy got to work, finding himself feeling quite marvelous as he cooked. There was something magical about nourishing the woman he loved; watching Valtora enjoy his cooking was one of the great joys of his life. It occurred to him as he cooked that Grandma Little must have felt the same, all those mornings she'd cooked breakfast for him. He smiled, remembering how she'd sat across from him, watching him eat with a contented smile on her face, even as she sipped her tea.

Loving you is the closest thing to magic I've ever experienced, she'd told him. *I just want you to feel that way toward someone too.*

He glanced back at Valtora, who was watching him cook from the kitchen table, a little smile on her lips.

I did it, he told Grandma silently. And in that moment, he found it quite strange that he'd never truly understood Grandma Little's love for him until he'd loved someone else. In that way, love was strange magic indeed…for it was felt far more powerfully when given than when received.

He swayed a bit as he finished cooking, giving Valtora a little show. For he was clad only in his chef's apron, per her request. His body had no magic for him, but to Valtora it most certainly did.

Having given Valtora a feast for the eyes, he finished his duties as chef, providing a feast for her mouth. They both enjoyed it, and afterward, they enjoyed each other. In the kind of way only a new-ish couple could. And while love was felt more powerfully when given, both got as good as they gave, and it was magical indeed.

Much later that evening, as Chauncy rolled over onto his side in bed, Valtora's diamond hand draped over him, he was struck with the feeling that everything in his life was finally *right*. After twenty-four years of waiting for destiny to come to him, he'd gathered the courage to go to *it*. And in saving magic, he'd saved himself.

"Love you baby," he murmured.

"Mmhmm," came her reply.

He smiled, knowing that she rarely said she loved him back. Not because she didn't, but because she – by her own admission – had *serious* commitment issues.

Had he only known just what those commitment issues entailed, Chauncy might have thought quite differently. But as they say, ignorance is bliss. And as Nettie had once said, nothing lasts forever.

Destiny, after all, had been *more* than patient. And honestly, it had had quite enough of being so rudely rebuffed by the rude women in Chauncy's life. It was, to be frank, rather pissed off. So it was that destiny decided right then and there that it needed to do something drastic about the whole mess…and it was very nearly time for Chauncy's ignorance – and therefore his happiness – to come to a spectacular end.

Chapter 2

The next morning, everything was back on track. Valtora was her usual bubbly, adorable self, and they went about their typical, wonderful routine. The customary metaphorical sizzling of the sausage, followed by the more literal kind. Then the donning of Chauncy's wizardly robe, the old grabbing of the staff, and off they went. Down to the city center at a stroll's pace, with the obligatory fisting of Archibald Merrick's statue, and finally the arrival at their destination: A Little Magic.

"After you," Chauncy prompted after popping the door open with his shoulder.

"What a *gentleman*," Valtora breathed. She grabbed his broomstick for him, and Chauncy got to work gathering up all the dust bunnies that had been birthed overnight. It was clear they were nocturnal animals, and quite busy bunnies indeed, for no matter how well he'd swept at closing the day before, there was always a fresh litter a half a day later.

That done, they flipped the sign to "open," and sat down behind the counter to await their first *dong* of the day.

Dong!

The door swung open, and a man came into the shop. Or rather, he didn't so much *come* in as he did *rush* in. And he wasn't any old man, but one of the city guards. He burst into the shop, sweating profusely.

"Evacuate!" he gasped, holding the door open. "Now!"

Chauncy and Valtora just stared at him blankly.

"Come on!" the guard urged.

Then a bell tolled in the distance. One that was instantly recognizable to Chauncy. For it was the Emergency Bell, a citywide alert that something extremely bad was occurring. And that they should seek safety immediately. Which meant, unfortunately, that the guard was not pranking them.

"Oh," Chauncy blurted out.

"Shit," Valtora replied, more appropriately.

When danger struck, it was common for heroes to burst into action, taking control of the situation from the get-go. It was, after all, what separated heroes from those they saved…the ability to realize their power in the face of danger, instead of cowering like pathetic little victims. Or just freezing, as slightly less pathetic, but definitely not heroic, people might do.

Chauncy and Valtora both stood there behind the counter, staring blankly at the guard.

"Come on!" the man repeated, gesturing for them to follow him. "We have to go, now!"

"What's happening?" Valtora asked, still staying put.

"The Gate," the guard answered. "We heard it unlock. It's going to open!"

"Oh," Chauncy repeated. "Shit."

For the last time the Gate to the magical kingdom of Pravus had opened, a swarm of goblins had…well, swarmed in and massacred a bunch of people. They'd of course been looking for Chauncy at the time, hoping to bring him to Valtora to fulfill his destiny. Which he'd done, eventually. King Pravus had vowed to keep the Gate closed from then on, so as to prevent the Republic of Borrin from invading. Chauncy had no idea why the Gate might be opening, but whatever the reason, it probably wasn't good.

"You have to leave," the guard insisted. "We have to bring everyone to the barracks!" The barracks were the most heavily fortified part of the city, a veritable fortress far from the Gate.

"Alright," Chauncy agreed, stepping around the counter and going to the front door. Valtora hesitated, then joined him. They stepped outside, and Chauncy closed the door behind him, fumbling with the key and eventually locking it. Then he turned around, seeing the Wall in the distance…and the silver double-doors of the Gate.

It was, to his surprise, closed.

"Oh," he said. For the third time. A moment later, the Emergency Bell stopped tolling, the last big *dong* echoing through the city a few times before everything went silent. Not long after, Chauncy heard a loud *thunk* echo through the city.

"Huh, must've been a false alarm," the guard declared.

"To be safe, we should probably move," Valtora said. "Come on Chauncy, let's go home and pack."

Chauncy blinked.

"Huh?" he blurted out.

"We need to move," she repeated, pulling him toward the street.

"Now." He resisted. "What are you talking about?" he demanded. "Why would we move?"

Valtora let go of him, putting her hands on her hips and glaring at him.

"You want kids, don't you?" she asked.

"Of course I do," he replied. Which was true. He'd been meaning to have that talk with her eventually, but it'd seemed a bit premature, considering he hadn't even given her the ring. "Eventually," he added.

"Well I can't raise them in a city that's constantly in danger of being attacked," she reasoned. "Do you *really* want your children to have to live in fear all the time?"

"Um...no," he replied. "But I'm not really sure we're *in* any danger," he added. "After all, you were the one who..."

"That's not the point!" Valtora snapped, glaring at Chauncy. Then eyeing the guard significantly, and not at all subtly. Then glaring at Chauncy again.

"It sorta is," Chauncy insisted.

"We're moving," Valtora declared. And promptly grabbed Chauncy's upper arm with her diamond-hand, hauling him across the street to the lawn of the commons...and toward the statue of Archibald Merrick in the distance.

"Hey!" he protested, trying to resist. But Valtora was surprisingly strong, particularly her diamond-grip. He thought as quickly as he could. "My staff," he added. "I left it in the shop!"

Valtora halted, taking a deep breath in, then letting it out. She turned to face him.

"Fine," she grumbled. And promptly towed him back to the shop. He went along, unlocking the door and pushing it open. They went inside, and Chauncy slammed the door shut behind him.

"What the hell?" he blurted out, glaring at her.

"What do you mean?" she shot back, glaring at him.

"Why are you acting crazy again?" he demanded. Her eyes widened, her pupils growing disturbingly large.

"I am *not* acting crazy!" she retorted. Stomping her foot on the floor for good measure.

"Are too," he insisted, with a bit less vigor than he would've liked. She clearly sensed his wavering resolve, and pounced on it.

"I don't feel safe here," she insisted.

"You did two minutes ago," he pointed out.

"That was two minutes ago."

"Right," he agreed.

"A lot's changed since then," she said.

"Like what?"

"Like that alarm going off," she replied.

"It was a false alarm."

"This time," she countered. "What about the next time?"

"Uh…"

"Exactly," she concluded before he could answer, crossing her arms over her chest and thrusting her chin up triumphantly.

"We're safe here," he insisted. "I'm a powerful wizard, and so…uh, are you," he added. "We have nothing to fear."

"I'm afraid of being afraid," she argued.

He blinked, trying to come up with a retort to that.

"Neither of us is powerful enough to beat that," she argued. "Even if we *are* strong enough to beat whatever might attack us, we're still not powerful enough to stop being afraid of being afraid of what might attack us."

"Uh…" he stammered. "I could make a wand that takes away your fear," he pointed out.

"Yes, but then I wouldn't be afraid of what I *should* be afraid of, even though I shouldn't be. And that's not right."

Chauncy blinked rapidly, repeating the sentence silently to himself a few times over, just to be sure he'd heard it right. Valtora took the opportunity to lean in close to him, wrapping an arm around his shoulders and staring up at him with soulful eyes.

"Do it for me, Chauncy," she urged, biting her lower lip. She put her other hand on his chest, then slid it down to his belly, and then further down still, until his breath caught in his throat. "I swear I'll make it worth your while," she added, flashing him a gorgeous smile. And then she began to play with his…

Dong!

Valtora cursed, letting go of Chauncy and turning around…just as the door to the shop opened.

"God *damn* it!" she snapped, punching the wall to her left. Her diamond fist smashed right through the wood, making a huge hole in it…and making a very surprised Mrs. Thimblethorp, one of Chauncy's best customers, nearly jump out of her skin.

"Oh!" the elderly woman gasped, clutching at her pearls.

"Mrs. Thimblethorp!" Chauncy exclaimed, digging deep to flash the biggest, warmest smile he possibly could at her. A skill he hadn't had to use since returning to Borrin. "Didn't mean to startle you," he added reassuringly, pulling Mrs. Thimblethorp into the store, past Valtora. "It's…that time of the month," he added in a rather loud whisper, giving the old woman a knowing wink and nodding at Valtora. The poor woman could barely hear, after all.

"Oh," she replied, glancing at Valtora with a rather appropriate level of fear.

"It's alright," Chauncy soothed.

"Better get her some chocolate," Mrs. Thimblethorp advised.

"And a bottle of wine," she added. She watched as Valtora pulled her diamond fist from the wall, hunks of plaster falling to the floor.

"Make that two," Mrs. Thimblethorp corrected.

"What can I get for you today?" Chauncy inquired, ignoring Valtora's glare. Mrs. Thimblethorp's eyes brightened, and she turned immediately to the Lotions & Potions aisle.

"Well, my girlfriend Mrs. Biggins told me about the 'Lotions & Potions' promotion," the old woman declared. "Fifty percent off, is it?"

"Um…" Chauncy began, glancing at Valtora. The promotion had ended yesterday. "The promotion ended yesterday, I'm afraid. But for you, I'll make an exception…if you promise to keep it a secret," he added, giving her a sly wink and a nudge. Her eyes twinkled; for if there was one thing Mrs. Thimblethorp loved, it was an exclusive offer.

"Your secret is safe with me, Chauncy boy," she vowed. "I'll take it to my grave!"

A trip she'd be taking rather soon, he suspected.

She rushed forward as quickly as her old legs would take her, gathering up a rather large number of lotion bottles. She paid for it – coin by slowly retrieved coin, in the manner of all elderly women, much to his dismay – then eyed the Lotions & Potions aisle critically.

"You're almost out," she notified him. Chauncy grimaced, suddenly realizing he'd forgotten to make more the night before. Which meant that he'd have to do it tonight.

"More coming tomorrow," he reassured as he helped bag her lotions.

"Mrs. Biggins said she'd be by to get that cure for her wrist you promised her," Mrs. Thimblethorp notified him. "You're a good man, Chauncy."

"Right," Chauncy muttered. "Thanks." And swore to himself, for he'd forgotten to do that too. Mrs. Thimblethorp hobbled out of the shop happily, her bag of lotions in hand. The door swung closed, and Valtora turned to Chauncy.

"Think she'll last long enough to use all of it?" she asked.

"Not a chance," he replied with a guilty little smile.

"Sorry about the wall," she offered. "I'll get the plaster."

She went to the broom closet, opening the door to it. It was more of a walk-in closet, and she found all the supplies he'd need to repair the wall. After a few months of living with her, Chauncy had learned to keep such supplies at home and at work. Valtora's temper was ultra-violent, but thankfully short-lived. If she held grudges, Chauncy hadn't noticed it yet. Her outbursts were far easier to endure knowing that they lasted seconds…and that the vast majority of the time, their time together was marvelously agreeable.

"Want me to do it?" Valtora offered. Guiltily.

"That's alright," he replied.

"Okay," she mumbled. She hesitated. "I'll make it up to you," she promised. "By doing that thing you like."

His eyebrows rose.

"*That* thing?" he asked, daring to hope. She grinned evilly.

"*That* thing," she confirmed.

And with that, he set about to fix the hole with gusto, secure in the knowledge that it would not be the last one that he'd get the opportunity to fill that day.

* * *

That evening, after closing the shop and strolling home, Valtora went right to their bedroom upstairs.

"What are you doing?" Chauncy asked from the foot of the stairs. She turned around, already halfway up.

"Packing," she answered. As if it were obvious.

"Packing?" he pressed. "Why?"

"We talked about this," she reminded him, turning about and going upstairs. He watched her disappear into the bedroom.

"Honey, we're not moving," he protested.

"Go make dinner," she called out. He hesitated, then crossed his arms over his chest.

"I'm not moving."

A moment passed. A very silent moment, which made Chauncy suddenly quite ill at ease. For he'd seldom said no to anyone in his life, least of all Valtora. But to be fair, she hadn't given him any opportunities to do so until now.

She emerged from their bedroom, standing at the foot of the stairs. To his surprise, her arms weren't crossed over her chest. Nor were her hands on her hips. She looked...defeated.

"What's wrong?" he half-asked, half-demanded.

She just stood there, staring at him.

"You're acting really *really* strange," he continued. "And I know it's not that time of the month," he added. A moment's reflection on the events of the day had made him realize that.

"Chauncy..." she began.

"No excuses," he interrupted. "Just tell me the truth baby. Whatever it is, we'll work through it together."

She sighed, her shoulders slumping.

"Okay," she muttered. She went downstairs glumly, standing before him. But her eyes were on her feet. "I...just want everything to be okay between us," she said.

"Everything *is* okay," he insisted, putting his hands on her shoulders and giving them a squeeze. "And it always will be, as long as we're honest with each other."

She looked up at him, a little smile on her lips.

"Wow, that was a really good line," she admitted. He smiled back.

"I know, right?" he agreed. "Kinda proud of myself for that one."

"You should be."

"I feel like I'm killing it in the boyfriend department," he confessed.

"You always do," she replied. "But that was above and beyond."

"I still want an answer."

"Damn," she muttered. "I was hoping you'd forget." He pointed at his own temple.

"Mind like a steel trap," he declared.

"You mean rusted shut?" she retorted. But she sighed again, nodding to herself. "Alright," she agreed. "I'll tell you. But you have to promise not to be too mad at me."

"I can't promise that," he replied. "But I can probably promise you I probably won't be mad for long."

She frowned, replaying the statement in her head a few times, then decided it would have to do.

"So, remember that whole thing about how I went to the Great Wood and the Cave of Wonder and Mount Thrall as a girl?"

"Yeah," Chauncy replied. It was standard Chosen One stuff. Valtora grimaced, wringing her hands a bit.

"Well, Imperius made me live with The Dark One for twenty-five years," she continued. "And…um…" She paused then, wringing a bit more vigorously, while biting her lower lip.

"It's okay," he soothed. "You can tell me."

"See, the thing is Chauncy, when a girl goes through…the change."

"Menopause?" Chauncy asked. Valtora gave him a withering look.

"Puberty!"

"Oh. Right," he mumbled.

"She gets urges," Valtora continued. "Strong urges. And you know me," she added. "My urges are…they're like my magic. Like, *fucking* powerful."

"…yeah," Chauncy agreed. Ish.

"So you can imagine how hard it was for me," Valtora told him. "Being up on that volcano for years and years, just *bursting* with needs. Pressure all building up until I wanted to just…unnghhh…explode. Gets to the point where you'd just hop on anything and…"

"Okay, I get it," he interjected.

"So anyway, you understand, right?" she asked.

"Of course," he replied with a smile. "I know what it's like to want that kind of thing and not have it."

"For decades," she agreed. "What would *you* have done, Chauncy?"

"Umm…pined from afar," he confessed.

"Well I'm not a pussy," she countered. He blinked. "No offense," she added. "But you are."

"I *was*," he countered.

"…yeah," Valtora replied. "So anyway, me being me, I took what was available," she concluded, crossing her arms over her chest. And glaring at him for some reason.

"Uh…fine?" he offered. Her expression softened.

"You're okay with it?"

"Sure," he answered with a shrug. "So I wasn't your first. No big deal."

"Oh," she replied. "Good." She broke out into a smile. "Well, I feel *much* better now. Thanks for understanding," she added, giving him a loving hug. He frowned.

"That was it?" he asked. She pulled away, giving him her gorgeous-est smile.

"Mmmhmm," she replied. "Pretty much. Yup."

"Well, that wasn't so bad."

"Good," she said. "Now, let's go pack together!" she exclaimed, grabbing his hand eagerly. "We need to leave before..."

And with that, destiny did its thing, knocking on Chauncy's door.

"Mother *fucker!*" Valtora snapped, chopping her diamond-hand down on the stair railing. It snapped in two, falling to the floor with a clatter. Chauncy jumped, making a squeaking sound. Valtora ran toward the kitchen, hauling Chauncy along with her.

"Where are we..."

"Go through the backdoor!" she cried.

"What..."

"Just do it Chauncy!" she pleaded. "For me!"

He did as he was told, much as he'd done the last time she'd made such a request. They reached the kitchen, bolting toward the door leading to the backyard. Valtora grabbed the doorknob, flinging the door open...

...and shrieked.

For there, blocking the doorway, was a woman. An elderly woman, short and robust. She wore a blue shirt and white pants, and her short arms were crossed over her considerable bosom. She glared at Valtora with glacier-blue eyes, frowning fiercely.

It was Nettie!

"You!" the old woman snapped, jabbing a finger at Valtora. An index finger, which – in Nettie's case – was not the one she was in the habit of using. Valtora flinched as if it'd stabbed her, letting go of Chauncy's hand and wringing her hands.

"Nettie-poo!" she gasped. "Oh my *god*, is that *you?*" She stepped in for a hug, but Nettie stopped her with an outstretched hand.

"Touch me and I'll drown you," Nettie warned. And to Chauncy's surprise, it seemed like Nettie actually meant it. The two had never gotten along, which was a shame. "Where d'ya think *you're* going, ya black-hearted hussy?" Nettie demanded, stomping into the kitchen. And slamming the back door behind her.

"Uh…" Valtora began.

"Nettie!" Chauncy blurted out, overjoyed at seeing his friend. He rushed up to her, giving her a big hug. And she hugged him back.

"Hey Chauncy," she greeted with a warm smile, pulling away and tousling his hair. "How in the hell are ya, kid?"

"Great actually," he replied. He looked Nettie up and down. "You look great," he added. For, despite being at least eighty, she looked spry as ever. Her short white hair fell in bouncy curls to just above her shoulders, contrasting nicely with her blue shirt. She wore an amulet around her neck, one with a small pebble made of blue quartz set in it. The Wetstone, one of the first magical items Chauncy had created.

"Like hell," Nettie replied, but seemed quite pleased.

Chauncy glanced at Valtora, who looked as pale as a sheet. Or rather, someone else's sheet, considering theirs – like just about everything else in the bedroom – was pink.

"Um, how are you?" he asked Nettie.

"Oh, just fine," she answered. "Finished orientation at the Order of Mundus a couple weeks ago." She gave him a look. "Boring-entation, if you ask me."

The Order of Mundus was a group of powerful wizards that…well, Chauncy wasn't quite sure what they did, other than that it seemed really important. Nettie and Harry had spent most of their lives trying to get into the exclusive club, and had only recently done so, by virtue of saving magic along with Chauncy.

"Everything was hunky-dory 'til this little harlot ruined things," Nettie added, shooting Valtora a glare. "Tryin' to skip town, eh?"

"Um…" Valtora began.

"She was worried about the city alarm going off," Chauncy told Nettie. "She doesn't want to raise kids in a dangerous city."

"Is that so?" Nettie shot back, putting her hands on her hips. Then she eyed Chauncy warily. "Please tell me you didn't put a bun in this idiot's oven," she pleaded.

"Not that I'm aware of," he replied. They'd specifically avoided that issue, favoring buns over ovens.

"Well don't," Nettie warned. "She's nothing but trouble, Chauncy."

"Nettie…" Chauncy began.

"You know what? I don't need to take this," Valtora declared, putting her hands on her hips. "Defend me Chauncy!"

"She's not an idiot, Nettie," Chauncy countered gently.

"Do better!" Valtora snapped. "Insult her!"

"…and that wasn't very nice," he added. Valtora groaned, burying her face in her hands.

"God you suck at this," she grumbled.

"Go ask your crazy girlfriend why I'm here," Nettie prompted. Chauncy turned to Valtora.

"Why is Nettie here?" he asked gamely. And immediately wished he hadn't. For now Valtora was glaring at *him*.

"So now you're taking *her* side?" she accused incredulously.

"Um…" Chauncy began. Then stopped, glancing at Nettie. Who stood there, arms crossed over her chest, looking rather amused at this turn of events. "Right," he decided. "I'll be upstairs. Be sure to lock up when you go."

And with that, he went right for the stairs, which were in the foyer by the front door.

"No, we're leaving *now*, Chauncy," Valtora declared, grabbing his arm and yanking him toward the door. She flung it open…and gasped. For a man was standing in the doorway, blocking it. A very old, very tall man. He wore a brown shirt and brown pants, with a vest made of interlocking stones and wood chips and such. He had wispy red hair with patches of white, and bright blue eyes that peered at Chauncy through a pair of slightly crooked silver glasses. The man grinned at him.

"Heya Chauncy," he greeted in an odd, warbly voice.

"Harry!" Chauncy exclaimed, rushing in for a hug. Harry chuckled, hugging him back…and nearly breaking his ribs in the process. The man's embrace was like a steel vise.

"Ack," Chauncy gasped. Harry released him, then turned to Valtora, his eyes twinkling.

"Heya gorgeous," he greeted. Which was exactly the right thing to say. Valtora's eyes lit up, and for a moment, she forgot she was in mid-escape.

"Harry-kins!" she gushed, rushing up to hug him. "Oh my god, it's so good to *see* you!"

"Same to you," he replied, giving Chauncy a sly wink. He hugged Valtora for a bit longer than was appropriate, then released her, and she beamed at him, squeezing his arms.

"Still hard as ever," she observed.

"Am now," he agreed.

"Quit being nice to her!" Nettie snapped from behind. "She's a bad girl, remember?"

"Well that's why I'm being nice to her," Harry pointed out.

"Shut up Harry!"

Chauncy glanced at the two elderly wizards, then put his hands on his hips.

"Alright," he declared. "Will somebody *please* tell me what's going on?"

"Sure Chauncy," Nettie replied. "See, your precious little psycho's been lying to you all along. She's not just the interim The Dark One, you see."

"She's not?" Chauncy replied.

"Nope," she confirmed. "Valtora spent a lot of time working under The Dark One…"

"In a lot of positions, actually," Harry added.

"Shut up Harry," Nettie scolded. But she smirked at the quip. "Good one."

"I thought so," Harry agreed.

"What do you mean?" Chauncy interjected, getting a bit irritated with the two. Valtora grabbed his arm.

"Chauncy, don't…" she began, but Nettie cut her off.

"Your girlfriend," Nettie replied, "…is The Dark One's wife. And if we don't get the hell out of here soon, everyone you know in Southwick is going to die."

Chapter 3

King Pravus the Eighth always felt absolutely marvelous after a good workout at the gym. The smell of sweat, the symphony of manly grunts all around him. The *clang* of weights striking weights, the *thump* of other weights hitting the floor. And the most wonderful feeling of all:

The pump.

That singular feeling of his big muscles practically bursting out of his skin, veins engorged with blood. Oh, it was *gorgeous*, this feeling. In fact, there was only one sensation he loved more...a feeling involving a rather different kind of pump. One that also involved the smell of sweat and a symphony of manly grunts, coincidentally.

He'd spent this morning like every other, getting up ridiculously early to go to the gym he'd founded in the center of the city. And an hour later, he found himself doing the post-leg-day waddle out of the gym toward his carriage, feeling drained but positively giddy. Even the obnoxious finery of his royal carriage ahead and the ridiculous number of guards surrounding him as he hobbled couldn't dampen his spirits. For as he'd often found, a good workout was like a vaccination against the evils of the world, albeit one that lasted a few hours at most. Which was why he typically insisted on a getting a good pump twice a day.

At length, he'd managed to limp up to the carriage, and his driver had already opened the door. To Pravus's delight, none other than his cousin Templeton – sweet Templeton! – was seated inside. He got into the carriage with a fair amount of effort, his legs wobbling under him. Then he didn't so much as sit as *fall* into his seat, wincing at his sore buttocks.

"Sorry I couldn't make it, my liege," Templeton apologized. For he was Pravus's usual gym-mate. "Affairs of state, I'm afraid."

"Quite alright," Pravus replied. "One must attend to one's affairs," he added. While wishing fervently that he could attend to an affair with Templeton. They were two peas in a pod, after all, and

Templeton's peas and pod had long been the objects of Pravus's desire. But while attraction was powerful magic indeed, what was magic for one could be mundane – or even grotesque – to another. And unfortunately, his cousin did not see any magic in him, other than that of their friendship. But a man was entitled to his fantasies, and King Pravus had enjoyed many a pump indeed in the pursuit of his.

"Dull affairs," Templeton replied, making a face. For as kin to the throne, Templeton was a lord, responsible for all sorts of ghastly things. Like servants and payroll and logistics of all kinds. Not to mention that he'd decided to have children. A brave man indeed to suffer so many obligations at once. Pravus suspected that Templeton's only respite from these noisy obligations was the time they spent together.

"Affairs should be anything *but* dull, eh cousin?" Pravus inquired with a twinkle in his eye. "Otherwise what's the point in having them?"

"Indeed," Templeton agreed with a smile. "You always do know just what to say, cousin."

"I've been told I have a spectacularly silver tongue," Pravus replied. Indeed, his orations were the stuff of legends among those who'd had the pleasure of experiencing them.

The carriage started off toward the castle, accompanied by a ridiculous escort of guards, of course. With his magical monarchal robes, Pravus hardly needed much protection. But a good show of power gave his citizens a kind of reassurance, he knew. If people thought their king was just like them, why, they'd lose all respect.

A wonderful idea, equality, but in practice, utterly disastrous. For when people were equal to each other, they had a terrible tendency to treat each other like freshly shat shit. Mostly because they all thought they were *better* than each other, and wasted so much of their time struggling to prove it.

"What now, my liege?" Templeton inquired.

"Meetings," Pravus answered, making a face quite similar to the one Templeton had made when regarding his affairs. "Terrible things, meetings," he mused.

"Awful," Templeton agreed.

"Wastes of time," Pravus continued, happy to step up onto this metaphorical soap box. "The more mouths that speak, the fewer ears listen."

"And the less brains work," Templeton added.

"Indeed," Pravus agreed. "Tell me cousin, what brilliant revelation was had by committee?"

"None, I daresay," Templeton replied at once.

"You daresay correctly," Pravus concurred. "Do you know what type of person finds magic in meetings?" Templeton shook his head. "Managers," Pravus answered with disdain. "The mediocre ones, anyhow. But the only magic being cast is an illusion," he added.

"Why's that?"

"Because meetings give them the illusion they're doing something terribly important," Pravus replied.

"I couldn't have said it better myself," Templeton declared.

"When it comes to tongues," Pravus stated, "...none is more skilled than mine."

"I've not had the pleasure of enjoying your orations," Templeton noted apologetically, utterly, adorably clueless of his unintended double-entendre. "But I hear they're quite stimulating."

"Indeed," Pravus agreed, doing his best to maintain his composure. Templeton rarely came to court. But Pravus was quite sure that if his cousin would only consent to experience his orations, he'd come quite frequently, so to speak. Pravus realized he was growing a bit too fond of the idea, and crossed his legs hurriedly, looking out of his carriage window at the passing scenery. It simply wouldn't do for his arousal to arouse suspicion, after all. For a man of his stature, his stature was a royal pain to conceal.

"What's on the docket for today, my good man?" Templeton inquired. Pravus sighed.

"The Dark One," he replied darkly, his expression darkening.

"Still rising, eh?"

"Indeed," Pravus confirmed. "It seems our Chosen Ones haven't defeated him yet."

"It's been quite a while," Templeton pointed out.

"Tell me about it," Pravus grumbled. He'd met the four Chosen Ones at the Great Wood six months ago. The heroes had stopped Gavin Merrick's wife Marie Merrick from felling it, and had made it quite clear that they'd take care of The Dark One next. Just a little break, they'd said. Can't save the world twice in one day. Or something to that effect.

"Where *are* the Chosen Ones?" Templeton inquired.

"Two are in Borrin, the other two at the Order of Mundus, or so I assume," Pravus replied.

"Shall we summon them?"

"We may have to," Pravus answered. "I can't say I appreciate them blowing me off." An act he usually *did* appreciate.

"Shall I get on it?" Templeton inquired. Pravus hesitated, then nodded.

"If you wouldn't mind, dearest cousin," he replied.

"Consider it done!" Templeton declared with gusto.

And with that, the carriage reached the tall walls surrounding the castle, crossing the bridge over the ridiculously wide moat to the raised portcullis beyond. They passed through it into the castle grounds, and Pravus sighed, dreading what was to come.

For while the gym had been a magical place indeed, now he was leaving its magic far behind.

Chapter 4

Chauncy blinked.

"What?" he asked, not quite registering what Nettie had just said. Nettie crossed her arms over her chest, Harry at her side…and Valtora looking like she was going to pass out.

"Your girlfriend's The Dark One's wife," Nettie repeated. "And if we don't get out of here soon, everyone you know in…"

"What?" he interrupted.

"She went and got married to the personification of evil," Nettie explained. "Got hitched to the biggest, blackest asshole in the world."

"A real stinker," Harry piped in.

"She married him, Chauncy," Nettie insisted. "Why else would he let her become interim The Dark One?"

Chauncy processed this.

"Oh," he replied at last. Then he turned to Valtora. His mouth worked, but words didn't come out. He felt utterly numb.

"Chauncy," Valtora began.

"Save it psycho," Nettie interjected. "We don't got time for your bullshit."

"No," Valtora shot back. "Chauncy, I can explain."

"That's what they always say," Nettie grumbled.

"Shut up," Valtora snapped. Nettie's eyebrows shot up, and she was about to lay into Valtora when Harry put a big hand on Nettie's shoulder.

"Ain't no harm in listening," he reasoned rather reasonably. Nettie glared at him.

"What part of the whole 'if we don't get out of here soon, everyone in Southwick is gonna die?' don't you understand?" she argued.

"We got a few minutes," he countered. She rolled her eyes, but held her tongue. A considerable feat, given how vicious and quick her tongue could be.

"Is it true?" Chauncy asked Valtora. Valtora sighed, her shoulders slumping.

"It's true," she confessed. "But we're separated," she added quickly. "I haven't...um, *been* with him for like, three years now."

"Uh huh," Nettie grumbled.

"He was desperate to get back with me," Valtora explained. "That's why he gave me the Amethyst Army."

"But you're married," Chauncy stated. Valtora grimaced.

"Technically," she admitted. "But we're separated, Chauncy. I was going to divorce him, but I couldn't."

"Well why the hell not?" Nettie inquired.

"Because I needed the Amethyst Army," Valtora answered. "And Imperius told me to stay on Mount Thrall until Chauncy got there. The Dark One would've kicked me out if I'd divorced him, and he would've taken the Amethyst army away from us. And honestly, he probably would've killed me."

"Why would he do that?" Harry asked.

"He already told me that if he couldn't have me, no one could," Valtora replied. "You know, typical evil awful asshole shit." She turned to Chauncy, grabbing his hands in her own. He resisted the urge to pull away, so pleading was her expression. "When I said I never wanted to go back to Mount Thrall, I meant it," she insisted, giving him a weak smile. "I came here with you to leave The Dark One behind forever. I came here to start a life with *you*."

"But you're *married*," Chauncy retorted, pulling his hands away from hers.

"I'm separated," she corrected. "I can't get a divorce without taking him to court. And if I do that, I'll have to see him again, and he'll try to kill me. And you too, Chauncy. He's the jealous type."

"So...you just stay married?" Chauncy pressed.

"What other choice do I have?" she retorted.

"But that means *we* can't get married," Chauncy realized. Valtora grimaced, and Nettie rolled her eyes.

"Oh *hell* no," she complained. "Don't do it Chauncy," she pleaded.

"She makes me happy," Chauncy countered.

"She's a lying, cheating, psycho bitch," Nettie accused. Valtora shot her a deadly glare.

"I am *not* cheating!" she insisted. "I'm separated!"

"Uh huh," Nettie grumbled.

"So this is why you're here?" Chauncy asked. "To ruin my relationship with Valtora?"

"A girl can dream, can't she?" Nettie replied.

"Don't need to," Harry answered, putting an arm around her shoulders. "I already made your dreams come true."

"You sure did, honey," Nettie agreed. She wrapped an arm around his waist, giving him a squeeze.

"So why are you here?" Chauncy pressed.

"We're here 'cause Imperius Fanning asked us to pay you a visit," Nettie answered.

Chauncy's eyebrows went up, and Valtora seemed to shrink a bit.

"Imperius Fanning?" he blurted out. He'd never met the man who'd come to this very house a quarter century ago. The man who he'd almost been destined to go defeat The Dark One with.

"The same," Nettie confirmed. "In fact, Imperius came to your house yesterday morning," she revealed. Chauncy's eyebrows shot up again.

"Really?" he blurted out. He'd always wanted to meet the famed wizard, but it seemed like he was destined to never do so. "Well darn," he added. "We must've been at the shop."

"Nope," Nettie replied. "You were home." She pointed a finger at Valtora. "*She* answered the door." Chauncy glanced at Valtora.

"Is that true?" he asked.

"Oh it's true," Nettie insisted before Valtora could answer. "Crazy tart threw Imperius out. Slammed the door in his damn face, just like your idiot grandmother."

"Rest her soul," Harry added, for politeness's sake.

"Why?" Chauncy pressed, frowning at Valtora.

"He wanted us to go back to Mount Thrall," Valtora revealed.

"But why?" he repeated.

"To kill The Dark One," Nettie answered. "Turns out that's your destiny. Yours and Valtora's both."

"But...I thought my destiny...uh, *our* destiny was to save magic," Chauncy countered.

"It was," Nettie agreed. "And you did that. But then Imperius's gut told him you weren't done...and that you were destined to fulfill the destiny we thought you were destined to do."

Everyone paused, trying to make sense out what she'd just said.

"So why'd you kick Imperius out?" Chauncy asked Valtora.

"Because I don't *want* to go back to Mount Thrall," she answered, grabbing his hands again. And holding on awfully tight. "I never want to see that asshole again."

"You saw his asshole?" Nettie asked. Valtora blushed, which was answer enough.

"The point is, I want to stay here with you," she insisted. "I want to be with *you*, Chauncy." She smiled at him. "Being with you has been the happiest six months of my life," she added. "If I never set foot on that damn volcano again, I'll…"

"Be hunted down by your black-hearted husband for the rest of your life," Nettie finished for her. Valtora blinked.

"What?" she asked.

"The Dark One's amassing his armies," Nettie warned. "The Order of Mundus has been tracking his movements. He's sending his forces across Pravus, and last I heard, they're coming for the Gate."

"You mean…?"

"If you don't go to Mount Thrall to defeat The Dark One and fulfill your destinies," Nettie concluded, "…then The Dark One's gonna come for *you*."

Chauncy swallowed in a dry throat, throwing Valtora a nervous glance. She grimaced again.

"That's why I wanted to leave Southwick," she admitted. "I wanted to get as far away from The Dark One as possible."

"Well, the way I see it, running ain't in the cards," Nettie declared, putting her hands on her generous hips. "The only way outta this mess is to get right into it."

"She's right," Harry agreed.

"But I don't want to get into it," Chauncy complained. "I like my life the way it is!" He paused. "Was!"

"Sorry kid, but it's your destiny to defeat The Dark One," Nettie told him. "You're a wizard, Chauncy. You have responsibilities."

"So I've been told," he grumbled. Then he frowned, glancing at Valtora. "But…what about the whole being married thing?"

"Well Chauncy, if you *really* wanna marry this psycho," Nettie replied, "…then your destiny's the answer. The only divorce The Dark One's gonna honor is the one he signs in his own blood."

"What's that supposed to mean?" Chauncy asked.

"'Till death do us part," Nettie replied. "Sorry to burst your bubble kid, but the only way outta this marriage…is murder."

* * *

And that was how Chauncy found himself compelled rather hurriedly and reluctantly to follow his destiny into a second adventure. For he of all people knew the folly of saying "no" to destiny. Thus, instead of packing to run away from danger – as he'd refused to do for Valtora – he packed in order to run toward it. Or rather, Valtora packed for him, almost certainly out of guilt. She was one to apologize not with words but with actions, mostly because if she didn't *say* she was sorry, she maintained plausible deniability. Something she'd probably learned from The Dark One. Her *husband*, he had to remind himself. And in reminding himself, he felt terribly depressed. But Nettie wouldn't let him mope, insisting repeatedly that they needed to hurry.

"Come on you idiots," she urged as they came down the stairs, luggage in tow. "Hurry it up already!"

"Calm down," Valtora grumbled.

"I'd be a lot calmer if we didn't have the damn The Dark One's army all the way up our asses," the old woman shot back. "No thanks to you, they know exactly where we are."

"Wait, what?" Chauncy blurted out.

"We had to beat off a small goblin contingent on the way here," Nettie explained. Valtora nodded sagely.

"That's one of the only ways to pacify them," she piped in. "Lot of work though."

Nettie blinked, her mouth hanging open. Then she paused, clearly deciding whether or not she wanted to touch that one.

"There's a story there," Harry noted.

"Shut up Harry," Nettie grumbled. "Let's just go already."

They left the Little residence quickly, Chauncy clutching his staff tightly, keeping his eyes on the sidewalk before him. Valtora offered to hold his hand, but he stuffed it in his robe-pocket instead, refusing to make eye contact with her.

"Honey?" she asked, glancing sidelong at him.

Chauncy resisted the urge to answer. To pretend that everything was okay. For it was his nature to take the path of least resistance, and he'd suffered most of his life because of it. Chauncy had always been a good little boy, according to Grandma. Never able to say no…just like his mother.

So instead of saying no, he decided to say nothing at all. Which was the closest to "no" he could manage.

Valtora fell silent, and the four of them set about on their usual route back to the courtyard in the center of the city. But not, as per their usual, at a stroll's pace. No, this was more of a brisk, grim march, a means to an end…whatever end destiny happened to have in store for them. And with this pace, Chauncy found himself settling into a familiar place in his mind, one he hadn't visited in quite some time. A place of preparation rather than participation. Of waiting for the present to end so he could get on with enjoying the future, whenever that came.

Or in this case, *if* it came.

He sighed, lifting his gaze to the huge silver double-doors in the distance. The Gate to the magical kingdom of Pravus. A place he didn't particularly want to be. For he'd had all the magic he needed here in Southwick. Or so he'd thought.

But, having no other choice, he followed Nettie and Harry past the magic shop, then down the street and through the Gate, which opened at their touch. Beyond, they found a black carriage waiting for them, with a very unusual-looking horse at its front. One blindingly white, save for its mane, which was long and luxurious and rainbow-colored.

"Oh," Chauncy blurted out when he saw it.

"Ooo!" Valtora exclaimed, rushing up to the horse and hopping up and down. After which she gave the horse's neck a big, non-consensual hug. "OhmygodI *love* her!" she exclaimed.

"Him," Nettie corrected.

Valtora frowned, leaning over to take a peek. Her eyes widened even further, and for good reason. For the horse was indeed a stallion, and was as long and showy down below as his mane was up above.

"Oh my," Valtora gasped, putting a hand to her mouth. "It's *beautiful*."

"Please tell me she's talking about the whole horse," Nettie pleaded. But it was quite clear from the direction of Valtora's gaze that this was not the case. And because she kept staring at it. Without blinking.

"I *so* want to ride him," she gushed.

"Let's get in already," Chauncy grumbled, pulling the side door open. Valtora blinked, then tore her gaze from the stallion, staring at Chauncy.

"Huh?" she asked.

"Quit dicking around," Nettie told her. "We got a job to do."

"I'm *going* to ride you," she promised the horse. After one final lingering glance, she complied, getting into the carriage. Chauncy sat by the leftmost door, Valtora at the right. And Nettie sat in the middle between them, for which Chauncy was grateful. Harry went to the driver's seat, pulling himself up into it rather stiffly, then snapped the reins.

"Ha!" he prompted.

The carriage rolled forward, following the wide dirt path forward into the kingdom of Pravus. And so the four Chosen Ones, most of whom would've chosen differently. Chauncy sighed, glancing back through the rear window at the closing double-doors of the Gate, profoundly depressed at the thought of leaving A Little Magic behind. He resigned himself to the fact that it was his destiny to confront A Very Big Magic instead.

Chapter 5

Gavin Merrick sat at his large desk in his office, staring at the stack of papers set upon it. Assets and liabilities. Endless numbers separated into neat little columns. He used to look forward to these reports, devouring them with glee whenever they graced his desk. Their numbers used to be as magical to him as any of the countless magical artifacts he'd acquired as the President of the Evermore Trading Company. Only one thing had been more magical: his wife, Marie.

She had, he realized only now, been the source of magic for him. For now that she was gone – murdered by King Pravus's wizards, by all accounts – the magic in his life was gone. Now the numbers on the pages before him were lifeless, mere ink on a page. They meant nothing to him, other than that they represented a task to be attended to. An obligation to continue the work of his father, and more importantly, his grandfather before him. The great Archibald Merrick, founder of the company that Gavin owned and ran. Its destiny was in Gavin's hands, and Gavin's destiny was to make it the most successful corporation in the land.

A destiny that had once been an asset, and now seemed nothing more than a liability.

Gavin stared at the stack of papers, the remainder of his work for the day. Suddenly, the thought of reviewing them was overwhelming, a task so monumentally difficult he couldn't bear to think of it, much less do it. He sighed, turning away from his responsibilities and gazing at a picture set in a small golden frame on his desk to his left. A tiny painting of his late wife, made for her when they'd first married. He gazed at it, drinking in all the little details. Her beautiful brown eyes. Her golden skin. Long black hair tied back into a ponytail. Full lips…lips that had kissed his countless times.

Yet, as many times as he'd kissed her – as he'd had her – it had proven never enough. For Marie had been one of the few things in

Gavin's life that he could never get enough of. And now that he couldn't have more, he'd had enough of everything else.

I'm sorry baby, he thought, touching the frame of the painting gently.

He never should have let her go off to the Great Wood alone like that. Sure, she'd led raids in countless other countries, but Pravus's most powerful magical wilderness had been different. Gavin should've been there with her. If he had, she never would have died. Or had he failed, they could've died together in a blaze of glory. He could've been there with her, instead of leaving her to die alone.

Gavin grit his teeth, tearing his gaze away from the painting. He slid his chair back, then stood up, bracing his palms on his desk.

King Pravus.

The idiot had almost certainly been responsible for Marie's death. And even if he wasn't, he at least had to know who was. It irked Gavin to no end that the man had nearly bested him in battle. He'd nearly been strangled to death by Pravus in the king's throne room, after all. Pure luck for the king, of course. Gavin had proven himself stronger than the man during their workout together, at the king's gymnasium.

And he knew that, without a shadow of a doubt, he could defeat the monarch if given another chance.

The problem of course was that, to exact his revenge on the idiot king, Gavin needed to get through the Gate. And the Gate, he knew now, could only be opened by a wizard. Wizards, unfortunately, were in short supply, particularly in the Republic of Borrin. And any that Gavin might find would hardly want to do anything to help him, not after what Evermore had done to them.

Unless…

He broke out into a grim smile, recalling the last shipment he'd received through the Gate, before King Pravus had shut off the magical kingdom for good. A shipment from Marie's second-to-last raid. She'd gotten scant few magical artifacts from the place, nothing of particular use to him.

Except, of course, one little wizard.

Gavin returned his gaze to the stack of papers on his desk, knowing with sudden certainty that he would never read them. The Evermore Trading Company was not only solvent, but marvelously profitable. Those reports simply revealed the degree. But the degree to which Evermore was succeeding was no longer important to

Gavin. For though he possessed the largest storehouse of magical artifacts in the world, owning them held no magic at all for him. Not anymore.

He turned away from his work, a stack of drudgery he was compelled to endure, and found himself gazing once again at his wife's portrait. There was something far more urgent to attend to than the work his obligations demanded of him. The one thing left that roused his spirit:

The destruction of his enemy. And vengeance for the cold-blooded murder of his one true love.

Chapter 6

The journey to Mount Thrall was a familiar one to Chauncy, or at least it was after a few hours. For he'd spent the very first part of his first journey tied up and tossed into the luggage compartment of the carriage Nettie and Harry had stolen the first time around. This time, from his more privileged position in the passenger compartment, he was able to witness the small town they passed through, bathed in silver moonlight. He was seated to the left, Valtora on the right and Nettie in-between.

"This is the town we dropped that girl off at the last time," Nettie told him as they went through it.

"You mean Addie," he replied.

It was a quaint little village, population fifty per the cute little sign he'd seen on the way in. The village square consisted of precisely three buildings flanking the road: an inn, a bar, and a grocery store. Which covered the basics of human experience quite well, Chauncy supposed. For eating, drinking, socializing, and sleeping were – along with work, at least according to Grandma Little – what life was all about. Or rather, what it was *only* about.

Chauncy found himself thinking of Addie. His childhood – and adulthood – crush, a sweet, gentle, shy woman who'd visited his shop often. She hadn't visited much since he'd gotten with Valtora, and he could hardly blame Addie for moving on. But now he found himself wondering what life would have been like if he'd chosen Addie instead. A lot less complicated, he supposed. For one, he wouldn't have to worry about Addie's husband, considering the man was quite dead.

He imagined still being at the shop, with Addie at his side. Or at her grocery store, him at *her* side.

He sighed, feeling suddenly enormously guilty at the thought. He gave a sidelong glance at Valtora, who was staring glumly out of her window. And then realized Nettie was staring at *him*.

"What?" he asked, guiltily.

"Just reminiscing 'bout the last time we were here together," she replied.

"All I remember is being tied up in the trunk," Chauncy admitted. Nettie chuckled at the memory.

"That's what I was reminiscing about," she replied. "Good times, eh Chauncy?"

"Eventually."

"Oh, come on," she said, punching him in the shoulder. Unlike Harry's stony flesh, Chauncy's was quite soft, and her little fists – toughened by punching Harry countless times a day – hurt like hell.

"Ow!" he complained, rubbing his shoulder gingerly.

"Still a little bitch," Nettie mused, shaking her head. "Never thought you'd actually make something of yourself."

Chauncy blinked, rather taken aback.

"Really?" he asked.

"Well sure," she replied. "Harry believed in you right from the start, but I sure as hell didn't. We even made bets."

"Bets?"

"He got his reward while you were in the Cave of Wonder," she told him. Chauncy frowned, then recalled what Nettie had said she'd done for Harry while Chauncy had been busy being reborn. An act that had, not to be *too* graphic, had never resulted in anyone being born.

"Oh *god*," he blurted out, turning away from her and shaking his head. She cackled…and so did Valtora.

"Go Nettie!" she exclaimed.

"Shut your mouth, hussy," Nettie snapped.

"Says the woman who kept hers open," Valtora retorted.

"Open yours again and I'll put my fist in it," Nettie warned.

"Not if I fist you first!" Valtora countered.

"No one's fisting anyone!" Chauncy interjected. And saw Harry twist around in the driver's seat to look at them through the front sliding window. Chauncy saw rather than heard the man chuckle. "Can't we just get along?" he pleaded.

"Nope," Nettie replied instantly.

"Not a chance," Valtora agreed.

Chauncy sighed, turning to gaze out of his window. And began to *thump* his forehead rather vigorously into the glass, over and over again. Respectable people, much less friends, would have made an attempt to stop him. So it was no surprise to him that no one did.

He gave up, staring out of the window at the passing scenery. They'd reached a familiar forest, the one he'd stared at the last time he'd made this journey. At the time, he'd found the sunlight playing with the leaves and forest floor magical indeed, but to his troubled mind, the moonlight bathing the forest now was merely light, and the trees were merely trees. For magic was one's relationship with the world, and at the moment he was somewhere in the world he'd rather not be.

He closed his eyes, resting his head against the window. And, seeing as it'd been a long day, he fell fast asleep.

* * *

"Shmookie tookums!"

Chauncy's eyes snapped open, and he blinked, realizing it was tomorrow. Or rather, that it was today, and that the today he'd experienced moments before was now yesterday. The sun was just starting to rise, and some fifty feet ahead, Chauncy spotted a familiar stone bridge spanning a wide river. The carriage reached the bridge, crossing over it, and Chauncy spotted a familiar figure standing in the middle of it. A twenty-foot-tall giant with stony skin and a big blocky head, charging right toward them.

"Oh my god oh my god!" Valtora blurted out, hopping up and down on her seat and pointing at Rocky. Harry stopped the carriage, and Valtora shoved her carriage door open, leaping down and sprinting toward Rocky just as fast as she could. "Tookums!" she cried, leaping at the giant and wrapping her arms around his upper leg. She held on tight, clinging to him…and wrapping her legs around his huge leg too.

"Huuuuy," Rocky greeted, smiling stiffly at her.

"Oh I *missed* you," she gushed. Then she detached from him. "We're going back to Mount Thrall to murder The Dark One," she told him. "Wanna come?"

"Yaaaah," Rocky agreed.

Valtora beamed up at him, clearly overjoyed at this. Then she turned to eye the rainbow-maned horse. She bit her lower lip, looking tremendously conflicted.

"Ugh, I wanna ride you so *bad* Rocky," she admitted. "But I wanna ride horsey too."

Nettie exchanged looks with Harry, who was still up in the driver's seat.

"I wish I could ride you both at the same time," Valtora complained, stomping her foot.

"Be a hell of a show," Harry mused.

"Nice to see you Rocky," Chauncy interjected hurriedly, exiting the carriage and giving the giant a smile. Rocky beamed at him, stomping up to him and reaching down. Rocky embraced him gently, lifting him bodily off the ground and giving him a little squeeze. Then he lowered Chauncy to the ground.

"Niiize...see yewww tewww," the giant replied.

"Aww!" Valtora cooed, clutching at her heart.

"Back to the riding thing," Harry prompted rather hopefully. Nettie elbowed him.

"Shut up Harry," she snapped. And Harry, being an agreeable sort, did just that. Still, he looked rather disappointed that this particular line of conversation hadn't been pursued.

"Can I take turns?" Valtora asked Rocky. "I can ride you for a bit, then I can ride horsey until he gets tired. Then I'll ride you again."

"Oookaaaaah," Rocky agreed.

"Yay!" she exclaimed, hopping up and down and clapping. Chauncy smiled despite himself, relieved at seeing her back to her usual effervescent – and rather un-self-aware – self. "Who wants me to mount them first?" she asked, glancing back and forth between the two. To Chauncy's surprise, the horse immediately neighed, rearing up on its hind legs for a bit. "Okay horsey-poo," she decided with a smile. "I'll ride you for a bit."

She skipped up to...uh, horsey-poo, mounting him in one smooth, practiced motion. Chauncy's eyebrows rose at the sheer athleticism of the maneuver, surprised at her skill. For, having mounted her stallion with ease, she rode him with expert technique, guiding the beast between her thighs toward their inevitable – and mutual – destination.

"Wow," Chauncy blurted out. "I didn't know you could ride."

"Clearly not her first time," Nettie grumbled.

"Pfftt, not even close," Valtora replied rather proudly, bouncing up and down a bit as she rode. "I've ridden *hundreds* of stallions."

"You don't say," Nettie said.

"Well, let's go," Chauncy prompted, turning right back to the carriage and getting in before anyone else could comment. Nettie joined him, and with that, they were off. They continued forward across the bridge, Rocky leading them. His big hard feet *thumped* on the dirt road beyond, the sound soon putting Chauncy in a kind of trance.

"How ya doin' kid?" Nettie asked. He blinked, turning to look at her.

"Um...not good," he admitted. "Seeing as how my awesome life was a lie."

"Sorry 'bout bursting your bubble," Nettie apologized, patting his knee. "I know how you feel about her. But I warned you," she added. "I told you right from the beginning she was trouble."

He sighed miserably, eyeing Valtora's back through the front window of the carriage. Her hair flowed gorgeously down her back, rippling in the breeze as she rode her stallion. Nettie was right, of course. She *had* warned Chauncy.

Suddenly he was so tired that he just wanted to close his eyes and fall asleep.

"It's all right," Nettie told him. He shook his head.

"No," he replied. "It's not."

"Well it will be," she insisted, patting his knee again. "Better to know the truth than to live a lie, kid. Believe me."

"I liked the lie better."

"Bet she didn't," Nettie retorted, nodding at Valtora. Chauncy grimaced. He hadn't really thought about how Valtora must've felt, knowing that she was keeping something from him. Something that would devastate him.

"She was protecting me," he realized. "She kept it a secret because she knew it would hurt me."

"Maybe," Nettie replied grudgingly. "Or maybe she was just protecting herself so she could get what she wanted."

Chauncy frowned, watching as Valtora bounced up and down a little on her stallion. She twisted around, flashed him an absolutely gorgeous – and delighted – smile, joy so pure that it made him smile despite himself. For it reminded him quite clearly of who Valtora really was. A bit evil, yes. Vindictive at times. Foul-tempered, in teeny-tiny bursts. But these defects in her character were things she didn't bother to hide. She was, unlike anyone else Chauncy knew, utterly herself, without apology. There was no way she would lie to get what she wanted, because she wasn't ashamed of what she wanted.

"No," Chauncy replied, watching as Valtora turned away from him, continuing to ride blissfully. "She doesn't need to protect herself. She doesn't care what anyone thinks."

Anyone, that was, except for him.

"You got me there," Nettie conceded.

"I used to care about what *everyone* thought," he told her. "Grandma and Addie. My customers. I did everything they wanted me to do and everything I *thought* they wanted me to do, so they wouldn't be disappointed in me."

"Terrible way to live, for everyone but yourself."

"It was," he agreed. "Magic was me doing what I really wanted to do."

Perhaps that was why Valtora was so magical to him. Because she *was* magic, doing whatever she really wanted, regardless of the consequences. And if that was true, then it meant that she'd wanted to protect him by not hurting him with the truth. It meant that she'd valued them being together so much that she was willing to keep a secret from him, one that had to have eaten at her, day after day. Keeping secrets was probably the most difficult thing for Valtora to do, after all. Especially being as impulsive as she was.

Harry steered the carriage to the left suddenly, turning off the main road and onto a narrow one that led toward a forest far in the distance. Chauncy frowned, not recalling having gone this way the last time. Nettie must have noticed his confusion.

"We met that goblin contingent on the main road," she said. "Gonna have to take back roads if we wanna avoid The Dark One's minions."

"Oh," he replied.

With that, he turned to look out of his window, telling Nettie that the conversation was over without having to say so. She took the hint, looking out of her own window. He gazed out at the landscape as it rolled by, feeling quite a bit better than he had before.

After defeating Marie Merrick, he'd realized that his destiny had been to be with Valtora and save magic. And it still was. For the only way to *be* with Valtora was to defeat The Dark One, so he could marry her one day. Something that Imperius Fanning's magical gut must've told the man.

He smiled, resting his head against the carriage window. A familiar feeling came over him then, the same feeling he'd had when he'd proclaimed his intentions before Marie Merrick. A feeling he'd rarely felt in his life…and one that felt so good.

Like he was a goddamn *badass*.

His name was Chauncy Little, and he was a great-ish wizard. He'd plunged deep into the Cave of Wonder to find the source of his magic, and by his hand, the Great Wood stood as tall as ever.

Now he would face his ultimate challenge: the biggest, blackest asshole that'd ever lived. And with his magical staff in hand – and with the help of his friends – he would beat The Dark One's dragon. Then he would reach that great crater beyond, with its stench of sulfur. He would penetrate The Dark One's defenses, plunging deep into the man's dark temple. And by golly, he wouldn't leave until he was good and finished.

Until he'd given The Dark One everything he had...and conquered him at last.

* * *

Chauncy woke up to the darkness of late sunset, starlight poking through the veil of night. And to the horse veering sharply to the right, nearly making the carriage tip over a bit in the process. He took a sharp breath in, bracing himself against the carriage door. But the carriage righted itself, falling back onto all four wheels. The horse stopped, rearing up on its hind legs and letting out a blood-curdling shriek.

"What the...!" Chauncy blurted out.

"Incoming!" Nettie warned. "Everyone out!"

Valtora leapt down from her horse, and Nettie shoved open her door, getting out. Chauncy hesitated, then opened his own door, stepping down from the carriage. They were on the narrow road Harry had taken them down earlier, dense forest on either side. A road that extended off into utter darkness.

There, standing in the middle of the road a couple hundred feet away, was a huge...*thing*. A dark, hulking shadow silhouetted by the stars. Humanoid, but as tall as Rocky. And much, much broader. Glowing white eyes glared at them, the awful gaze making Chauncy's hackles rise.

"What the hell *is* that thing?" Nettie asked.

And then it *roared*.

"Oh *shit*," Valtora swore...just as the thing charged toward them.

The horse reared again, letting out another shriek, and tried to bolt. But Harry slipped down from the driver's seat, landing feet-first on the ground with a grunt. Bare-feet-first, Chauncy noted. The man yanked the reins, forcing the horse down.

"Harry!" Nettie blurted out.

"Gotta hold your horses," he replied. And then he did just that. Fingers of earth shot up around the horse, trapping it in place. Then he turned to face the charging…thing. It was, Chauncy realized, a bald giant with black skin and massive, veiny muscles. And it was closing in fast, only fifty feet away now.

Thirty.

"Chauncy, blow that guy!" Valtora cried.

Chauncy grimaced at the wording, but gripped his staff tightly, winding up and swinging it hard at the charging beast. A blast of wind shot forward from the staff, striking the huge humanoid. It stumbled in surprise, but recovered quickly, the blast barely slowing it. And it closed in on them rapidly, leaping forward through the air at Chauncy.

"Crap!" Chauncy blurted out.

A huge stone fist shot up between him and the creature, uppercutting it right in the chin. It shot upward and backward, its head snapping back viciously. Flying through the air, it landed on its back with a loud *whump*, a good twenty feet away from them.

"Yeah!" Valtora exclaimed. "Way to go, Harry!"

"What the hell is that thing?" Chauncy asked. The giant black humanoid groaned, then started to sit up.

"Obsidian Ogre," Valtora answered grimly, her hands on her hips. "One of The Dark One's minions." With that, she strode toward the beast, even as it struggled to its feet.

"Valtora!" Chauncy blurted out. "What are you doing?" But she ignored him, walking right up to the Obsidian Ogre and glaring up at it.

"What the hell?" she demanded, putting her hands on her hips. Chauncy thought he noted a signature jawline-ripple, but it was hard to tell in the darkness. The ogre rose to its full height, glaring down at her. "Don't you know who I am, idiot?" she asked.

The ogre lifted both fists above its head, then brought them smashing down on Valtora.

"Bitch!" she cried as she flung herself out of the way at the last moment. The ogre's fists pulverized the road, sending dirt flying upward from the impact…and incidentally, some of that dirt shot right into the ogre's eyes. It roared, clutching its eyes and shaking its head violently…and Valtora took the opportunity to run back to Chauncy and the others.

"What were you thinking?" Chauncy demanded. "You could've died!"

"I thought he'd recognize me," Valtora retorted, clearly insulted that the thing hadn't.

"I'm sure he did," Nettie shot back. "That's why he wanted to kill you."

"Shmookie, smash!" Valtora ordered, pointedly ignoring Nettie.

Rocky grunted, stomping toward the ogre, who'd finished wiping the dirt from its eyes. Rocky broke out into a charge, closing the distance quickly and ramming his big blocky shoulder into the ogre's chest.

Or at least he tried to.

The ogre swung one big fist, smashing it into Rocky's shoulder...and sending the rock-giant flying into the trees to the right of the road. Rocky smashed into the tree trunks, snapping them like twigs and landing with a crash in the forest.

"Oh," Chauncy blurted out.

"Tookums!" Valtora gasped, sprinting after the poor giant.

"Harry," Nettie prompted, turning to glare at her husband. "You gonna kill that thing already?"

"Anything for you, darling," Harry replied.

The old man limped toward the huge ogre, and it turned to glare down at him as he strolled toward it, its huge hands clenched into fists. Normally, Chauncy would've been terrified by the thought of a poor old man facing such an enormous, powerful creature. But this wasn't just any old man.

It was *Harry*.

So, instead of being afraid of what might happen to the old man, Chauncy found himself wondering just how epic an ass-kicking the Obsidian Ogre was about to receive.

Harry stopped a good ten feet from the ogre, smiling up at it with his hands stuffed in his pants pockets.

"Hey there fella," he greeted. "Looks like we got off to a rocky start."

The ogre swung a fist at Harry, smashing him right in the face.

Now Harry should've careened backward, his face a bloody pulp. Instead, he merely floated backward with the blow, his body flattening and wrapping around the ogre's fist as if Harry were a big handkerchief. The ogre blinked in surprise, and Harry un-flattened himself, falling onto his back on the dirt with a grunt. The ogre took the opportunity to lift one big foot up to stomp the life out of Harry.

A stone fist shot up from the ground in front of Harry, punching the ogre right in the nuts.

The ogre squeaked.

Harry chuckled, getting to his feet just as Rocky burst through the forest onto the road, crashing into the ogre. The ogre fell on its back, and Rocky leapt atop it, pummeling it with his stony fists.

"Yeah shmookie tookums!" Valtora cried exuberantly. "Pound his ass!"

And Rocky did pound the ogre. His face, anyhow. Over and over again, until his fists were bloody, and the ogre's face was quite a bit flatter than it'd been moments before. Eventually Rocky tired, standing up from the ogre and glaring down at it. And spitting on it.

Harry stuffed his hands into his pockets again, hobbling back to Chauncy and Nettie. He beamed a smile at his wife, who gave him a hug…and a squeeze on the butt, to Chauncy's dismay.

"Good work hon," she told Harry.

"Do I get a reward?" he asked hopefully.

"Might get more than one," she answered. He grinned, waggling his eyebrows suggestively. And threw Chauncy a wink. Chauncy ignored it as best he could, turning back to the carriage.

"We should get going," he reminded them. "There might be more."

Rocky dragged the ogre off into the woods to clear the road, and Chauncy and Nettie and Valtora went back into the carriage. With that, they continued their journey, passing the pummeled ogre and leaving it far behind. But Chauncy didn't fall back asleep, and took to biting his nails instead. For it was clear now that The Dark One was after them…and that while they were leaving his first minion behind, what lie waiting in their future might be far, far worse. His Staff of Wind had been useless against the ogre. No, *he'd* been useless. If he was going to face The Dark One – and have any chance at defeating the bastard – he'd need far better magic than he had.

For as it stood, Chauncy Little, one of the four Chosen Ones destined to defeat the very source of evil itself, was clearly not up the task.

Chapter 7

King Pravus drummed his fingers on the oversized armrest of his oversized throne, gazing across his oversized throne room at the oversized double-doors leading out of it. Everything far bigger than it needed to be, for the sole purpose of making everyone else feel small. People were, after all, relative thinkers. Everything in comparison to everything else. Which was why his throne was set on a raised platform, so that he would seem taller than anyone who beheld him. And why he sometimes wore a spectacular cape if he *really* wanted to shrink someone down to size. Though he hardly needed this, considering that, as a consequence of his favorite hobby, he was quite a bit larger than anyone else.

"Desmond!" he barked. At the top of his lungs.

"Right here, sire," Desmond replied. For the old man was standing right beside his throne. And had been for some time. Sixtyish years old, his trusty servant was a bit younger than he used to be, on account of the potion of youth he'd quaffed. But still old enough to irritate Pravus. The man wore a very expensive-looking suit of gold and black. But on his pudgy, smudgy frame, not even its finery could elevate his appearance much.

"I'm in a bad mood," Pravus informed.

"You don't say," Desmond replied dryly.

"Well I don't like it."

"No one does," Desmond agreed.

"Are you implying that I'm unpleasant to be around?" Pravus inquired, suddenly itching for a fight.

"Only when you're working."

"But I only interact with you when I *am* working," Pravus pointed out.

"Indeed sire."

Pravus glared at the old man.

"Now you're starting to irritate me," he muttered.

"Only now, sire?"

"More so than you normally do," Pravus corrected. "You know, I cannot for the life of me understand why I feel any sort of affection for you, but I do."

"You sound like my wife, my liege."

Pravus frowned at him.

"You have a wife?" he asked.

"Regrettably," Desmond confirmed.

"Do you have children?"

"Regrettably," Desmond repeated.

"My god Desmond," Pravus exclaimed. "Is there anything in your life you don't regret?"

"I regret not."

Pravus's eyes narrowed, and he peered at his servant suspiciously.

"Are you screwing with me, Desmond?" he inquired. "Or is your life really that sad?"

"Yes," Desmond answered.

Just then, the double-doors to the throne room opened, and none other than Templeton strode through. Pravus shot up from his throne, breaking out into a smile.

"Cousin!" he cried, filled to the brim with elation. For Templeton never failed to raise his spirits.

"My liege," Templeton greeted cheerily, striding confidently up to the throne. In a marvelously masculine sort of way, so *bro*, as the conventional men in the gym were fond of saying. Pravus almost forgot the little mission he'd given Templeton.

"How goes the mission?" he inquired. "Have you found our naughty little Chosen Ones?"

"In a way," Templeton replied, stopping a few yards away. He was wearing a tight black and gold uniform, quite similar to the one Desmond was wearing, in fact. But on Templeton's sculpted frame, the finery looked fine indeed, and Pravus gobbled up the visual smorgasbord provided to him, his infinite appetite hungry for more.

"Do tell," he requested eagerly, rubbing his hands together.

"It appears the Chosen Ones have been visited by none other than Imperius Fanning," Templeton declared triumphantly. "Of the Order of Mundus," he added, which of course was entirely unnecessary. Everyone knew who Imperius was, after all. The most famous wizard in all the land and such. Still, it added a bit of drama for Templeton to include that little bit extra, and Pravus appreciated all the "extra" he could get.

"Go on," he urged.

"Imperius left for the Isle of Mundus," Templeton revealed.

"And the Gate to the Republic of Borrin opened the day after."

"And?"

"Well, we assume the Chosen Ones went through it," Templeton answered. Pravus's eyebrows furrowed.

"You *assume?*" he pressed with a flash of irritation. Which irritated him even more, for he rarely felt irritated with his cousin.

"Only wizards and yourself can open the Gate," Templeton pointed out. "And your ambassador to the Order of Mundus assures me that the Chosen Ones are on their way to defeat The Dark One, as was prophesied."

"Ah," Pravus replied, feeling much better. "Good work, dearest cousin! I can always count on you to get the job done."

"I am but a tool of the king," Templeton declared valiantly, executing a most impressive bow.

"Speaking of tools," Pravus said, settling back onto his throne. "Has there been any headway regarding one Gavin Merrick, Desmond?"

"None sire," Desmond replied.

"Well that's *irritating*," he grumbled. For, after Gavin had attacked Pravus – in this very chamber, no less – Pravus had set quite the bounty on the man's head. One that should have appealed to all sorts of murderous fellows and femme fatales. And yet to his dismay, none had come forward to take him up on the offer to open the Gate to go after the colossal prick. "Why in the hell not?"

"Something about him being rich and nigh-invincible, sire."

"Pah!" Pravus retorted. "Invincible my ass!"

"Everyone appears to be afraid of him," Desmond stated.

"They should be afraid of *me*," Pravus retorted.

"You haven't threatened anyone."

"Yet," Pravus grumbled. He sighed, drumming his fingertips on his armrest. The fact that Gavin was still alive was suddenly profoundly vexing to him. "Well, double the bounty," he ordered.

"At once your Worship."

"Can't have people attacking the king and getting away with it," Pravus reasoned. "Sends the wrong message."

"Quite," Desmond agreed.

"Do you require anything more of me, King Pravus?" Templeton inquired quite formally. Pravus turned to him.

"No," he lied. "Thank you, dearest cousin. You're the only one who never disappoints me."

"Duly noted, sire," Desmond grumbled.

"It is forever my pleasure," Templeton replied with the grandest of bows. With that, he turned crisply, leaving the throne room. Pravus watched him go, then sighed again, eyeing Desmond. Who was still standing there.

"Didn't I give you something to do?" he grumbled.

"Sorry to disappoint," Desmond replied.

"*Are* you though?"

"No sire," Desmond replied. He paused then. "I believe I've just discovered something I don't regret."

"Just go," Pravus muttered, waving him away. Desmond bowed dutifully, exiting the room in his usual way. All old and stiff and tottering and such. It was monumentally depressing for Pravus to watch, in keeping with the rest of the man. He imagined himself getting old and feeble for a moment, then decided he didn't like it.

He sighed, watching the double-doors to the throne room close. All he could do now was wait for his next meeting, which was in five minutes. His day was filled with the dreadful things, one after the other. For with The Dark One rearing his ugly head, the Lords and their citizens were all in a tizzy, carrying on about doom and gloom and the end of the world and such. And there was even a religious sect called Dark Awakening that welcomed such premonitions, practically salivating over the thought of being lorded over by the evil bastard. They targeted the stupidest, most gullible, and impulsive people in existence: teenagers.

It wasn't long before the doors opened, and Pravus began the rest of his day. He tolerated each as best he could, but time seemed to drag on into infinity, endless drudgery that was dreadful to his soul. Something to endure, as all compulsory activities seemed to be. But with each passing minute, Pravus reminded himself that every minute that passed was one minute closer to sweet, sweet freedom. To the magical light that twinkled at the end of this awful tunnel: his next workout at the gym.

Chapter 8

A few hours after the sun set, Harry stopped the carriage at the side of the road, lowering himself down from the driver's seat rather stiffly, then opening the carriage door for Nettie.

"Thank you hon," she said, letting him help her down. He grinned at her.

"Anything for you, angel."

"Okay Rocky," Valtora said from atop Rocky's broad back. When she'd tired of riding her stallion, she'd ridden Rocky instead, having him walk on all fours while she sat on his back. He lowered himself to a push-up position, and she hopped down, beaming at him. "Thanks tookums," she cooed, blowing him a kiss.

"Yaaaaaaah," Rocky replied with a stiff smile.

Chauncy opened his own door, stepping down from the carriage and joining the others. Valtora glanced at him nervously, and he glanced back, also nervously.

"Hey," she mumbled, waving her diamond hand at him. Then she glanced at it instead, grimacing and hiding it behind her back.

"Hi," he replied. "Um…sorry," he added, clasping his hands in front of him.

"For what?" Valtora asked.

"For being mad at you," he explained.

"You were mad at me?" she pressed, her eyes widening in horror.

"In my head," he confessed. "But I'm better now."

"Oh," she replied, brightening instantly. "Good." She paused then. "Can I hug you?"

"You'd better," he replied with a smile.

She ran up to him, leaping into his arms. And promptly knocked him over, because he hadn't been expecting that. He landed on his back with a *whump*, the air blasting from his lungs. She fell on top of him, then sat up, straddling him.

"Sorry!" she blurted out.

"Get a room," Nettie grumbled.

"Way I see it, the horse and Rocky got a turn," Harry reasoned. "Only fair for Chauncy to."

"Go set up camp ya big lout," Nettie ordered. Harry saluted stiffly.

"Yes ma'am," he replied. And with that, he did just that. Chauncy went to help the old man, gathering sticks for a fire. Nettie started rooting through the packs in the luggage compartment of their carriage, retrieving some rations. Valtora went to help her, but Nettie shot her a deadly glare. Right between the eyes, in fact. Valtora backed away, while Nettie seemed a bit disappointed that her glare hadn't been as deadly as she would've liked.

Soon the campfire was crackling merrily, and everyone sat around it. Valtora next to Chauncy, of course. She reached for his hand with her non-diamond one, and he took it in his own. Which made her smile adorably. Nettie sighed, stretching her legs so her feet were close to the fire.

"I missed this," she admitted.

"Missed what?" Chauncy inquired.

"This," she answered, gesturing at him. "Going off on an adventure. Spending time with you and Rocky."

"And me?" Valtora piped in. Nettie ignored her, saying nothing for a long enough time for it to be quite clear what the answer was. "Bitch," Valtora muttered. Loudly.

"Harlot," Nettie shot back.

"Hag!"

"Whore!" Nettie retorted. Valtora scoffed.

"Whores get paid," she retorted. "I do it for *free*."

"Uh huh."

"Harpy!" Valtora snapped, clearly excited by the opportunity to find as many insults that started with an "H" sound as possible. She had a habit of turning fights of all kinds into a game. To the point where the only reason she ever started a fight was for entertainment purposes. Including more than a few wrestling matches with him.

"Blow it out your ass," Nettie grumbled.

"I will blow it *in* my ass!" Valtora shot back, really getting into it now. Nettie raised an eyebrow at her, then at Chauncy, and Chauncy blushed.

"So!" he interjected hurriedly. "What's for dinner?"

"The usual," Harry answered, passing around some bread and soup. And, busy with chewing bread instead of chewing each other out, Nettie and Valtora fell mercifully silent. Afterward, Chauncy realized that both of the women must've been a bit hangry, for with their bellies filled, their dispositions were vastly improved. Valtora snuggled up against Chauncy's shoulder, and Nettie against Harry's.

"Thanks for the fire hon," Nettie told her husband.

"Anything for you," he replied. Which made Chauncy smile. For it was as true as true could be. Harry had all but given his life for Nettie, turning himself to stone to save her from Magmara, The Dark One's lava dragon. And Chauncy knew that the old man would do it again in a heartbeat. He was a good man, Harry. Perhaps the best man – and wizard – that Chauncy had ever met.

He realized that Valtora was gazing at him, a big smile on her lips. Her gorgeous eyes twinkled in the flickering light of the fire.

"What?" he asked.

"I just love you," she replied. "Can't I love you?"

"Um…yes?"

"I don't need your permission, you know," she retorted, shooting him a glare. "I'll love who I want."

"Uh…"

"You men are all the same," she complained, standing up and continuing to glare down at him. He blinked rapidly, then frowned, crossing his arms over his chest.

"You *want* to argue," he realized. "You're just mad because Nettie wouldn't keep insulting you."

Valtora's eyes widened with indignation.

"I can't *believe* you'd accuse me like that!" she almost shouted. Chauncy rolled his eyes.

"Come on poopy-dooz," he pleaded, patting the grass beside him. "It's been a long day, and I'm tired."

Valtora's face fell, and she pouted at him.

"Aww," she complained. But she sat down, snuggling against him again. Nettie and Harry stared at her, then at each other, then back at her.

"There's something seriously wrong with you," Nettie told her.

"Hack," Valtora shot back. Nettie's eyebrows rose.

"Hothead," she retorted.

"Hypocrite!" Valtora cried out gleefully.

"Hellion!"

"Ooo," Valtora exclaimed, breaking out into a smile. "Good one!"

"Go eat lava," Nettie grumbled.

"I can't," Valtora replied. "Only Magmara and The Dark One can do that."

"Well you got some of him inside you, don'tcha?"

"Not anymore," Valtora retorted, crossing her arms over her chest. "I'll have you know I haven't had The Dark One inside me for three *years*."

"Uh huh."

"That's like, a *century* in Valtora years," she added. Chauncy grimaced, not wanting to imagine The Dark One inside of his girlfriend.

"Right," he interjected, standing up suddenly. "I'm going to bed."

"Gotta pitch a tent first," Harry countered. Which was true, Chauncy realized with dismay.

"Can I help?" Valtora asked. Harry grinned at her.

"Sure can," he replied. Nettie swatted him with the back of her hand. And then swore, shaking her hand out.

"I always forget how damn hard you are," she muttered.

"Wait till you see me pitch a tent," Harry replied with a wink. Nettie ignored him, while Chauncy tried in vain not to visualize what Harry was insinuating. He distracted himself by helping Harry erect the tent, and Valtora helped out as well, with her usual gushing gusto. Chauncy found himself smiling at her, for despite everything, she was back to normal again. An explosion of noise and color in an often subdued and gray world. Someone who wasn't afraid to be utterly, ridiculously herself. Nettie and Harry had packed two tents, as it turned out, and they pitched them both, with a good distance between them. Nettie said it was because she didn't want to be tempted to put a pillow over Valtora's head while she slept, but Chauncy suspected there were other…compelling reasons. Reasons that, it turned out, turned out to be quite compelling to Valtora. For when they settled into their tent, she immediately pounced on him, a devilish gleam in her eye.

"Let's *do* it," she whispered. Loudly, as usual.

"Do what?"

"It," she answered. And performed a bit of her standard pantomime.

"No way," he retorted. "They'll hear."

"So?"

"It's…I can't," he protested.

"I'll be *super* quiet."

"You *can't* be quiet," he shot back. "You always get carried away." Which was true.

She sighed, her shoulders slumping. Then her eyes lit up. "How about *this*?" she inquired. And promptly started doing what it was she was proposing she should do.

"Oh," he blurted out. "Wow."

And in a testament to her remarkable skill, it wasn't very long after that Chauncy fell into a fast – and very content – sleep, Valtora snuggled up against him. He as the little spoon, she as the big. It was almost as if they were still home in Grandma Little's house. But in a way, Chauncy *was* home. For home was wherever Valtora was, and as long as she was with him, there was no place else he would rather be.

**

The next morning, Chauncy woke up inside his tent to find Valtora outside of it.

He sat up just as she came inside, a pack in her arms. She threw it down unceremoniously on the floor beside him, then squatted before it, rummaging through its contents.

"Morning," he mumbled, rubbing the sleep from his eyes. "Whatcha doing?"

"Getting you dressed!" she exclaimed cheerily. For Valtora was a morning person. And an evening person. In fact, she was a person pretty much all of the time. The only thing that ruined her mood for more than a few seconds was hunger.

"I've got my robe," he pointed out.

"But you need undies."

"I packed some," he said, standing up and stretching. In fact, it was all he'd packed, because she'd packed the rest out of guilt. Valtora made a face.

"I *saw*," she replied, opening her mouth and sticking out her tongue. Then shoving a finger in it and pretending to gag. "I threw them all out when you weren't looking," she confessed.

"You what?"

"Well, seeing as we're going on a trip, I thought we should bring the *special* ones, from our special drawer," she reasoned. "The ones mama *likes*." And with that, she held up an article of clothing that made Chauncy's eyes widen in horror.

"You didn't!" he gasped.

"Put it *on* already," she ordered, dangling it before him. And doing a little sashay while she was at it.

"No!"

"Come *on* baby," she insisted. "Do it for *mama*."

"I'm not wearing that!" he insisted.

"Well you'll have to," she shot back. "It's all I packed."

And with that, she withdrew five articles of underwear from the pack that positively shimmered in the light, and – in terms of square inches of cloth – together were equivalent to perhaps a half of a pair of his normal underwear. From experience, Chauncy knew that each struggled mightily to contain the front, so much so that they almost had no energy – or fabric – left to cover the back.

"That's it," Chauncy muttered. "I'm wearing the underwear I wore yesterday." He looked around the tent for them, but to his increasing frustration, he couldn't find them. "Where are they?" he demanded. She giggled.

"I threw them out."

"You *what*?"

"I threw them out," she repeated. "Tossed them in a river while you were sleeping."

"What river?!"

"It's three miles away," she told him. He stared at her incredulously.

"You woke up in the middle of the night to take my underwear and walk six miles so I'd have to wear *these*?" he pressed, gesturing at the semi-underwear.

"Barefoot," she confirmed.

His mouth fell open, and he just stared at her.

"You *could* go commando," she offered. "But with that silky-ass robe, gosh, it's just gonna show *everything*."

"I hate you," he muttered.

She beamed at him, leaning forward and pecking him on the cheek. Then she turned about, exiting the tent. And leaving Chauncy to do what he had to do. He sighed, then slipped the underwear on, putting his wizard's robe on afterward. Despite the fact that the robe hid the underwear completely, he still felt utterly ridiculous – and exposed – wearing it. For it was quite tightly-fitting, in an invasive sort of way, making itself impossible to forget about.

"Great," he muttered. "Just great."

He exited the tent, seeing Harry and Nettie already up. They were breaking down their tent and lugging it back to the carriage. Harry waved good-naturedly, and Chauncy waved back...and then promptly glanced down to make sure the man couldn't see through Chauncy's robe. Then he sighed, getting to work breaking down his own tent so they could continue their journey.

Given that it was a bit chilly, Valtora decided to ride her stallion first, on account of his flesh being warmer than Rocky's. Plus, Rocky was a lot harder, and after hours of riding him last night, her butt was a bit sore.

So it was that Chauncy found himself once again in the carriage with Nettie, Harry in his customary place in the driver's seat. Valtora vaulted onto the rainbow-horse's back as impressively as she had the first time, slipping into the saddle with ease.

"Ha!" she cried. "Onward, Peter!"

"Peter?" Chauncy asked, glancing at Nettie. She gave him a look, rolling her eyes. Chauncy sighed, settling in mentally for a long ride. For it would be many days before they reached Mount Thrall.

"All right Chauncy," Nettie stated. "Guess we better figure out how we're gonna beat The Dark One. Whatcha got?"

"Um..." Chauncy began. "As far as weapons?"

"Or defenses," Nettie added.

"Not much," he admitted. "Almost everything I've made since going home was for my customers. To make their lives better."

Nettie smiled, patting his knee.

"You're a good guy, Chauncy," she told him. Then she sighed. "Well, guess we better get crackin' then."

"How?" Chauncy asked. "My magic just kinda comes to me. I can't just think of a weapon and make it, it has to...I don't know, inspire me."

"Don'tcha think I know that?" Nettie replied. "On the next stop, we'll start sparring, and that'll put your mind in a fighting mood. I'd bet you'll start seeing weapons and stuff everywhere."

"That's actually a good idea," he admitted. She smirked.

"Of course it is," she replied. "I came up with it, didn't I?"

Chauncy had to smile at that.

"All right kid," she stated, stifling a yawn and resting her head back. "I'm gonna take a nap."

"Already?" he asked. "We just woke up."

"Didn't sleep well."

"Why not?" he pressed.

"Harry's reward," she answered, cracking an eye open and waggling her eyebrows at him. While smiling devilishly. His eyes widened.

"Oh god!" he blurted out, burying his face in his hands. "Please don't put any more images in my head!"

Nettie cackled, and Chauncy turned to look out his window, trying in vain to distract his overly imaginative mind's eye by giving his real eyes something to look at. With not nearly as much success as he'd hoped.

Thankfully, Nettie fell silent, and shortly thereafter, fell asleep. Chauncy fell into the familiar trance of travel, watching the world go slowly by. After six months of his usual routine, it was strange to be sitting around doing nothing. And with nothing to do, he soon joined Nettie and went to sleep.

Chapter 9

"All right Chauncy," Nettie declared. "Ready?"

They stood a good twenty feet away, facing each other. Chauncy with his Staff of Wind in hand, and Nettie with her Wetstone. Valtora and Harry stood by the carriage a good thirty yards away, watching both of them. Nettie had insisted they spar, seeing as how Chauncy had been utterly useless against the Obsidian Ogre. He faced her with a sort of resignation, not particularly wanting to spar her.

"I guess," he replied.

"You guess?" she shot back. "Don't guess. Fight!"

And no sooner had the F-word left her mouth than she grabbed the Wetstone, squeezing it. A stream of water crawled up her hand and arm, wrapping around her upper back, then streaming over her other arm. She pointed this arm at Chauncy, and a column of water shot outward at him with sphincter-spasming speed.

Chauncy froze, and the water struck him right in the chest, sending him flying backward onto his butt. He gasped, the icy water chilling him to the bone instantly.

"Pffftttppthh!" he spat, wiping the water from his eyes. He stood up, rubbing his sore chest while Nettie cackled. "Ha ha," he grumbled. "I wasn't ready!"

"You think The Dark One's gonna attack you when you expect it?" she shot back. "You gotta be ready all the time, kid. If you ain't ready, you're dead."

She threw a small thread of water to the puddle around him, using it to draw the water she'd used right back into her Wetstone...and drying Chauncy completely. For her magic was her connection with water. As long as she was touching water, she could control it.

"Kick her ass, Chauncy!" Valtora shouted from the sidelines, pumping her diamond fist in the air.

"Give it your best shot kid," Nettie told him. "You ready now? Or should I wait?"

"Ready," he grumbled.

She attacked again, using the same tactic. This time, Chauncy swung his staff right at her. Having absorbed months of breezes and stormy gusts, the magical staff released some of this power, sending a blast of wind Nettie's way. It slammed into her water-attack, sending water spraying right back at her.

She shaped that water into a sphere in front of her, then shot *this* out at him, connected to her by a thread of water. Then she flash-froze it in mid-flight, making a huge ball of ice.

That flew right for his face.

"Gah!" he cried, leaping out of the way. The ball of ice whizzed past his head, missing him by inches. He fell to the ground, watching as Nettie melted the sphere in mid-air, then sucked it back to herself, sending it into the Wetstone. He got to his feet, shooting her a glare.

"What the *hell?*" he blurted out. "You could've killed me!"

"Keep that in mind," she replied with a vicious grin.

"It's not funny," he insisted.

"It's a little funny."

"You need to be more careful," he pressed. Nettie crossed her arms over her chest.

"You need to suck less."

"I'm rusty!" he argued.

"Uh huh. Sure."

"Fine, damn it," Chauncy grumbled, clutching his staff tightly and glaring at her. "You want a fight? You *got* one."

"Oh ho ho!" Nettie exclaimed, rubbing her palms together eagerly. "All right kid. Let's do this!"

She clutched her Wetstone, and Chauncy whipped his staff at her, sending another blast of air her way. Then he immediately thrust the butt of his staff at her, making a wind-bullet that shot out behind the initial blast. At the same time, Nettie made a hollow sphere of water around her, flash-freezing it.

His wind-attacks struck the sphere, the first attack scattering off its curved surface, the second shattering it. But the ice-sphere absorbed the blow, leaving Nettie unscathed.

"Ha!" she cried, sending another stream-blast of water at him…and freezing it to form an ice-spike.

Chauncy slammed the butt of his staff on the ground, sending a blast of wind downward…one that shot him up into the air. The deadly icicle missed him by a few yards, passing under his feet.

"Ha ha!" he cried triumphantly. He swung his staff down at her in a vicious arc while still in mid-air, sending a blast of wind her way. And sending *himself* flying backward.

"Crap!" he blurted out, flailing his arms and legs madly. He fell to the ground with a *whump*, the air blasting from his lungs. He laid there for a moment, trying desperately to breathe.

He heard cackling, followed by wheezing. Then a fit of coughing, followed by more cackling. And what was almost certainly knee-slapping.

Chauncy sighed, getting to his feet. He'd dropped his staff a few yards away, and went to retrieve it, stomping back to his original position. While pointedly avoiding looking at Nettie. At length – far too long a length for Chauncy – she stopped laughing. She wiped tears from her eyes, and Chauncy grimaced, meeting her gaze reluctantly.

"Never gonna get anywhere beating yourself," Nettie teased.

"Worked for him for thirty-four years," Valtora shot back. In a particularly unhelpful attempt at trash-talking Nettie. Chauncy blushed furiously.

"Go ahead," he grumbled. "Keep making fun of me."

"Nah," Nettie replied. "That was actually pretty good."

"Good?"

"You experimented," she explained.

"Didn't work."

"So what?" she retorted. "At least you're *doing* something. You started to play. Remember what I told you about fighting?"

"It's play," he recited, breaking out into a reluctant smile. "Like magic. I forgot about that."

"That's why I had to get you fired up," she told him. "So you'd feel yer shriveled-up oats and wanna kick some ass already."

"They are *not* shriveled," Valtora interjected. "They're smooth and *cute* and *this* big," she added, moving her thumb and forefinger apart a disturbingly accurate distance.

"Not helping," Chauncy grumbled. But he nodded reluctantly at Nettie, realizing she was right. Magic was play, and fighting with magic was no different.

Go play, he told himself.

"Ready?" Nettie asked. He nodded.

"Ready."

Nettie pulled water from her Wetstone, shooting a powerful stream of water his way. Instead of swinging his staff, he spun it like a top. This created a miniature tornado around him, and Nettie's stream struck it, spiraling around and up until it sprayed high in the air.

"Ha!" he cried.

She flash-froze her stream, sending another icicle flying at him. He grabbed his staff, slamming the butt of it into the ground and shooting upward again. The icicle flew by beneath him, and he swung his staff at her like he had the last time, sending a blast of air her way. She created a wall of water to block it, which blasted away on impact, but left her unharmed.

And he flew backward as before, falling as he did so.

"Counter-thrust!" he shouted, thrusting the butt of his staff downward and backward. It shot a bullet of air that mostly neutralized his momentum, and he landed gently on the ground.

"Arc-blast!" he cried, winding up and swinging his staff as hard as he could at her.

Nettie created a sphere of water around her, one that rapidly expanded until it was the size of a house. The arc-blast smashed into it, blasting away a good third of the sphere in a fantastic spray of water.

But it left Nettie entirely intact.

She sucked the water back into her Wetstone, beaming at Chauncy.

"Now that's more like it!" she exclaimed. Chauncy grinned, holding his staff in a rather heroic pose. And feeling pretty damn good about himself. "But next time, don't tell me every damn attack you're gonna use," she added.

"Otherwise they'll know what's coming," Harry added.

Chauncy grimaced, feeling himself deflate a bit.

"Sorry," he apologized. "Got carried away."

"Don't be sorry 'bout getting carried away," Nettie countered. "Just trash-talk by telling me how bad I'm doin' rather than telegraphing all your moves."

"Oh. Right."

"Good job baby!" Valtora yelled. "No one blows like my Chauncy!"

"She really has no idea, does she," Nettie realized.

"Nope," Chauncy confirmed.

"Well all right then," Nettie declared, walking back toward the carriage. "That's enough for now."

"Aw," he complained. "I was just getting into it."

"We gotta keep moving," she counseled. "We'll keep practicing, don't you worry. At some point," she added, reaching Harry and Valtora, "...you're gonna have to spar Harry here."

"Oh boy," Harry replied with a gleam in his eye.

"Oh no," Chauncy said, feeling the blood drain from his cheeks. For while Nettie was plenty powerful in her own right, Harry was easily the most impressive wizard Chauncy had ever met.

"Don't worry," Harry told him, patting Chauncy on the shoulder. "I won't hurt'cha. Too much."

"Still worrying," Chauncy notified him. Harry chuckled.

"That's healthy," he replied.

With that, they resumed their usual travel positions, Chauncy and Nettie in the carriage, and Harry in the driver's seat. Harry slid the sliding front window between the cabin and Harry open a bit, letting in some fresh air, and Valtora mounted Rocky, riding the giant gleefully beside them. Chauncy watched her, unable to help smiling at her joyful abandon. Nettie eyed her through the window.

"She's cracked, you know that?" she asked Chauncy.

"Yup."

Nettie watched for a while, then sighed, shaking her head.

"Whatever floats your boat," she decided.

"She doesn't make much sense," Chauncy admitted. "And she's wild and crazy and free. But when I look at her," he added, "...magic is what I see."

"Oho!" Nettie exclaimed, nudging him painfully in the ribs. "Starting to rhyme, eh?" Chauncy frowned. "Sign of a wizard," she told him. "Magic is play, and wizards play with language."

"You don't rhyme much," he pointed out.

"Only the awkward ones do," she clarified.

"Ah."

"Well Chauncy," Nettie stated, "...if she's magic to you, don't listen to an old fart like me."

"What do you mean?"

"Remember what I told you 'bout magic, Chauncy: it's your relationship to the world. What's magic for me ain't magic for you, and that's just the way it's gonna be."

"So...you're okay with me dating Valtora?" he asked. She sighed then nodded.

"She ain't my cup of tea, but she is yours. Much as I hate to admit it, you seem happy with her, Chauncy," she answered. "And believe me, if you can find someone that makes you happy – and they're still making you happy a few years down the line – then you're luckier than most."

"Thanks Nettie," he replied with a smile.

"Just don't put a bun in her oven for a few years," she warned. "If you two go sour, a kid'll tie you to that misery forever."

"Right."

"Obligations you want have hardly any weight at all," she lectured. "Obligations you don't want are the heaviest of all."

Chauncy raised an eyebrow.

"You rhymed," he noted.

"It ain't rhyming if you use the same word at the end twice," she retorted. But she smiled at him. "Maybe I'm a *little* awkward. But all wizards are, thank heaven. Being regular is boring," she added.

"And it gets harder the older you get," Harry piped in from the driver's seat.

"Shut up Harry," Nettie shot back, sliding the window between them shut.

Chauncy chuckled, shifting over to the middle seat, then putting an arm around Nettie's shoulders. He supposed she was right. For wizards were those who rejected the mundanity of the world, and saw the magic in everyday things. To those who didn't, wizards would seem odd indeed. For being odd meant being different, and so many people struggled mightily to be anything but. To be oneself was the only path to magic…to play while others toiled, and to be faintly – or in Valtora's case explosively – ridiculous. But being ridiculous meant taking a risk…that others wouldn't accept the *you* that you really were.

Nettie patted Chauncy's knee, and they rode ever-forward through the magical kingdom of Pravus, toward Chauncy and Valtora's destiny.

Chapter 10

Skibbard sighed, sitting cross-legged on the cold stone floor of his cell. A box six feet squared, with a cot and a pot and not much else. Prison bars extended from the floor to the ceiling in front of him, and beyond that, a short hallway with a door at the end.

Rectangles and squares, boxes within boxes, everything awfully organized. And gray, all of it. Not a splash of color at all.

Skibbard stared at it all glumly, absolutely hating it…and the humans who'd created it.

Strange creatures, humans. Although he was one, Skibbard considered himself quite reformed. For his home had been a forest in the land people called Pravus. A magical place without a single square or rectangle in sight. It was the bizarre compulsion of humanity to desperately want to make the world into boxes, to obsessively order everything around them. Flat walls, flat floors, flat ceilings. Flat lives and then flat deaths, laying in flat boxes buried in rectangular pits in the ground.

He'd left it all behind when he'd fled to the forest so many decades ago. When he'd rejected the compulsions of his fellow man and decided to live *with* the world instead of walling himself off from it.

Then his home had been burnt to the ground, by that horrible woman and her army of thugs…and that awful lich, an undead wizard bound in servitude to evil.

Traitor, he fumed.

Skibbard sighed again, lowering his gaze to his lap. For months he'd been kept here, like an animal in a zoo. That woman Marie had seen to it…after torturing him for having the gall to fight for his home. She'd told him that she'd make an example of him, with a message that'd been branded into his memory:

Don't. Fuck. With. Evermore.

To ensure that he wouldn't be able to do so, she'd promised to cut off his…branch. And to his horror, she'd made good on that promise.

So, with no release in sight, Skibbard was stumped, for there was nothing at all he could do.

And then there was a *thunk*, followed by a *shing*, and the door to the hallway beyond his cell opened.

Skibbard lifted his gaze, seeing a man step through the doorway into the hallway. A tall man with long golden hair falling to just below his shoulders, framing a wide, chiseled jaw and eyes as green as spring leaves. He wore an equally green suit that fit tightly to his muscular frame, and a golden tie that contrasted sharply with it. The same uniform Skibbard had seen on the men who'd attacked his forest.

The man stepped up to the bars, eyeing Skibbard silently for a long moment. No stranger to silence, Skibbard eyed him back, still seated cross-legged on the hard floor.

"The wizard Skibbard, I assume?" the man inquired.

Skibbard said nothing.

"I am Gavin Merrick," the man introduced. "President of the Evermore Trading Company."

Still, Skibbard said nothing.

"I understand you were taken from your home by a few of my…overzealous employees," Gavin stated. Skibbard raised an eyebrow at that. "Regrettably, I learned of your interment here only an hour ago," Gavin lamented. "Had it been brought to my attention earlier, I would have had you freed immediately."

"Theaarrrkkk," Skibbard began, then fell into a fit of coughing. He cleared his throat, which he hadn't used for speaking in many months. "Then free me now," he demanded.

"At once," Gavin replied. And with that, he produced a golden key, inserting it into the lock and twisting it. There was a *click*, and the cell door swung open.

Skibbard sat there, eyeing the open door, then Gavin. He got to his feet. Considerably shorter than his captor, he was forced to look up to him. But only figuratively. For fancy clothes and good looks didn't fool Skibbard, any more than colorful feathers on a bird, or pretty flowers. Ornamentation for mates…and since Skibbard was not particularly interested or capable in that regard, he found Gavin's decoration decidedly unimpressive.

"Where am I?" he inquired.

"In the Republic of Borrin," Gavin answered.

"R.O.B.?" Skibbard pressed. "Seems right."

"I've arranged for transport back to the kingdom of Pravus," Gavin informed, ignoring Skibbard's quip. "As a token of apology, I will accompany you myself, and provide you with enough money to keep you comfortable for the rest of your life."

"I'd be more comfortable without money," Skibbard grumbled. But he stepped out of his cell, eager to leave it behind.

"I'll have one of my employees bring you your clothes," Gavin told Skibbard. "We'll leave for Pravus tomorrow."

Then the man stood there, clearly expecting Skibbard to thank him. Skibbard just stared at him. Silently. Eventually, Gavin cleared his throat, turning around and walking back down the hallway toward the door.

"Follow me," he told Skibbard. And Skibbard did, not once looking back at the cell he'd spent half a year in. For though his home in the forest had been destroyed, the trees burnt to a crisp, he would soon find a new home where he could rest. For there was nothing more magical to him than plants, and in Pravus, plants were in marvelous abundance.

Home was just a few seeds away, and with their magic, he would grow roots in fresh soil. And, nurtured by the warmth and light of the sun, Skibbard would leave the sterile boxes of Man behind, and allow the world in instead of shutting it out.

Chapter 11

After what seemed like an interminably long ride, Chauncy spotted something rather spectacular in the distance. Grassland gave way to the tree line of a forest of truly massive proportions, with trees that grew hundreds of feet tall, and were as thick around as any Chauncy had ever seen. Actually, they were precisely as thick as the thickest trees he'd seen. So much so that he frowned, glancing at Nettie, still seated in the carriage to his right.

"What the hell?" he blurted out.

"It's the Great Wood," she confirmed, smiling at the majestic forest. Countless trees with silver bark like elephant skin greeted them, massive branches extending horizontally for dozens of feet in either direction before plunging back into the earth. And forming more trees wherever they plunged. It was a sight immediately recognizable to Chauncy, for he'd seen it precisely twice before.

"What the hell?" he repeated. "Why are we here?"

"We have to go here," Nettie explained.

"But we've already been here," Chauncy retorted.

"Even so," Nettie insisted.

Their rainbow-maned horse – still ridden with considerable expertise by Valtora – led them into the Great Wood, and they were soon surrounded by forest-ial majesty.

"What are we doing here?" Chauncy pressed. "We're supposed to go to Mount Thrall!"

"We have to go through the Great Wood first," Nettie explained. "And through the Cave of Wonder."

"We already did that," he protested.

"We have to do it each time," she insisted.

"But why?" he pressed.

"Have you ever defied a prophecy before?" Nettie retorted. Chauncy frowned.

"Does delaying it count?"

"No," she answered. "Now shut up Chauncy," she added. Chauncy's jaw snapped shut, unaccustomed to the treatment that had typically been limited to Harry. Still, his thoughts continued unabated, questioning the logic of going through the whole rigmarole once again. But despite his silent protestations, they made their way to the edge of the Great Wood, until their carriage could go no further. They exited the carriage, unhitching the horse from it. The menfolk got the packs from the luggage compartment, loading them onto Rocky's back, and then everyone climbed aboard Rocky…save for Valtora. Having mounted her stallion, she made it quite clear that she preferred riding him to joining the others.

With that, they entered the Great Wood, the oldest of the kingdom's magical forests. It was a place plucked out of a fairy tale, with the biggest beech trees Chauncy had ever seen. Magnificent silver trees that had bark like elephant skin, with copper-colored leaves forming a marvelous canopy high overhead. One that shimmered as the leaves danced in a warm breeze, sending spots of sunlight twinkling on the forest floor.

It'd all been magical the first time around, but now Chauncy found them mundane. Mere scenery to be passed through on the way to his grim task.

"I still don't understand why we have to do all this," Chauncy grumbled from atop Rocky's back.

"It's like, *prophecy* and shit," Valtora reminded him.

"That's what I said," Nettie agreed. And then looked irritated that she'd agreed with her.

"It doesn't make any sense!" Chauncy insisted.

"Magic doesn't have to make sense," Nettie shot back. "If you want things to make sense, try engineering."

"Ugh," Valtora said, making a face.

"Or plumbing," Harry added helpfully. Valtora's eyes brightened.

"That's better," she opined.

"So what, we go back to the Cave of Wonder?" Chauncy pressed, irritated with all of them now. He threw up his hands. "This is ridiculous! We're wasting time!"

"Shut up Chauncy," Nettie snapped.

"Yeah, stop being such a little *bitch*," Valtora piped in.

Chauncy blinked in surprise, but found Valtora smiling happily. She loved a good roasting nearly as much as a heated argument, and one often led to the other. At the moment, he didn't want to give her the satisfaction of either, so he kept quiet. Much to her disappointment, to *his* satisfaction.

"Bitch-ass bitch," Valtora added hopefully, but fell silent as soon as it was clear that Chauncy wasn't going to take the bait. Everyone fell silent then, Rocky bringing them further into the woods, and Valtora riding beside them. And in that silence, Chauncy found his mind free to wander. But minds only wandered when generally happy, or at least at peace. Troubled minds, in contrast, tended to ruminate. Which is exactly what Chauncy found himself doing. Mostly about The Dark One and Valtora, and their secret union. Which unfortunately conjured up visions of them…unioning, in a variety of grimace-inducing ways.

He sighed, tearing his mind from his morbid thoughts and focusing instead on what exactly he was going to do to beat The Dark One. For other than his staff, Rooter, and the Wetstone, he had no new weapons to speak of. And if he didn't make any more before they reached Mount Thrall, they were all going to be in deep trouble.

Onward they went, minutes passing into hours. At length Chauncy felt the air grow a bit chillier, even though it was only a little past noon. He soon found the reason: they were nearing a large lake within the forest, one quite familiar to him. It was the same lake he'd come to with Nettie and Harry six months ago, during his first date with destiny. After standing destiny up for a good twenty-four years.

But what a date it'd been.

He gazed at the lake's shimmering surface, ripples glittering like diamonds in the sun, and realized he was smiling. For the sight brought back fond memories of his adventure with Nettie and Harry. An adventure that'd helped him find himself. Heck, even the lean-to they'd built a ways from the shore was still there, though the roof had collapsed.

"Lean-to leaned a bit too much," Harry mused, eyeing the shelter. Nettie rolled her eyes.

"You come up with that all by yourself?" she asked.

"I thought it was pretty good," he admitted.

"Now that's why you only get a penny for your thoughts," she retorted, glaring at him. Then she broke out into a chuckle, and he did too.

Chauncy smiled at the two, shaking his head.

"Brings back memories, eh?" Nettie mused, elbowing Chauncy and giving him a little smile. He smiled back.

"Sure does," he agreed.

He took a deep breath in, enjoying the aroma of flowers and trees and the crispness of nearby water. As they passed the tree line and made their way toward the lean-to, he felt his worries slip away. And in that moment, he was *in* the moment, without a care in the world. The future faded, replaced by the now, and he found it utterly delightful. For the forest encircling the lake was simply bursting with color, bright green moss covering the thick roots of the trees, orange mushrooms clinging to the trunks. Wildflowers grew in clusters, all purple, pink, and blue. Even the sky seemed to burst brighter blue, puffy clouds a happy white high above.

"There's the Chauncy I know," Nettie said, her smile broadening. She patted him on the shoulder. "Welcome back, kid."

"Thanks," he replied. "Sorry for being…"

"A little bitch?" Nettie guessed. He nodded reluctantly.

"It's been a long couple of days."

"Don't I know it," Nettie agreed. "Nothin' like worry to take the magic out of life," she mused. "Your head's a horrible place to spend too much time in."

"It'd rather spend time in you," Harry said, waggling his eyebrows at her suggestively.

"Not that head, prick," she retorted.

"See, now that's the one I was talking about."

"Hardy har har," Nettie grumbled. "All right Chauncy, go have fun in the Cave of Wonder. We'll wait for you here."

"Oh boy!" Valtora exclaimed, grabbing Chauncy's hand and pulling him toward the lean-to. She reached it, and promptly bent down to pull up the fallen roof. "Come on Chauncy, help me get it up."

"Uh…" Chauncy began, staring at her.

"Come *on*," she urged, giving him a devilish smile. "They said they'd wait for us."

"Not *that* Cave of Wonder, idiot!" Nettie yelled. Chauncy grimaced, blushing a bit, and Valtora's face fell.

"Oh," she mumbled, standing up and brushing her hands on her thighs. "Fine." Then her expression brightened. "Maybe after?"

"Definitely," Chauncy agreed. Valtora beamed at him, skipping to his side and giving him a kiss. The kind of kiss that no respectable woman would give in public. But Valtora was far from respectable, having chosen to be exceptional instead. Which was, Chauncy realized in that moment, one of the things that made her so magical to him.

"You enjoy that cave, lover boy," she purred. "But when you're good and finished, come back to me so I can *reclaim* you."

"Um…?" was all he could say.

"I'm practicing," she told him. He frowned.

"For what?"

"You'll see," she promised with a naughty gleam in her eye. Then she waved at him. "Bye-bye now."

He waved back, which was silly, seeing as they were standing a foot away from each other. Then he turned, walking away from her toward the shore, going rightward along it. There was a cliffside on the other end of the lake, where the entrance to the Cave of Wonder could be found. He glanced back, seeing Valtora blowing a kiss at him. He pretended to catch it, then blew a kiss back. Valtora's head snapped back, and she flew backward, falling onto her back on the ground. Chauncy gasped, freezing in place…but Valtora sat up, giving him a big grin and a thumb's-up. He chuckled, shaking his head…and saw Nettie slamming the palm of her hand into her own forehead. Over and over again. Harry rubbed her back, apparently in an effort to console her.

"All right," Chauncy told himself, facing forward once again. "Let's get this over with."

* * *

The entrance to the Cave of Wonder was barely more than a narrow slit in the vertical rock wall of the cliffside on the opposite end of the lake, so narrow that at first pass, Chauncy missed it entirely. He went too far around the shore, then circled back, studying the rock wall more carefully this time. And that's when he found the entrance, just wide enough for him to squeeze through. Or at least it had been six months ago. He'd gained a bit of weight since then, what with all the breakfasts he'd been eating. Still, he gave it a go, turning to the side and shoving himself in, grimacing at the uncomfortable pressure. He was struck with a sudden fear that he'd get stuck and not be able to go all the way in…or pull himself out.

"Crap!" he grunted, sucking in his belly as best he could and forcing himself in. The rock walls on either side scraped his belly and back, but he popped through into the tunnel beyond. And promptly realized he hadn't brought a torch like Harry had last time.

"Crap," he repeated. Then he thought about having to go back out of the cave. "Crippity-crap crap!"

He sighed, then had a bright idea. The Sunstone! Reaching into his right robe pocket, he retrieved the fist-sized hunk of yellowed quartz. It absorbed light, and then when activated, released it. With a thought, it glowed quite brightly, illuminating the tunnel. The tunnel was still quite narrow, but not as much as the entrance had been, and he made his way forward. The tunnel went straight for a long ways – far longer than he remembered from his first venture – and with every step, he found himself becoming more anxious. The last time he'd been here, he'd fallen abruptly down a shaft, gravity had shifted, and he'd entered into a bit of a feverdream of sorts, yelling at a chair and such.

But instead of all that, the tunnel just kept going. And in fact, instead of a sudden drop, it angled slightly upward.

"Maybe I went in the wrong hole," he thought out loud. A mistake he'd made in the past, though it'd turned out all right in the end. The tunnel made a sudden turn left, continuing onward for a while, then turned left again. And then *again*. He paused, scratching his head and glancing backward. "I *definitely* went in the wrong hole," he muttered.

And then the Sunstone winked out, plunging him into utter darkness.

"What the...!" he blurted out, freezing in place. He gripped the Sunstone tightly, willing it to turn on again. But instead of it doing so, he saw a different sort of light. A thin rectangle a few yards ahead, like sunlight peeking from around the outside of a door. He hesitated, then walked up to it, reaching out to where a doorknob would be...and found that there was one there. He twisted it, and the door swung open, revealing a blinding light.

Chauncy squeezed his eyes shut, waiting for them to adjust, then peered out, using his hand as a visor...

...and found himself standing behind the counter of A Little Magic.

Dong!

The door opened, and an elderly man stepped inside. A terribly familiar old man, tall and thin, and sporting thick glasses. It was Mr. Schmidt, the creepy old man who loved Valtora's lotion.

"Morning," Mr. Schmidt greeted, waving a hand. That glistened in the light, Chauncy noted. From Valtora's lotion, he hoped. The old man reached the counter, extending a hand for Chauncy to shake.

"Um...morning," Chauncy replied, grimacing at the offered hand. He shook it reluctantly, as it'd be rude not to, and found the old man's hand disturbingly slick. Moist. Soft. His grip was quite firm, but not painfully so. Chauncy pulled out of it, which was easy to do.

"Where's all the lotion?" the old man demanded. Chauncy blinked, then turned about, looking at the Lotions & Potions aisle. It was utterly empty of Mr. Schmidt's preferred product.

"Um..." Chauncy mumbled.

"You promised to make more!" Mr. Schmidt accused.

"I know," Chauncy replied apologetically. "Things came up."

"They always do," the old man replied. Creepily. "You should keep your promises," he chided.

"I'll do it tonight, Chauncy promised. And felt rather awful about it, knowing that it was a lie. But seeing as this was the Cave of Wonder, and therefore not at all real, it didn't really matter. Mr. Schmidt nodded, then left, and Chauncy sighed. He nearly wiped his hands on his robe, then thought better of it, wiping it on the counter instead.

Then he froze

For while his hand was now mostly lotion-free, it was also free of color. Utterly gray...and while he could move his fingers, they had no feeling at all.

"Huh," he muttered, sliding his numb fingertips over his...

Dong!

The door swung open, and an elderly woman came in. It was Mrs. Biggins, he realized. She squeezed her wide hips through the doorway, then immediately glared at him, looking as if she'd just bit into a cow pie.

"Mrs. Biggins!" he greeted, hiding his numb hand under the countertop.

"Where's my healing magic?" she demanded.

"Um..."

"Did you make it?" she pressed, waddling up to the counter. Chauncy grimaced.

"Well, something came up," he admitted. "My..."

Dong!

Another customer entered the shop, but Mrs. Biggins snapped her fingers in Chauncy's face.

"Chauncy!"

"It was an emergency," he insisted.

"My *wrist* is an emergency!" she retorted, showing him her wrist. In a way that, had she extended her finger, would have communicated precisely how she was feeling.

"Sorry," he replied. "I'll get on it."

"That's what you said before," she pointed out. "Being a wizard comes with responsibilities, Chauncy," she reminded him, jabbing an arthritic finger into his breastbone. Using her bad hand, he noted.

"Don't I know it," he grumbled.

She gave him a nasty look, then turned about, leaving the shop. And nearly knocking over the other customer in the process. A very tall man. A very *muscular* man. A man in a black and gold uniform, a golden crown on his head.

"King Pravus!" Chauncy blurted out.

"Indeed," the monarch replied. He arched an eyebrow. "Have you defeated The Dark One yet?"

"Um…no," Chauncy confessed. "But I'm…"

"What?!" Pravus replied incredulously. "Chauncy, you're a Chosen One!"

"I know," Chauncy stated. "I…"

"You're a wizard, Chauncy," King Pravus chided, putting his hands on his hips. And flexing his enormous lats. "You have responsibilities."

"I know," Chauncy repeated. King Pravus shook his head disapprovingly, then blinked, staring at Chauncy's chest.

"What's wrong with you?"

"Pardon?"

"Your chest," the man clarified. "What's wrong with it?"

Chauncy looked down, and his eyes widened. For just like his right hand, a large spot on his chest was gray, the color sucked right out of it.

"Oh," he mumbled, clutching his gray hand to his gray chest. And turning a bit gray in the face at the sight of it.

"Better get going," King Pravus warned. "You don't have much time left."

Then the man left, and Chauncy felt a sudden pain in his chest. It was an awful, twisting pain, and he gasped, clutching at his breastbone.

"Son of a…" he blurted out, gritting his teeth. The pain grew, spreading across his whole chest and radiating to his back. He looked down, seeing the grayness spreading across his chest and up his shoulders, as if all the color were being sucked out.

Dong!

The door swung open, and Chauncy looked up, seeing Valtora standing there. Her eyes lit up.

"Baby!" she cried.

"Valtora!" he blurted out, relieved to see her. "What're you doing here?"

"Oh *baby*," she repeated, her eyes twinkling. "Give it to me."

"Um...right now?" he asked. The pain in his chest started to lessen, and in fact his whole chest became numb, like his right hand. That numbness spread up to his shoulders gradually, going wherever the color left.

"Yeah baby," she cooed. "I'm coming."

"Come on in," he prompted. For she was still in the doorway.

"I'm coming!"

"I heard you the first time," he stated, a bit irritated now.

"Oh god!"

"Valtora," he began...and then stopped. For he realized that there was someone behind Valtora. *Right* behind her. A figure shrouded completely in shadowy fog-armor, twin red eyes seeming to bore into his very soul. A chill ran down his spine, and his eyes widened in horror.

The Dark One!

"Come on, Hubby!" Valtora urged. "Get it!"

And Chauncy realized quite suddenly that The Dark One was, in fact, in the very midst of following Valtora's commands. And that like with Chauncy, her color was slowly fading, grayness spreading across her body until it enveloped everything but her diamond hand.

The evil bastard roared, and Valtora's diamond hand dimmed, turning utterly gray. And as it did so, the color in Chauncy – and the shop, and everywhere – vanished.

The Dark One's black fog-armor billowed outward, flowing in a never-ending stream from him in all directions. Into the shop it went, filling it completely, until only darkness remained.

Chapter 12

Immersed in utter blackness, Chauncy did the only thing he knew how to do in such a situation:
He panicked.
First he hyperventilated, his heart threatening to burst out of his chest. Then his lips and fingers turned numb. He sank to his knees, clutching them and feeling like he was going to die. The numbness that'd claimed his hand and chest earlier receded, the pain in his chest returning with a vengeance. A pressure unlike anything he'd ever felt, as if Rocky had stepped onto his chest.
"Oh god," he gasped. "Oh god!" All while hoping beyond hope that the blackness would go away. That the light would somehow return.
But it didn't.
Minutes passed. Then what felt like hours. And, as a candle burning brightly couldn't burn for long, his panic gradually subsided. It was replaced by sheer exhaustion. An acceptance of things. For, unable to do anything to change his situation, he had no choice left but to accept it.
Only then did the light return.
He found himself in a large circular chamber with walls made entirely of huge amethyst crystals, with a domed amethyst ceiling high above his head. Magnificent wooden bookshelves were arranged in a spiral configuration in the chamber, with occasional breaks to allow people to pass through. The bookshelves were at least a foot taller than Chauncy, their beautiful dark wood polished to a mirror-shine. And upon their shelves were countless wonderful books. Not the kind of books you'd find in Borrin, of course. Those books were purely functional, with boring covers and spines, and plain white paper. Made purely for the purposes of information storage and transfer.
But *these* books...
Their spines were beset with jewels, their titles embossed with gold and silver leaf. Their paper had golden edges, and their scent

screamed – from his previous experience – of ancient important tome.

After the gray-on-gray of his previous experience, the sheer intensity and variety of color in this cavern was mind-blowing. A feast for starving eyes. Chauncy broke out into a relieved smile.

"Hello you," he told the place.

He strolled along the outer portion of the spiraling bookshelves, studying the spines of the tomes. "Bless to Become Your Best," one read. "Robes and Globes," read another. "Liches are Snitches," read a third. They all had fun little titles, bedazzled with playful colors. It was all faintly ridiculous, and a few of the titles made Chauncy chuckle. "Mods for Rods." "Love Potions & Love Lotions."

He pulled out "Mods for Rods," cracking the book open. Any reasonable wizard would've imagined the book to be about magical rods, but this book was clearly not. For it showed rather lovingly crafted illustrations of magical codpieces. And, as he turned a few pages, little helmets for, ah, little heads. Ones that would most definitely not offer any protection at all, at least from blows to the skull.

"This is stupid," he blurted out incredulously. He flipped a few more pages, and saw one that looked like a little unicorn head, complete with a very sharp looking horn. One that he couldn't imagine would ever be permitted in a…Cave of Wonder. He imagined himself wearing it, and Valtora's inevitable reaction. Which made him giggle rather stupidly.

He shook his head, putting the book back on the shell.

Chauncy strolled around the perimeter of the bookshelves, which naturally led him through the spiral toward the middle. "Hexes and Exes." "Devils of a Time." "The Magic of Magic."

He stopped at this last one, eyeing it curiously.

Pulling it from the bookshelf, he found that it was possessed of an absolutely ridiculous purple cover. The title was embossed with gold, and so pointlessly over-fancy that it was nearly impossible to read. And the letters were so big that some fell off the page. The purple glittered precisely like Chauncy's robe, and the amethyst ceiling above his head. And – this was very odd – its weight was sideways. Meaning that instead of being heavy down, it was heavy *right*. He nearly dropped it in surprise, and if he had, it would've fallen to the rightmost wall.

"The hell?" he blurted out.

He rotated his body ninety degrees, but still, he felt its weight going to his right. So its weight was relative to him, and no matter where he was facing, it was right.

"Guess I picked the right book," he joked lamely.

He flipped the book open, then gasped. For the letters on the page tumbled right out, falling rightward to strike the bookshelf to his right. The letters scattered across the spines of the books there, while others landed on the floor, all jumbled up.

Crap!

But a few of the letters hadn't fallen out: the title of the first page. "How to Deal With Weighty Text," it read. And unfortunately, the instructions of how to do so had just fallen out.

"Well how in the hell?" he wondered, staring at the mostly-blank page, then at the scattered letters. For the book had posed an impossible problem, in that the solution to the problem was the problem itself.

Then his eyes widened.

The solution to the problem is the problem itself.

His mind blew open, and he felt quite suddenly that he was *here* and *now*, this moment crystallizing in his consciousness. And whereas before this cavern had been mere scenery, a passing-through kind of space, a step on a staircase, a means to an end, in this moment it *was* the end.

He was *here.*

Chauncy gazed all around him as if seeing the underground library for the first time. He felt the space within the chamber as well as its substance, each glittering facet of the amethyst ceiling a world unto itself. His gaze fell to the amethyst floor, and he was struck with amazement, for he knew with sudden certainty that he was not being pulled down to it, but that it was pressing up on him. Holding him up. And the fact that the world would do such a thing for him was profoundly comforting. He felt the weight of the air upon his skin, and knew that without it, he would explode.

The universe was holding him up and keeping him together, so by golly, everything was going to be alright.

Chauncy broke out into a goofy smile, feeling positively giddy at the revelation. But it wasn't long before the feeling passed, and as it did, revelation transformed into information, losing its power. And without feeling, knowledge had no magic at all.

He sighed, looking down at the book. And then did a double-take, for the words had returned to the page. But the words were utter nonsense, letters arranged haphazardly in no particular order. Chauncy supposed it didn't matter what the words said, for what they'd done had done more than enough.

He closed "The Magic of Magic," and was about to put it back on the shelf when something made him pause. He stuffed it into one of the large pockets of his wizard's robe instead…the right one. But it pulled to the right, making his robe bulge out weirdly. So he switched the book to his left pocket, and the book "fell" against his hip instead, resting there weightily.

He resumed his walk, feeling a bit lighter as he strolled around the bookshelves, eventually reaching the center. He eyed more of the books, but after the last one, he didn't feel the need to read them.

"Well then," he told himself. "Better get to work."

So he made his way from the center of the chamber, toward the far wall. And promptly tripped, landing on his hands and knees on the floor. He grunted, looking back what he'd tripped on. It was, he found, a word. The word "word," actually.

"Huh," he muttered, getting to his feet. He resumed walking, and then tripped *again*, falling onto his chest. Air blasted from his lungs, and he gasped, looking back. He'd tripped on the word again, for it'd moved. Apparently to trip him up again. "Cut it out," he scolded it. And then felt rather ridiculous, realizing he was using words against a word after tripping over words. He shook his head, then blinked, staring down at the floor. Millions of crystalline facets greeted him, glittering like diamonds. And, being translucent, he could see *beyond* the surface, deep into the floor itself. More facets gleamed under the surface, getting dark and deeper purple the further down he looked. And the deeper he looked, the deeper he saw.

He moved his head from side-to-side, watching the facets glimmer as his perspective changed. And with each change in perspective, more beauty was revealed to him.

It was, he found, simply *marvelous*.

Chauncy crawled on his hands and knees, studying the floor, getting lost in its infinite details. Until the aching of his knees and shoulders pulled him reluctantly from his sudden obsession. He got to his feet, glancing back at the word he'd tripped over. But it was gone…and he suspected it'd returned to "The Magic of Magic" after having tripped him up.

"Huh," he murmured, pulling the book out of his pocket partway. Its cover glittered identically to the floor. As if the magic of this chamber was the magic of the book. As if the book and the chamber were one, their magic shared. "The magic of magic," he murmured, smiling at the book, then returning his gaze to the floor. "Okay," he told it. "I think I get the point."

For the point was to not have one. Only in these moments had Chauncy found any magic at all.

The solution to the problem is the problem itself.

And while he didn't understand quite what that meant, if felt somehow right, as if it were what he'd come here to discover in the first place. To the point where Chauncy didn't feel like staying here for a single second longer. So with that, he made his way out of his little library and down the tunnel toward his destiny. And though he left the cave behind, he took a bit of its wonder with him.

Chapter 13

King Pravus was having a positively piss-poor day. He'd received word from one of his lords that the kingdom had been attacked the night before, an army of goblins and zombies and such descending upon one of the towns some fifty miles from Mount Thrall. The awful army had decimated the town, massacring its poor citizens and burning the buildings to the ground. It was all-too-clear who was responsible for the attack, of course. It could only be one person. Or rather, personification. The personification of evil itself.

The Dark One.

"Desmond!" he barked, whilst slumped miserably in his throne. He'd started off perky enough, ramrod straight as was his favorite posture. But, having been forced to skip his morning workout for an emergency meeting with the aforementioned lord – and then travel by dragon to the town that'd been razed – he found he just wasn't in the mood for monarching. Thus his current flaccid state. A state he rarely found himself in, particularly in the evening.

"Desmond!" he barked.

"Yes, sire?" the old-ish man replied. For, as usual, his faithless but loyal servant was standing at his side. Pravus eyed him irritatedly, noting the man's forward-slumping shoulders. Poor posture, a sign of weak scapular muscles. Which of course put undo tension on the muscles of the back of the neck, and caused headaches. Indeed, just looking at Desmond was giving *Pravus* a headache.

"I'm irritated," Pravus announced.

"Would it help if I left?" Desmond inquired. For the man knew very well that his being alive, much less in close proximity, was irritating to Pravus.

"I'm willing to try it," Pravus replied. Desmond gave a bow, and Pravus sighed again. "Bring me food, Desmond. And wine."

Desmond raised an eyebrow. For as a rule Pravus didn't drink, for fear of alcohol stunting his muscle development.

"At once, sire."

"I'll be in my office," Pravus declared.

With that, the man left, and Pravus was alone in his throne room. Save for his ridiculous number of royal guards. And a few servants at the ready, cowering in the back of the room. But they were all but invisible to Pravus, as they were always there, and rarely moved. As such, they might as well have been furniture. He sighed for the umpteenth time that day, standing up from his throne and making his way down the fancy-shmancy red carpet to the double-doors at the end. These opened for him, of course, and he made his way through the labyrinthine hallways of his ridiculously enormous castle, trailed by his usual contingent of personal guardians. All *thumpity-thumping* in step. All of them marvelously fit men with big spears and swords ready to penetrate anyone who dared to penetrate Pravus.

Without his permission, anyway.

Unfortunately, his unexpectedly sabotaged day had necessitated that he forgo permissible penetration, which didn't help Pravus's mood one bit. He needed a pick-me-up, he realized. A ray of sunshine to cut through the dark clouds that'd conspired to blacken his day. There was nothing quite as frustrating as unmet expectations, and today, not a single one had been met.

"Someone!" he snapped. "Get me Templeton!"

Someone left to do just that, naturally.

Pravus made his way to his office, a room far larger than necessary for its function. Bookshelves bursting with books lined the walls, an oversized chair set before an oversized desk upon which oversized stacks of papers had been placed. By people whose sole purpose in life was to torture Pravus, if you asked him. For while his father had found the duties of being a monarch magical, for Pravus, they were merely mundane. Chores to endure, as evidenced by the fact that he checked the time constantly to see if his obligations were complete. Something he never did in the gymnasium, of course. For when it came to doing what one loved, there was never enough time in the day to do it, but when doing anything else, it seemed like the time spent doing so would never end.

Pravus slumped into his chair, drooling down to a slouched position within it. He stared at the stacks of paperwork nagging him, and glared at them petulantly.

"Shut up," he told them. But being paper, they were unimpressed with his title as king, and stayed right where they were. There was a knock on the door, and Pravus felt a burst of hope. "Enter," he ordered. And the door opened, and Templeton entered.

"My liege," Templeton greeted. His tone was subdued, and he gave a more formal bow than normal. Clearly he'd heard of the tragedies perpetrated by The Dark One.

"Have a seat, dearest cousin," Pravus prompted. Templeton complied, sitting on a chair opposite his desk.

"I heard the news" he stated. "Terrible."

"I've sent two legions to the area to defend the surrounding towns and help survivors," Pravus told him.

"A sizable force indeed," Templeton replied.

"I fear it may not be enough," Pravus warned. "Survivors say The Dark One's minions numbered in the tens of thousands, if not more."

"Are they sure?" Templeton inquired.

"They seemed sure," Pravus answered. "But the truth is often not what it seems to be."

"Indeed."

"But if it *is* true, then we're in deep trouble," Pravus muttered, leaning back in his chair and sighing heavily. "Where are those damn Chosen Ones?"

"We're not sure," Templeton admitted with a grimace. "I have scouts on the main road to Mount Thrall, but there's been no sign of them on it."

"That doesn't make any sense," Pravus complained irritably. After all, if those damn wizards had just done their jobs six months ago instead of dicking around in Borrin, those poor townspeople wouldn't have been massacred, and their town would still be standing instead of burnt to a crisp. "*They're* to blame for this," he accused.

"You're not wrong," Templeton agreed, if reluctantly. For it was poor form to think badly of Chosen Ones. They were heroes, after all. The finest people of their generation, chosen by fate itself to rise above their fears to defeat evil so that good might triumph.

Or at least they were *supposed* to be.

"Chosen Ones don't just run away from their destinies," Pravus stated. "Why, it's unheard of!"

"I've never heard of it," Templeton concurred.

"Because it's never happened!" Pravus agreed. With himself, as he always did. For, being king, few had the testicular fortitude to disagree with him. And he found it disagreeable indeed to disagree with himself.

In fact, the only man he knew that dared to challenge him on a regular basis was Desmond…and that was the very reason the oldish man had been promoted to an advisor. And Desmond had been *quite* helpful in unmasking Gavin Merrick's little plan to plunder Pravus's people of their magic power.

"Desmond!" he barked, to no one in particular. But of course there were guards just outside of his office that would rush to fulfill his every need. And a select few guards that had agreed to fulfill some very specific needs, now that he thought about it. In absolute secrecy, of course. Except when in groups. Sometimes more than one was far more fun.

The door opened, and Desmond's horrific comb-overed head popped in.

"Yes, sire?" he inquired, stepping into the room and closing the door behind him.

"Come in and put on your advisor's hat," Pravus prompted. For most of the time, Desmond was merely his long-suffering servant.

"I never got one," the old man replied.

"Metaphorically-speaking," Pravus corrected.

"Very well."

"Desmond, I have a big problem," Pravus declared.

"Just one, sire?"

"One pressing one," Pravus corrected.

"Then split them up," Desmond offered.

"I was speaking metaphorically," Pravus grumbled. "What idiot would say that one problem was pressing against another one?"

"I mean split up the problem," Desmond countered.

"Explain."

"You have a big problem," Desmond pointed out. "So cut them up to make a few little ones."

"My problem is The Dark One," Pravus explained. "And while I would *love* to cut him up into little pieces, the fact that I *can't* is precisely my problem."

"So cut up cutting him up into little pieces into little pieces," Desmond replied instantly. Pravus blinked. Then blinked again, as did Templeton. Which made Pravus feel better, because they were both quite intelligent men, as they'd told each other on many an occasion. Yet Desmond's sentence completely baffled them.

"Pardon?" Templeton asked. Far more politely than Pravus would have, bless his heart.

"What do you need to do to kill The Dark One?" Desmond inquired. Like a patient teacher trying to draw an answer out of a particularly dense child, to Pravus's irritation.

"Chosen Ones," Pravus answered.

"And how do you get Chosen Ones?"

"I'm not supposed to get them," Pravus snapped. "The Order of Mundus is!"

"Indeed," Desmond replied. And then just stood there, staring at him. Pravus narrowed his eyes at the man.

"Are you suggesting I put some pressure on the Order of Mundus?"

"Quite."

"Then why are you still looking at me like that?" Pravus inquired.

"What's the first rule your father taught you?" Desmond asked.

"Trust no one," Pravus recited. "Especially yourself."

"Indeed," Desmond confirmed.

"So you're telling me not to trust the wizards in the Order?"

"Are they no one?" Desmond shot back.

"No, they're definitely someone," Pravus grumbled.

"The only one who can be trusted is no one."

"Right," Pravus muttered, rubbing his ridiculously broad and chiseled chin with one hand. "Templeton, what do you think?"

"That a single stick is easily snapped, but many held together are not," his cousin replied.

"So trust no one…means don't trust only one?" Pravus asked.

"Indeed sire," Desmond answered.

"So I can't just trust the Order," Pravus reasoned. "And I can't trust these idiot Chosen Ones," he added. "But if I go after both of them, and look for *other* wizards in my kingdom, and use my army," he continued, feeling a spark of hope. He realized he'd stood from his chair, and was pacing in front of his desk. He stopped, turning to Templeton. "Why, that might just work!"

"It's our best chance," Templeton agreed. "Throw everything we've got at the enemy, all at once."

"An orgy of violence," Pravus mused. "What other choice do we have?"

"Dying horribly," Desmond answered unhelpfully. "And cursing the world for all eternity."

"Cheery thought," Pravus grumbled. "Always so delightful to have you around, Desmond. Your wife must eagerly await your return each and every night."

"Quite the opposite, sire."

"What a sad little life you live, old boy," Pravus mused, shaking his head. "Why on earth do you go on?"

"Hope," Desmond replied.

"That it'll get better?"

"That it won't get any worse," the servant-advisor corrected.

Pravus and Templeton stared at the old man for a while, and then Pravus dropped his face into his hands, rubbing vigorously. At length, he sighed.

"Thank you for your service, Desmond."

"May I leave now?" Desmond inquired. "I have to disappoint my wife."

"How?"

"By coming home," he answered.

"Ah," Pravus replied. "Wouldn't want to not disappoint the old lady, eh? By all means," he prompted, waving the man away. Desmond bowed stiffly, then left, closing the door with a *click* behind him. Templeton eyed the door, then turned a quizzical eyebrow in Pravus's direction.

"Do you suppose he's fooling with us?" Templeton inquired.

"I have no idea, actually," Pravus admitted.

"He can't possibly have *that* terrible a life."

"Don't be so sure, Templeton," Pravus countered. "Desmond has every reason to hate his life."

"Why?"

"Because he's spent it doing what other people want him to do," Pravus explained. "Which is the exact opposite of living, so I'm learning."

"Hmm."

Pravus stood there for a bit, then plopped back into his chair, mulling quite sullenly. Templeton frowned, and then his eyes brightened.

"Say, I know what'll brighten your spirits," he declared. "What say we do some pushups?"

Pravus gave his cousin a sour look.

"Not in the mood," he muttered. Templeton blinked. For while Pravus had been not in the mood for many things, exercise had never been one of them. "In fact, I think I'll turn in," Pravus added.

Not because he had any intention of going to sleep, but because at the moment, he didn't feel like entertaining company any longer. Templeton took the hint, rising from his chair and bowing.

"Then good night, my king," he stated. And walked out, closing the door gently behind him.

Pravus sighed, irritated that his conversation with his cousin had gone the way it had. He'd summoned Templeton to escape his responsibilities for a while, not to have company ruminating over them. His work had spilled over into his relationship with his cousin, and he didn't like it. Not one bit.

He sighed, staring at the mountain of paperwork stacked on his desk. Before all of this, he would've simply ignored it, or thrown it in the trash. Or better yet, had it burned in his bedroom fireplace for a bit of mood-lighting. After all, he was king, and if he didn't want to do something, he very well didn't have to do it.

Except if he didn't do *this* particular work, he likely wouldn't be king for long, which meant he wouldn't be able to do what he wanted. Because he'd be dead.

Pravus had a sudden yearning for the gym, to cast his worries aside and lift a far more manageable weight. A tangible one, one he could see and smell and use his remarkable muscles to challenge. But he simply didn't have the time for it.

And so, confined to his office until late into the night, the weight he hadn't lifted weighed heavily on his mind.

Chapter 14

Chauncy emerged from the Cave of Wonder, passing from dark into light. And as all things were relative, in comparison to the darkness, the light was bright indeed. The sky shone the most brilliant blue Chauncy had ever seen, though it itself had not changed since he'd seen it last. Clouds glowed puffy white, and the lake ahead of him sparkled like a bed of the most precious jewels. Trees in the distance were so deliciously green that it made Chauncy's mouth water to look at them. And even the warm breeze felt marvelous on him, a current of air that caressed his skin and made his silky robe flow sensually around his frame.

He basked in the sunlight, marveling at the sight. And knowing that it'd been there all along, waiting for him to see it.

"I missed you," he told it. The sky, the water, the trees. The universe, in fact. And most of all, the feeling that he was part of it. He took a deep breath in, filling his lungs with the sweet scent of fresh air, then letting it out. Then he strolled onto the shore of the lake, going leftward around the perimeter, back toward the camp on the opposite side. But this time, it was a stroll rather than a walk. A moment in and of itself, rather than an intermission between moments. Much like his trip and fall onto the floor of the cave of wonder, gazing in wonderment at its endless crystalline depths.

This, he realized, was as good as it got. A moment between moments, the *now* in which everything occurred. This was it. And it was always there, waiting for him.

This is where magic comes from, he realized. Not a power drawn from the world, but in moments of clarity, when he felt in relation with it. Magic was connection...and his connection with Valtora was as magical as his staff, or his robe.

Chauncy smiled, his eyes on the glittering surface of the lake. Bedazzled with its own kind of magic...and that magic was itself.

It was a long while until he reached the refurbished lean-to under which Nettie and Harry were seated. Harry with a huge smile on his face, and Nettie with a mischievous twinkle in her eyes.

"Hello," Chauncy greeted, feeling quite alright indeed.

"You're alive," Nettie declared, shooting Harry a glare. "Guess you won that bet, hon," she grumbled. Chauncy blinked, his feeling of ease rapidly retreating.

"Consider it paid," Harry replied with a sly wink.

"Damn right it was," Nettie agreed. "Brings back memories, doesn't it?"

Chauncy frowned, recalling what awful things they'd admitted to doing whilst he'd delved into the Cave of Wonder a half-year ago. And then he tried desperately not to visualize it, with absolutely no success whatsoever.

"Urrgghhhh," he blurted out, retching a bit.

"It wasn't *that* bad," Nettie retorted.

"You're taking it worse than she did," Harry noted.

"Just…stop," Chauncy pleaded. "Where's Valtora?" he inquired, desperate to change the subject.

"She wanted to ride Peter for a while," Nettie stated, pointing off into the forest. "Went that way."

It took a moment for Chauncy to remember that Peter was the name she'd given the horse. The one blessed with a generous endowment.

"I'll be back," Chauncy grumbled, trekking off in the direction Nettie'd pointed. For he had little desire to spend any more time with the elderly couple, what with the horrible images they'd forced into his brain. Luckily, it was easy to see where the stallion – Peter – had gone, as the steed's rainbow-colored dandruff littered the forest floor in its glitter. He left the shore behind, winding through the woods until he spotted Valtora. She was standing next to Peter. Or rather, leaning against his broad, muscled shoulder, stroking his mane rather lovingly while gazing into his eyes. Also lovingly. And with her face and shirt smudged with rainbow-dandruff. Chauncy felt the wonderful calm he'd acquired in the Cave of Wonder break, pierced by irritation, and a stab of jealousy. He strode up to them, making sure to stomp a bit to get their attention. And to break the eye contact.

"Oh!" Valtora blurted out, jumping a bit. And taking a quick step away from Peter. She clutched her hands in front of her lap, giving him the guiltiest smile he'd ever seen. "You're back so soon!"

"Um…yes," Chauncy replied, frowning at her. "What are you up to?"

"Peter was a little stiff and antsy just standing there back in camp," she explained. "So I rode him to help him blow off some pent-up energy."

"Oh."

"How'd it go?" she asked. "Did you find what you were looking for?"

"I think so," he answered. "I..." He stopped, realizing that Peter now had a rainbow-colored horn jutting out of his head, like a unicorn. Then Chauncy's eyes were drawn to Peter. More specifically, Peter's...peter. It was as spectacular as ever, but now it, like his mane and horn, was rainbow-colored. And it positively shimmered in the sunlight. "What the hell?" he blurted out.

"What?"

"Did you...?" he began, looking at her, then at Peter. "Did you bedazzle him?"

"Oh," Valtora mumbled, her gaze drawn to her...handiwork. "Well *yeah*," she answered. "I mean, come on, he was just *begging* to be bedazzled." She smiled, turning to gaze at Peter. "He was beautiful before, but now he's fucking *gorgeous*. And a unicorn!"

"Yeah, okay," Chauncy conceded. Because it was true enough, much as he hated to admit it. "But don't you have to...touch things to bedazzle them?"

"So?"

"His..." he began, then stopped, gesturing at Peter's colorful undercarriage. While giving Valtora a look. She frowned prettily at him.

"Huh?"

"You know," he pressed, gesturing at it again. She just stared at him blankly.

"Huh?"

He heard the *thump, thump* of heavy footsteps behind them, and turned, seeing Rocky stomping up to them, Rooter perched on his shoulder as usual.

"Foooood," he notified them.

"Oh boy!" Valtora exclaimed, grabbing Peter's reins and hauling him back toward the camp. "I'm frickin' *starving*. Come on, Chauncy!"

Chauncy hesitated, still rather irritated, and wanting to finish their conversation. But his stomach was even more irritated, and he sighed, trudging behind them. Eventually they made it back to camp, and found Nettie and Harry sitting by a merrily crackling campfire.

Harry was busy scaling some fish, and looked up from them, smiling at Chauncy and the others as they arrived.

"Have a bite," he offered, offering Valtora a fish. She took it, giving Harry a peck on the cheek as thanks. "Not in front of your boyfriend," he warned, eyeing Chauncy. "He's the jealous type."

"I am not," Chauncy grumbled, glaring at Harry. Then at Valtora. And then glancing at Peter, who was standing awfully close to Valtora. *Obnoxiously* close. Chauncy grimaced, sitting by the fire and crossing his arms over his chest. Harry handed him a plate of fish, but it was still steaming, and he had to blow on it to cool it. Then he ate it…and realized with sudden clarity that he'd been famished. Devouring his meal, he ate a second helping, then a third, until he was sated at last.

It occurred to him then that, despite thirty-four years of life, he still didn't really know when he was hungry. And now that he was full, his irritation with Valtora – and Peter, and pretty much everything else in the world – vanished as if by magic. Perhaps that *was* food's magic, to make everything seem better, even though everything was the same.

"Huh," he mumbled to himself, considering this. For with a full belly and sunlight baking his skin, and the sight and sounds and smells of wondrous nature all around him, he found himself in a philosophical kind of mood. With all of his needs temporarily taken care of, he could truly enjoy the moment.

"Mmm," Valtora said, devouring her own fish. Rocky ate as well, requiring considerably more than everyone else. So much so that Harry ran out. Nettie used the Wetstone to send a stream of water shooting out far over the shoreline, arcing down to the lake. It struck the water…and promptly reversed course, flowing back to Nettie. And, Chauncy found with surprised delight, it brought dozens of fish back with it. They fell onto the ground before Nettie, flip-flopping as violently as a politician during election season before relaxing into their fates. Harry got to work cleaning and cooking, and soon even Rocky's mountainous appetite was sated. For Peter's part, the unicorn ate dull, plain grass. Which served the steed right, in Chauncy's opinion.

With that, everyone sighed contently, sitting by the fire and staring into the flames. Chauncy felt Valtora snake her hand into his, and he glanced at her. She was smiling at him.

"Hey you," she said. He smiled back, giving her hand a squeeze. It was a bit sticky, and still covered in rainbow colors, but he didn't mind.

"Hey *you*," he replied. And leaned in, giving her a kiss. To his delight, she gave a *real* kiss, one that made everyone else groan, and Peter snort.

"Get bent," Valtora grumbled, pulling away.

"Already there," Harry replied with a grin. For he was nearly a hunchback at this point.

"Go blow yourself then," she shot back.

"Halfway there," Harry countered with an even bigger grin. Nettie rolled her eyes at him, but didn't say anything. Which disappointed Valtora, who'd clearly been hoping for a good argument.

"Alright idiots," Nettie declared, standing up with Harry's help. "Time to get moving."

Everyone got up, and Valtora mounted Peter with her customary agility, riding him behind Nettie. Everyone else got on Rocky, and with that, the Chosen Ones – and their friends – continued their journey. For, having reached the Great Wood and plunged into the Cave of Wonder, it was their destiny once again to travel to Mount Thrall.

And this time, they were going to kill The Dark One well and good, so that Chauncy could return to the most magical thing of all: the life *he* wanted to live.

* * *

Mount Thrall was a good week's journey away, or at least it had been the first time Chauncy had taken it. Rocky brought them back to their carriage, and Chauncy and Nettie rode inside, with Harry resuming his customary role as driver. Valtora mounted Peter, and Rocky walked ahead of the carriage to stand guard. Harry brought them to another secret path the Order of Mundus had told him about, one that would lead them to Mount Thrall without attracting any attention from The Dark One's minions.

Valtora rode Peter for a while, then switched to riding inside of the carriage in the middle seat after a bathroom break, much to Nettie's irritation. Valtora smiled at Chauncy, sidling up to him for a bit of shoulder-on-shoulder snuggling. Chauncy smiled back, wrapping an arm around her shoulders.

"Hey babygirl," he said rather sexily.

"Ooo," she replied, her eyes brightening. "My *man*." She rested her head on his shoulder. "I missed you."

"I was right here," he replied.

"Look at you, being all *smooth* and shit," she murmured, eyeing him hungrily. "God, I could just take you right here."

"Please don't," Nettie pleaded. "My heart can only take so much."

"Mine can take a lot," Harry ventured, twisting around to grin at them through the front window. Nettie glared at him, then broke out into a smirk.

"Sure can," she conceded.

"Well we're just a bunch of horn-dogs, aren't we?" Valtora mused. "Like four peas in two pods."

"We ain't like you, hussy," Nettie retorted.

"Mmmhmm," Valtora replied.

"Maybe a little," Nettie conceded.

"Probably a lot," Harry opined.

"Shut up Harry," Nettie grumbled.

"I think he's on to something," Chauncy piped in. "We're both so wrong that we're right."

"*Damn* right," Valtora agreed, giving him the happiest smile he'd ever seen.

"Well *you* certainly are," Chauncy admitted. "You're the wrongest person I know."

"Pretty much," she agreed. Then she paused. "Except maybe The Dark One."

Chauncy felt his mood instantly sour.

"What's that supposed to mean?" he asked.

"Well, he's wrong, but he's supposed to be," she reasoned. "He's everything wrong about the human soul. All of the wrongnesses, you know? And nothing else."

"Oh."

"That's why I ended up hating him," Valtora confessed. "I wanted him to be something more than he was, but he couldn't be. He…he said I completed him, because I made him want to be something more. But he is who he is, and he can't be anything else."

"But you liked him," Chauncy pointed out.

"Once," Valtora admitted. "But I was a teenager when I met him. He was big and strong and authoritative, and *powerful*. I guess I fell for the ultimate bad boy."

"What happened?" Chauncy asked.

"It was great at first," she answered. "I mean, to a teenager, bad boys are the frickin' *bomb*. But in my late twenties, I started to realize that a bad boy was all he was. And when I hit my thirties?" She scoffed. "I mean, *forget* about it."

"So...you don't want him now?"

"Hell no," she confirmed. "I mean, don't get me wrong, I had fun. But The Dark One's an empty bastard. It's *just* fun. And after a while, just fun is no fun at all."

Chauncy frowned, processing this.

"You're what I want," she assured him, kissing his cheek. "I like you just the way you are, and you like me just the way *I* am."

"Well that's true," Chauncy admitted with a smile. "You're the right kind of wrong for me."

"And you're the right kind of right for *me*," Valtora replied. They kissed, and she melted into him, using her tongue with abandon. And almost immediately began to moan, becoming increasingly aggressive.

"Whoa!" Nettie snapped. "Break it up!"

They did so, and Chauncy gave Nettie an apologetic look.

"Sorry," he mumbled.

"I get carried away," Valtora explained.

"Well carry yourself back," Nettie grumbled. "We gotta figure out how we're gonna beat The Dark One."

"Got it," Valtora declared. Her eyebrows furrowed as she went immediately into planning mode. Evil planning mode, as it turned out. For she'd clearly learned a thing or two from The Dark One. "Okay, first we need to deal with his goblins."

"By beating them off?" Harry inquired from the driver's seat.

"No, takes too long," Valtora replied instantly. "Even between the five of us, it'll take hours to pacify them that way."

Nettie buried her face in her hands.

"No, we need to straight up *murder* the bastards," Valtora stated. "They're weak one-on-one, but overwhelm with numbers. So we need a way to kill lots of them at once."

"Like my staff," Chauncy reasoned.

"Or a flood from my Wetstone," Nettie offered.

"Right," Valtora replied. "Wet is better. We'll go with Nettie on that one." She frowned then, rubbing her chin with her diamond hand. "Next we'll need to deal with the lava elementals."

"Flooding again," Nettie stated.

"It'll take a lot," Valtora warned. "Most of the time, when they get wet, things just get hot and steamy."

"I see what you did there," Harry piped in.

"Shut up Harry," Nettie grumbled. "She didn't do anything. She's oblivious."

"So we'll need a lot of water," Valtora continued obliviously, proving Nettie's point. "And then of course there's Magmara."

"The lava dragon," Chauncy realized. "I forgot about her."

"She's a real bitch," Valtora said. "But you beat her the last time."

"True," Nettie replied. "But Harry had to choke that damn dragon, and it nearly killed him."

"I got very hard," Harry agreed. For he'd turned to stone making a giant rock-hand to strangle Magmara.

"Well I'd like you to not get so hard choking The Dark One's dragon, thank you very much," Nettie shot back.

"Now who's oblivious?" Chauncy inquired, raising an eyebrow at her. Nettie grimaced.

"Shut up Chauncy!"

Chauncy smirked, glancing at Harry, who smiled back. He thought back to the last time Harry had talked about him and Valtora. How he'd said that Nettie hated Valtora because they were so much alike. Bat-shit nuts, he'd said.

The right kind of wrong indeed.

"Well, all our powers are the same as the last time we fought that dragon," Harry pointed out.

"Which means *you* need to figure out how to beat that dragon without choking it," Nettie declared, eyeing Chauncy critically.

"A gentler touch might work," Harry agreed.

"That's not what I meant!" Nettie complained.

"No, I think she's right," Valtora interjected, her eyes widening.

"Of course I am," Nettie replied irritably. Then she frowned. "Tell me why I'm right," she ordered. "I like hearing it."

"Never gets tired of it," Harry mused.

"Why beat The Dark One's dragon when you can be nice to it?" Valtora asked. Everyone else joined Nettie in frowning. "Me and Magmara are like this," she added, crossing her fingers. "She's sick of having to pretend to nearly kill Chosen Ones all the time, then pretend to get beaten at the last minute. I mean, The Dark One barely even talks to poor Maggie anymore."

"Maggie?"

"That's her nickname," Valtora explained. "I gave it to her."

"You nicknamed The Dark One's dragon?" Nettie asked.

"Well yes," Valtora confessed, giving Chauncy an apologetic look. "But I'm not talking about Gigantor."

Chauncy blinked.

"Gigantor?" he blurted out.

"I mean, yeah," Valtora replied, her cheeks flushing a bit.

"Why Gigantor?" Chauncy asked. "Wait, never mind," he added immediately. "I don't want to know."

"The point is, The Dark One treats his dragon terribly," Valtora explained. "Just abuses her and expects her to take it...and like it. And I don't think she does."

"So you're saying we should try to make friends with her?" Nettie asked.

"Right," Valtora confirmed.

"And how in the hell do you expect us to do that?" Nettie inquired.

"I'll talk to her," Valtora answered. "We're both super tight."

"Alright," Nettie stated before Harry could comment. "Say we deal with...Maggie. We still gotta beat The Dark One. And that's gonna be real hard if we don't know what he's capable of."

"Pfft," Valtora scoffed. "I know *exactly* what The Dark One's capable of. And with my helping hand," she added, holding her diamond one up, "...we're gonna finish him off once and for all!"

Chapter 15

That evening, long after the sun had gone to bed below the horizon, Rocky stopped at last. He went to the side of the road, well out of sight of any travelers that might use it while they slept. For the surest way to win a fight was to avoid fighting in the first place, according to Harry. With The Dark One's armies on the prowl, avoidance was the most prudent strategy. The Obsidian Ogre was only one of the many awful, powerful minions The Dark One employed. Still only armed with his staff, Chauncy was hardly looking forward to another fight, at least until he made himself a few more weapons.

So, after helping Harry set up the campfire, surrounding it with rocks to absorb and radiate heat for the rest of the night, Chauncy decided he'd better get to magicking, and quick.

"I'm gonna go for a walk," Chauncy notified everyone. Valtora perked up. "For magic," he added hastily.

"Oh," she mumbled. For she knew that, when it came to magic, magic came to him when he was alone. Most of the time, anyway. "Bye," she offered.

"Be back sometime," he promised.

With that, he left the camp, heading off into the starlit wilderness. It was mostly rocks and grass, and a few hills here and there. It reminded him of the walk he'd taken before reaching Mount Thrall, when he'd found Rooter and the Sunstone. He smiled at the memory, stuffing his hands in his robe-pockets.

And found the book he'd taken from the Cave of Wonder still there in his left pocket.

Chauncy pulled it out, surprised as before that it tried to fall rightward instead of downward. He accounted for this awkwardly, then stared at the glittering purple cover. "The Magic of Magic," it read. He smiled again, for it was the Cave of Wonder itself that had taught him the truth he'd forgotten as a child…that magic was magical to him. For the magic of magic made the mundane extraordinary, and in a way, that was his power. With it, a stick could become the Staff of Wind, after all. And suddenly, he felt quite giddy imagining what other ordinary things he would make exceptional.

A world of black and white, waiting to be filled with color! He gazed off at the dark landscape bathed in silver light, and saw that it *was* black and white. Except, he realized, for the book he held. For it appeared somehow as if it were in sunlight, giving off no light itself, but deep, sparkling purple as if brightly lit...like Chauncy's robe.

"Huh," he murmured.

For though he'd worn his robe every night whilst walking home from work with Valtora, he'd never seen his robe light up like this. Color against the dreary darkness, "The Magic of Magic" was a perfect match for him. Nettie connected with water, and Harry with rocks and cloth. Valtora connected with beauty, and Chauncy...well, he connected with the magic in things. Or rather, by connecting with things, he made them magical.

"Connection *is* magic," he realized, his eyes widening.

He looked up from the book, gazing out at the silver-hued landscape. And then upward still, to the starlit sky above. Infinite space, or so he'd been told. But space was supposed to be nothing, and that simply couldn't be true. For nothing couldn't have distance or volume, but space did. It was far *from* nothing. It was almost everything...a vast *thing* that connected everything to everything else, and through which everything was allowed to be.

"Well I'll be," he blurted out. And in that moment, he felt connected to the space around him, that unknowable nothing that was truly something. And through it, he felt connected to the universe, and they were one.

He gasped, a chill running through him, reveling in this sudden revelation. But nothing lasted forever, and the feeling gradually passed. Everything was once more as mundane as it'd been, only the knowledge of the truth remaining. But knowledge was nothing if it wasn't felt...and in not feeling it, Chauncy felt his sense of wonder fade as well.

"That's that," he supposed. And he tried not to be too disappointed. For magic was felt in fits and starts, and wisdom was felt this way too. Nothing was forever, as Nettie had taught him. He'd have to be grateful for having felt it at all.

He sighed, suddenly done with his walk. Turning about, he strolled back toward the camp, following the flickering flames of the campfire. And when he got there, he found his friends seated around it, enjoying its warmth. He sat down beside Valtora – and opposite Harry and Nettie – warming his hands near the flames.

"How'd it go, kid?" Nettie inquired.

"I'm not sure," Chauncy admitted. "I felt magic, but I don't know what it did."

"Well, that's how it is sometimes," Nettie replied. "I'm sure you'll figure it out soon enough."

"Maybe," Chauncy mumbled.

"You always have," Harry pointed out. Chauncy smiled reluctantly.

"True," he conceded. "So far."

"So far so good," Harry replied with a wink. Chauncy chuckled, marveling at the man's constant good nature. Nothing seemed to rattle Harry. The old man was ever-hopeful, and never wavered in his resolve. He was Nettie's rock…and Chauncy supposed that Harry had more in common with the minerals he loved than Chauncy would ever know.

Chauncy stared into the fire, and everyone settled into a comfortable silence. Even Valtora, who leaned against him, enjoying his warmth as much as that from the flames. He settled into a kind of trance, his thoughts scattering like leaves in the wind. Swirling about without aim or purpose, neither worrying nor plotting nor calculating. And in this way, he found himself merely *experiencing*. Wasting his time, and having a wonderful time doing it.

He caught Harry looking at him from across the flickering flames, and the old man smiled, his eyes twinkling from behind his silver-rimmed glasses. He inclined his head, and Chauncy smiled, returning the gesture. Harry didn't need to say anything, because he'd said it before.

I'm old, he'd told Chauncy by the fire, the first time they'd gone to the lake in the Great Wood. *And this is about the best you get.*

And as he eyed the light reflecting off Harry's glasses, Chauncy reflected on the truth of this. It wasn't being by a campfire that made this wonderful, for the flames were just hot gas and light. And it wasn't the darkness of night. No, the magic *was* the moment…and in being *in* it.

"This is magic," he realized, staring into the fire. "Right now."

"Yep," Harry agreed.

"Damn tootin'" Nettie concurred.

"Sure is," Valtora piped in.

Peter whinnied, and Rocky grunted, and even Rooter nodded, the plant atop his head bobbing cutely.

"Ugh, *so* adorbs," Valtora cooed. "I just wanna squeeze your widdle body till you *die*."

"See, that's not a good thing," Chauncy told her.

"Huh?" she asked.

"It sends the wrong message," he explained.

"It's a message of love," she countered.

"It's a message of murder," he retorted.

"It's called hyperbole," Valtora argued, her eyes lighting up. For she'd been itching for an argument. "Idiot," she added, just to stoke the metaphorical flames a bit.

"Yeah, but see, the thing is, you always choose violent metaphors," he reasoned.

"What's that supposed to mean?" she demanded. "Moron!"

"That's not what heroes do," Chauncy told her, ignoring her insults.

"Maybe I don't want to be a hero," she shot back. "Hypocrite!"

Chauncy grimaced. It was true, after all. He was a hypocrite. He wasn't going on this journey because he was a hero...he was doing it for Valtora. For his own selfish reasons.

"What'd'ya gonna say about that?" Valtora pressed. "Thickskull!"

"Thickskull?" Nettie interjected, raising an eyebrow.

"It's all I could think of that started with 't-h,'" Valtora explained.

"She reads the dictionary so she can know insults that start with the same letters," Chauncy informed Nettie.

"And the thesaurus," Valtora added. "Really helps when I'm in a word-finding bind."

"Gotta admit, that's pretty dedicated," Harry told Nettie, giving her a nudge.

"I'll give ya that," she agreed reluctantly. "So toots," she added, eyeing Valtora. "Probably gonna regret asking this, but what's your story?"

"What'd'ya mean?" Valtora asked.

"Well, how'd a...formerly nice girl like you end up married to an asshole like The Dark One?"

"Wow," Valtora breathed, clutching at her heart. "That's the nicest thing you've ever said to me. And you've said a lot."

"Sure have."

"Well, I was ten when Imperius came to me," Valtora began, settling into a storytelling voice. She gazed up at the stars philosophically. "I was young and naïve, just a girl eager to escape her life and find a better one." She sighed. "When Impy came and offered me a chance to be someone…to *matter*…I couldn't say no."

"Didn't have a problem this time," Nettie quipped.

"Shut up Nettie," Harry scolded. Nettie's mouth snapped shut, and she shot Harry a surprised look. But he only chuckled.

"So I went off to the Great Wood and the Cave of Wonder, while Impy showed me my power. The incredible art of bedazzling, of finding beauty in everything…even the things others cast aside."

Rocky thumped a fist on his chest, smiling down at Valtora.

"Like you, tookums," she agreed. "Anyway, I made it to Mount Thrall, and Magmara tried to kill me. But I just…connected with her, you know? I thought she was just gorgeous, and I told her that. I talked, and she grunted, and we became best friends right on the spot. I even bedazzled her tail," she added proudly.

"Like you bedazzled Peter?" Nettie asked.

"Mmhmm," Valtora replied obliviously. "Then Maggie just *had* to bring me to The Dark One, because she thought I was *perfect* for him. Because I could see beauty in everything, you know? Even the most horrible person of all."

"The personification of evil," Chauncy murmured. "You thought he was…beautiful?"

"I saw that he *could* be beautiful," Valtora corrected. "Sure, he was dark and evil and murdered and destroyed shit. But he was also like, *totally* badass, and confident, and fucking awesome, or so I thought at the time."

"So you married him," Nettie stated.

"Not at first," Valtora countered. "I mean *he* wanted to marry me, believe me. Kept hounding me about it, actually. 'Cause honestly, he knew what a hot damn ticket I was," she added, tossing her gorgeous hair gorgeously. And no matter how many times Chauncy had witnessed this display, it never ceased to impress him…or anyone else who beheld it. Even Nettie seemed captivated by it, at least momentarily. She blinked rapidly, then recovered, clearly hating herself for having been so easily hypnotized.

"Then what?" she grumbled.

"Well, I was young," Valtora continued. "And The Dark One knew exactly how to woo me. He was the ultimate bad boy, telling me exactly what I wanted to hear. And honestly, he made it clear that the only way he'd help me fulfill my destiny was if I married him. Otherwise he wouldn't have given me his goblins to make the Amethyst Army, or helped all of you when Evermore attacked."

"Bull," Nettie retorted. "Evermore threatened magic. The Dark One would've helped no matter what."

"Well I know that *now*," Valtora shot back. "But I was young and stupid at the time. Like, fourteen."

Chauncy's eyes widened, his eyebrows shooting up.

"You were *fourteen* when you married him?"

"Uh huh," Valtora confirmed. "Now that I look back, I think I was a little too young to make that kind of decision."

"You don't say," Nettie stated drily.

"It was great at first," Valtora admitted, giving Chauncy an apologetic look. "I mean, who wouldn't love the idea of being married to the personification of evil?"

"Um…everyone?" Chauncy replied.

"But it got old quick," she continued, ignoring his comment. "The Dark One is one-sided, and that one side is dark. And…after a while, I yearned for something more." She smiled at Chauncy, putting a hand on his and squeezing it. "Someone who could bring out the best in me, not just the worst."

"A connection that was beautiful," Harry offered.

"Yeah," Valtora agreed. "I wanted someone to bedazzle…and who would be bedazzled by me, just the way I was. The Dark One never saw the beauty *in* me. Just the stuff on the outside. And don't get me wrong, my outside is *spectacular*," she added rather unnecessarily. For everyone knew damn well how spectacular her outside was. "But my insides are even better."

"I can vouch for that," Chauncy agreed.

"For the love of Pete!" Nettie stated exasperatedly. Peter swung his head to look at her. "Not you," she added. Peter snorted.

"The only reason I strung The Dark One on for three years after we separated was to fulfill my destiny," Valtora concluded. "I pretended to hem and haw, and made it seem like I might come back, and all that. For three frickin' years. When you guys came, it was like *ugh*, finally!" she exclaimed. "Now I don't have to deal with that big ol' dick anymore."

"It was…big?" Chauncy inquired.

"Figure of speech," Valtora answered. "But yes."

"Really?"

"Really," she confirmed.

"Like, for example…" he prompted. She put her palms together, then pulled them apart in what could only be described as a profoundly distressing distance. Chauncy stared at the great, yawning chasm between her hands, his shoulders slumping. Suddenly, space didn't seem quite so magical to him. She followed up by making a modified "OK" sign, but one that required two hands to form.

"Sweet mother of god," Nettie blurted out.

"Wowee," Harry breathed. Even Rocky seemed impressed, and a bit dismayed. And Rooter's plant wilted a bit. Only Peter seemed unimpressed, snorting and tossing his mane rather proudly.

Chauncy's shoulders slumped further, and he suddenly regretted ever asking. Ignorance was bliss, they said. And whoever they were, they were absolutely right.

"You asked," she accused.

Chauncy didn't have the strength to answer.

"I don't get it," Nettie stated. "Why'd The Dark One wanna marry you so bad anyway?"

"Well obviously because I'm awesome," Valtora answered, tossing her hair again. Which helped her case considerably. "When we married, I got some of his essence," she added.

"Ugh," Chauncy said.

"The whole The Dark One fog armor stuff," Valtora clarified. Nettie frowned.

"So that's a part of him in you?" she asked.

"Well…maybe," Valtora answered with a shrug. "I don't know."

"*Neeeeeaaaaaaaooooowww!*"

The screech echoed through the night air, so shrill it send a chill down Chauncy's spine. The hairs on the nape of his neck shot upright, and he shot to his feet.

"What was that?" he blurted out. Valtora stood up, and Nettie and Harry stood as well, with considerably more difficulty.

"*Neeeeeaaaaaaaooooowww!*"

"Damn," Valtora swore, peering up at the starry sky. "Harpies!"

"Harpies?" Chauncy asked.

"Minions of The Dark One," she explained, grabbing his arm. Dark fog swirled around her, forming black armor, complete with a vicious-looking helm, and awful red, glowing eyes peered through it.

"Gah!" Chauncy blurted out, averting his eyes. For to look into those awful orbs was to be filled with terror.

"READY YOURSELVES!" Valtora boomed in The Dark One's voice.

"Neeeeeaaaaaaaoooowww!"

And then Chauncy spotted something swooping down toward the camp, underlit by the flames of the campfire. It was a rather robust woman, with large, dirty-brown wings and long dirty-blond hair. She had the head and torso of a human and the legs of a bird of prey, and a vicious glare that made his sphincter snap shut.

"Holy!" he gasped, ducking down reflexively.

The harpy flew past him overhead, missing him by mere yards, the wind of her passage whipping through him. It landed a few dozen feet away with a *thump*, turning to glare at him again.

"Stay back!" Valtora warned, moving so that she stood between Chauncy and the harpy. Which was comforting on the one hand, and a bit emasculating on the other. But on balance, he was happy to be emasculated, as long as it was for a good cause.

"Valtorrrrrahhhh!" the harpy hissed, its voice making Chauncy's skin crawl. Valtora cast away her fog armor, revealing her gorgeous self.

"Damn right," she confirmed. "What's your stank ass doing here?"

The harpy pointed one long, sharp fingernail at Valtora.

"We're here for *you*," she hissed. "Betraaaaay-YER!"

"Betrayer?" Valtora retorted.

"Fooornicate-OR!" the harpy cried. "Breaker of the sacred vows of matri-MONY!"

"Oh *please*," Valtora countered, her voice dripping with disdain. "Like I started it!"

"Adulter-ER!"

"He screwed six succubi at *once*," Valtora shot back. "On our wedding day!"

"Returnnnn to The Daaaark One," the harpy commanded, "...and faaace your destinnnny!"

"Oh I'll return all right," Valtora countered, making her diamond hand into a glittering fist. "And finish off The Dark One once and for all!"

The harpy blinked.

"By killing him!" Valtora clarified.

"Ahhh," the harpy replied. Her glaring eyes turned to glare at Chauncy then, and her nasty, pointy fingernail pointed right at him.

"Thissss is your fault," it accused. "You dare violate The Dark One's wiiiiife?"

"Um...it's not my fault," he replied. "She didn't tell me."

"Chauncy!" Valtora complained.

"Honestly, I like, just *just* learned," Chauncy insisted.

"Oh my god," Valtora groaned, burying her face into her hands. "You're *such* a pussy."

"I'm just telling the truth," Chauncy countered rather indignantly. "There's nothing...female about telling the truth."

"Uh oh," Harry warned. "Now he's done it."

"SILENCE!" the harpy cried. Its shrill voice cut through Chauncy's flesh and into his soul, and he shuddered, his sphincter spasming again. The vile creature flapped over to Valtora, landing before her. It pointed at Valtora, its finger an inch from her chest. "Abandon these fools and return to your hussssband!"

Valtora replied by sucker-punching the harpy in the face. With her strong hand. The harpy flew backward, landing right in the campfire. And, being quite oily, ignited instantly.

It *shrieked*.

Everyone backed away from the howling harpy, covering their ears. Except for Valtora, who seemed to rather enjoy the sound of the harpy's shrieks. The harpy flapped its burning wings, rising into the air like a phoenix, then flew away from the camp.

"Wait for it," Valtora prompted giddily.

The harpy fell to the ground in a flaming heap, then moved – and screamed – no more.

Valtora cackled.

"Honey, that's terrible," Chauncy admonished. "A living being just died!"

"Terribly," Valtora agreed with a grin.

"It's not funny," he insisted.

"Hate to say it, but I'm with Valtora on this one," Nettie admitted. "That was pretty funny."

"Harry, help me out here," Chauncy pressed, throwing a glance the old man's way. Harry put a hand on his heart.

"A tragedy," he concurred.

"Thank you," Chauncy said.

"Reminds me of an old flame of mine," Harry mused. He nudged Nettie. "She was a harpy too, in a way."

Chauncy sighed, rolling his eyes. And then widened them.

"Uh...guys!" he blurted out.

"*Neeeeeaaaaaaaoooowww!*"

The combined shriek of dozens of harpies pierced the night air, and everyone cowered, covering their ears again. A good thirty of them appeared, underlit by the campfire, their unpleasantly naked bodies diving down at them.

"We're up!" Nettie told Harry.

She grabbed the Wetstone at her bosom, squeezing it. Water exploded out of it in a rapidly expanding sphere, forming a huge, humanoid water elemental easily thirty feet tall. Its chest cavity was hollow, and Nettie floated within it, protected by a windshield of water. She extended both of the elemental's watery hands, shooting powerful jets of water at the harpies.

The harpies dodged as they dived toward Harry, Chauncy, and Valtora, the water jets striking a few of them and sending them hurtling backward the through air.

"Ha!" Nettie cried. "Take that!"

But the other harpies dive-bombed Chauncy and the others, extending their vicious-looking talons to rake at them. Chauncy cried out, ducking down and covering his head as one of them flew right at him. Its claws raked down his back as it flew by, like knives slashing his flesh.

Chauncy bit back a scream.

Valtora, on the other hand, used her diamond fist to punch the harpy attacking her right between the legs. It grunted, flipping head-over-heels through the air before landing in some bushes.

Chauncy recovered, his back hurting terribly. Hot wetness spilled down his back, making his robe slippery there. He spotted more of the awful things diving at Harry and Rock. A few struck Harry, raking at his face and chest. Which did nothing at all, of course, seeing as the man's skin was as hard as a rock. Harry grabbed one by the neck, tossing it into the campfire, then bopped a second on the head with one big fist.

"Honey, are you okay?" Valtora asked Chauncy, rushing to his side. He grimaced.

"I'll live," he replied. "Duck!" he cried, following his own advice as more harpies dove at them. One clipped his shoulder, sending him onto his back on the ground. The impact made his wounds hurt terribly, and this time he did scream.

"Chauncy!" Valtora gasped.

"Meee huuuulp," Rocky declared, stomping over to them. The big stone giant bent over Chauncy, protecting him from the harpies with his broad, stony back. The harpies swarmed over them like a flock of awful pigeons, swooping by to try and claw at them. But their claws were no match for Rocky's thick skin…or Harry's, for that matter. Nettie was just fine in her water elemental, but Peter…

"Peter!" Valtora gasped.

One harpy swooped down, slashing at the stallion's flank. The claws tore his flesh, leaving long, gaping gouges that poured blood down his white coat. He shrieked, rising up on his hindlegs and kicking wildly with his forelegs, but the harpy flew away…while another landed on his back, raking madly at his hindquarters.

Valtora rushed to Peter's aid, but a harpy intercepted her, slashing at Valtora's face. Her head snapped back, and she fell to the ground, clutching at her face. Blood spurted from between her fingers.

She *screamed*.

The harpy circled around, then landed before Valtora, grasping her under the armpits with its talons.

"Chauncy!" Nettie shouted from within the water elemental, even as she blasted at the dozens of other harpies still circling in the air around them. "Do something!"

And in that moment, with the love of his life on the line, Chauncy did just that.

He leapt for his staff, laying on the ground near the campfire, then thrust the end of it at the harpy grabbing Valtora. A missile of pure air struck the harpy in the chest, startling it…and making it stumble backward, letting go of Valtora.

"You want a fight?" he proclaimed, holding his staff out before him. "You *got* one, bitch."

And then he wound up, swinging his staff at the harpy just as hard as he could.

A burst of wind shot outward from the staff, blasting the harpy backward…and making the campfire flare up brilliantly. The harpy – and many of its sisters flying nearby – hurtled backward through the sky, landing with a series of *thumps* on the ground far away. Two more harpies were ignited by the campfire's suddenly roaring flames, burning brilliantly against the darkness of the night. Even Nettie's water elemental suffered the blow, its legs rippling madly and nearly tearing apart under the force of it.

Chauncy gave a grim smile, eyeing the remaining harpies flying above them.

"My name is Chauncy Little," he declared valiantly. "And I'm about to make you bitches *my* bitches."

He slammed the butt of his staff on the ground, wind blasting him straight up into the air a good twenty feet. On a whim, he spun his staff like a top, creating a tornado around him…and making *him* spin too. He grabbed the staff, then used the centrifugal force to swing it like a bat, more powerfully than he ever could have on his own.

And aimed it right at the bulk of the swarming harpies.

Wind shot outward at them in an eardrum-bursting *boom*, so powerfully that it send them flying hundreds of feet backward, tearing the feathers from their bodies and snapping their wing bones with a sound like firecrackers popping. They vanished into the night, screaming shrilly…and Chauncy hurtled backward in equal and opposite force to that which he'd created. But instead of panicking, he played.

"Wooo!" he cried out gleefully.

He thrust the butt of his staff backward and downward, reversing his course, for a moment levitating a good twenty feet above the ground. Then he fell straight down, thrusting his staff downward in the process to slow his fall. He landed quite gently, with hardly a bend of the knees required, and stood there quite valiantly, staff in hand, his magical robes glittering in the night. And for perhaps the second time in his life, he felt a feeling that destiny was right.

"I *am* the Chosen One!" he declared triumphantly.

Chapter 16

Gavin Merrick leaned back in the plush seat of his carriage, watching the horse pulling it through the large front window. The midnight-black horse was a magical creature called a Shadowsteed, one he'd owned for decades. It was able to set its shadow anywhere it wanted, keeping it in place while it traveled wherever he told it to. The shadow would remain behind, pinned in place, but extending outward to wherever the horse was. The Shadowsteed's magic was to recall itself to its shadow's position with dizzying speed on command, a useful ability for a man as busy as Gavin. For with the Shadowsteed's magic, he could vastly reduce the amount of time traveling from place to place, and therefore conduct business at a faster pace.

And in business, the faster the pace, the greater the profit. For efficiency was the key to success in beating one's competitors, and Gavin had bested them all.

But while this fact had once brought him a smug satisfaction, now it meant nothing to him. A hollow victory, an accomplishment composed of the acquisition of sterile, meaningless numbers that – no matter how large he made them – possessed no magic at all. For whereas once he'd taken these carriage rides with Marie at his side, now he was alone. Or rather, he was seated next to Skibbard, the odd little wizard Marie had captured in The Wilds and held captive in Borrin.

Gavin glanced at Skibbard, eyeing the man. He was barely five feet tall, rather squat, and had long, curly black hair and a very long black beard and mustache. His skin was heavily tanned from a life spent in the sun, and lined with deep wrinkles. He wore a simple robe of sorts, one made of animal skins and furs that draped over his body.

In short, he was a very strange – and short – man.

The wizard hadn't spoken a single word to Gavin since they'd started their journey through the various towns of Borrin toward Southwick and the Gate. He was a man completely at ease in silence, more interested in gazing out of the carriage at the passing scenery than at interacting with humans. What the wizard could possibly see in a bunch of trees and spindly shrubs was beyond Gavin. But Gavin knew from experience with the few wizards he'd dealt with over the centuries that wizards were strange people. He'd never met a single one that was normal...not that he'd had the occasion to meet many. And he'd never really talked with one before. Not really.

With no interest in thinking about business, he found himself curious about Skibbard.

"What are you looking at?" he inquired. Skibbard blinked, then turned to look at Gavin with a rather irritated expression.

"What?"

"What are you looking at?" Gavin repeated.

"I'm not looking," Skibbard retorted. "I'm experiencing." And promptly returned his gaze to look out of the window.

"What's the difference?" Gavin asked.

"You wouldn't understand," Skibbard replied dismissively. Gavin suppressed a surge of irritation. After all, he'd saved the man from a life of imprisonment.

"Try me."

"You live a life of symbols," Skibbard told him. "I live a life of experiences."

"Explain," Gavin requested.

"Business," Skibbard stated. "Money. Words," he added, using his hand to mimic a mouth blabbering. "All symbols."

"Businesses aren't symbols," Gavin countered.

"They're imaginary," Skibbard shot back. "Make-believe bodies with make-believe names, symbolized by boxy buildings and logos that are symbols, obsessed with collecting imaginary numbers so it all works."

Gavin processed this, and found it to be technically true.

"I was a businessman once," Skibbard declared, gazing out of the window at the passing trees. Gavin's eyebrows went up.

"Really? Which business?"

"Banking," he answered. "I owned the biggest bank in Grissam. Grissam Accretive Bank."

Gavin blinked. For he'd heard of the bank, of course. It was a large, successful, and highly respectable institution, one he'd done business with personally in the past. He still had several accounts with them.

"What happened?" he asked.

"I got sick from symbols," he replied.

"Why did you get sick of symbols?"

"Sick *from* symbols," Skibbard corrected. "Because they're not real. So my life didn't feel real, so I didn't feel real."

"Huh."

"You know how banks work," Skibbard told him. "Fractional reserves!"

Gavin nodded. Banks worked on the concept of fractional reserves. Essentially, if a customer deposited a gold coin, the bank could lend the equivalent of ten gold coins to other customers…nine of which didn't exist. They were purely imaginary…but the banks could charge interest on that imaginary money. So in countries that used fractional reserve banking – which was all of them, except for Pravus – ninety percent of all money loaned and spent wasn't real.

"Money is a symbol," Skibbard stated. "Fractional reserves are symbols of symbols. Making profits of symbols of symbols so people can spend their symbols of symbols to get real things that distract them from the fact that they spend most of their lives working at something they hate to make more symbols so they can pay back the symbols of symbols they borrowed!"

Gavin frowned, processing this. And again, he found it accurate. Technically.

"So you quit?" he asked.

"Got so sick from symbols that I went into the woods to kill myself," Skibbard confessed with a smile. "And found me waiting for me there instead."

"I…don't follow."

"The real me," Skibbard clarified, turning to eye Gavin with a conspiratorial twinkle in his eye. "Not the me others told me to be, but the me I was meant to be."

Gavin frowned, then turned to look out of his own window at the passing scenery. But all he saw were trees. There was nothing else there for him…nothing else *anywhere* for him. For without Marie, he had nothing left.

"Transactional relationships with compulsion to profit from them," Skibbard mused. Gavin turned to eye the man. "A hard habit to break…especially when that's your relationship to yourself."

"Pardon?"

"You do things to get things from yourself," Skibbard translated. "Exercise to get more life. Eat to be healthier to get more life. Learn a skill to become more valuable. Work to become richer. Always doing to profit from the doing. Never for the doing itself."

Skibbard rolling down the carriage window, a breeze whipping through the carriage. He took a deep breath in, then smiled. And that was the end of their conversation.

Gavin stared at the man for a while, then turned to look out of his own window, picking at his lower lip. He stopped himself, knowing that the act betrayed nervousness. And while he didn't particularly care about what Skibbard thought of him, in business, showing weakness was forbidden. Old habits died hard.

Transactional relationships with compulsion to profit from them.

It was true, he had to admit. Every relationship he'd ever had had been transactional. Except for his mother...and Marie. He'd loved them merely for being them, without getting anything in return except for *their* love. A transaction of love, he supposed. But he didn't give love to get love. He'd given love because it'd been a pleasure to give, not because he'd wanted something in return.

And in his love for Marie, she'd suffered no symbols. No love letters, holiday cards, or gifts of any kind. She'd always considered these with contempt, far preferring *real* love to mere stuff.

Marie had always only wanted *him*. Everything else she could have gotten for herself.

He'd loved her for the love of doing so. For the doing itself, as Skibbard would say.

Gavin spotted the skyline of a great city ahead, and knew that it was Southwick. It wouldn't be long before they reached the Gate, and Skibbard – through his abilities as a wizard – got them through. That fact reminded him of why he'd taken this journey in the first place.

Pravus.

He pictured the man, feeling a familiar anger grow within him. The thought of Marie dying because of the cocky king. Of her taking her last breath alone, without him at her side...

Gavin gripped the armrest of his seat until his knuckles turned white, staring at the cityscape ahead.

I'll avenge you, Marie, he vowed silently.

For though he was Gavin Merrick, owner of the largest supply of magic in the known world, none of that magic had been magical to him. Only Marie had held such power for Gavin, and King Pravus had taken that from him. Now, all the imaginary numbers he'd accumulated, all the *things* he'd hoarded, were as empty and lifeless as her corpse.

And Gavin was going to spend everything he had – including his life, if necessary – making Pravus and the Chosen Ones pay.

Chapter 17

After their harrowing battle with the harpies, Rooter sucked the life out of the few maimed harpies that had any left to give, transferring their life force to Chauncy and Valtora. Thus, Chauncy's back was completely healed, as was a vicious gash on Valtora's forehead. One that'd ruptured her left eyeball, not to get too graphic. The harpies' talons had proven as sharp as their tongues, and if it hadn't been for Rooter, Chauncy's mission would've ended right then and there.

Of course, seeing as how Chauncy had helped defeat the majority of the awful creatures, and had made Rooter's healing magic possible, Valtora saw fit to reward him in grand fashion, after Harry had helped him pitch the tents around the campfire. So it was that Chauncy found himself quite blissfully content within one of those tents, Valtora lying by his side. They were both hot and sweaty, having performed a bit of magic themselves.

"Sorry," he offered, giving her an apologetic look.

"It's okay," she reassured, smiling back. For in the heat of the moment, he'd chosen ovens over buns, and this was a most dangerous decision indeed. A decision that had the potential to perform the most powerful magic of them all…a blessing and a curse, with a heavy emphasis on the 'curse' part, if others were to be believed. "Thanks for saving us," she told him, not for the first time.

"My pleasure," he replied. "Those harpies were terrible."

"Tell me about it," she agreed. "Never could stand them."

"What was that thing they screeched?" he asked. "The 'Neeeeeaaaaaaaoooowww' thing."

"Oh, that's what *all* harpies screech," she answered. "They're saying 'now,' like, '…do it neeeeaaow, bitch!'"

"Oh."

"That's why I never nag you," she told him. "Only harpies do that."

"I suppose you're right," he agreed.

"I find the carrot works much better than the stick," she admitted, eyeing his. "Men are much easier to manage if you know how to incentivize them."

And with that, she demonstrated her management technique. Which was masterful, of course. She was clearly upper management, given how quickly she was able to coax Chauncy to his very highest level of performance.

"Oh," he murmured.

"See?" she replied with a grin.

"I'll do anything you like," he vowed. And in that moment, he meant it.

"Me first," she replied. And showed remarkable insight into his mind, doing just that. A few minutes later, they laid facing each other, in precisely the same position as before.

"Thanks," he told her.

"My pleasure," she replied. He grinned, running a hand through her perfect hair.

"I'm the luckiest man alive," he declared.

"I know, right?" she agreed.

"Ha," he replied. Then he paused. "Do you feel lucky?"

"I just got lucky," she offered.

"I mean, to be with me," he clarified.

"Aww," she cooed, giving him a smooch. But she didn't say anything else. He gave her a look.

"See, you're *supposed* to say 'yes,'" he grumbled.

She just stared at him.

"Ass," he muttered.

"Next time," she agreed. "Less risky."

"That's it," he grumbled, rolling away from her. "Goodnight Val." She snuggled up to him, being the big spoon, as usual.

"Night Chauncy."

And with that, in the arms of an ass – but easily the best, if only, ass he'd ever had – Chauncy fell fast asleep.

* * *

The next morning, Chauncy and Harry got to work packing up, while Nettie cooked breakfast. Soup and bread, along with some salted fish they'd saved from the lake back in the Great Wood. It was quite good, if a little plain, and everyone enjoyed it whilst sitting around the fire. When they were done, Nettie stood up, brushing grass and dirt off her clothes and fixing Valtora with a stern look.

"You," she declared. And pointed at Valtora, so there could be no doubt whatsoever as to whom she was speaking.

"Huh?" Valtora replied, giving a gorgeously innocent look. It was her default expression when accused of anything, whether she was guilty or not.

"First that Obsidian Ogre found us," Nettie stated, "...on a secret dirt path in the middle of nowhere. And now a whole flock of harpies finds us on *another* secret path."

"Guess you can't call them secret paths anymore," Valtora reasoned. "Not if lots of people know about them."

"Not people," Nettie retorted. "Minions! Of The Dark One!"

"What's your point?"

"What are the chances they'd find us over and over?" Nettie inquired.

"Well seeing as they *did*, one hundred percent," Valtora calculated. Nettie rolled her eyes.

"They're tracking you," she accused.

"Huh?"

"The Dark One," Nettie clarified. "I'd bet my left boob he's tracking you. You're the one who said he can sense any of his minions."

"That's a big bet," Harry noted.

"Yeah, but I'm not a minion," Valtora pointed out.

"But you have his essence in you," Nettie countered.

"That was three years ago," Valtora shot back.

"I mean his fog-armor!" Nettie snapped. "He gave you a part of his power, and I bet that's how he knows where you are. Where we *all* are."

"Nettie..." Chauncy began.

"How else would he know you were in Southwick?" Nettie inquired, arching an eyebrow. Chauncy blinked, then grimaced. She had a point. "Right," Nettie concluded.

"I still don't think he can track me," Valtora insisted.

"It's obvious he can," Nettie shot back.

"Look, it doesn't matter," Chauncy interjected. They both turned to him. "So what if he can track her?" he added. "It's not like we can do anything about it. If we leave her behind, he'll find her and kill or kidnap her. If we bring her with us, at least we'll have a fighting chance fighting together."

"Ooo, that was a good one," Valtora told him.

"Sure was," Harry agreed.

"Thanks," Chauncy replied, feeling quite proud of himself.

"Like hell," Nettie interjected. "It *does* matter. It means we can send little Miss Hussy out there as bait, and surprise attack The Dark One's minions when they close in on her."

"She has a point," Valtora admitted. "It's like, classic evil tactics."

"It's a *good* tactic," Nettie countered.

"Evil," Valtora argued, her eyes lighting up. Nettie was about to reply when she realized what Valtora was up to.

"I'm not arguing with you," the old woman muttered.

"Yes you are," Valtora shot back.

"No I'm...shut up!"

"That's not nice," Valtora snapped. "It's evil...like the rest of your tactics."

Nettie opened her mouth, then closed it. Then lowered her face to her hands, rubbing vigorously. Then she took a deep breath in, letting it out...and turned to Harry.

"Let's go," she prompted.

"Awww," Valtora pouted.

With that, the conversation was over, and they all got up, cleaned up, and resumed their journey. Valtora hemmed and hawed, finally choosing to mount Peter, while Chauncy, Nettie, and Harry resumed their usual positions in the carriage. Rocky led the way, Rooter perched on the stone giant's broad, blocky shoulder. Chauncy glanced at Nettie, hoping to start a conversation with her, but she promptly closed her eyes for a nap. This time, he didn't dare ask her why she was so tired after a full night's sleep, for fear that she hadn't gotten one.

Instead, Chauncy retrieved his book, The Magic of Magic, opening it to a random page. Page 5,201 in fact.

Chauncy blinked, double-checking the number. For there couldn't possibly be enough space between the front and back covers for that many pages. Still, when he flipped through the book, he found the numbers going down reliably to page one.

Huh.

He went to the sixth page, seeing as how that was his favorite number. It showed a picture of a spectacularly obese vampire, sucking the life out of a poor, hapless peasant man. The bodies of similarly sucked men were piled in heaps on either side of the vampire, drained of every last drop of their blood.

"The Vile Lord Shuud," read the caption below this grisly scene. Chauncy studied this, not quite knowing what to make of it. Then he skipped to page nine – the last digit of Valtora's favorite number – and saw something quite different. It was a poem, written in the floweriest, most magnificent calligraphy he'd ever seen. So complex with its twirls and whirls and hoops and swirls that it was nearly impossible to read. But he found himself determined to penetrate its mystery, tracing each letter carefully, until at last he'd figured it out:

To Before and After it
Will never bow,
For The Magic of Magic is
Here and Now.

Chauncy frowned, reading it a second time, then a third. Then he closed the book, rubbing his aching eyeballs. He put it back in his robe pocket, then sighed, glancing at Nettie. She was fast asleep, her head resting against her window.

"Good idea," he murmured.

With that, Chauncy closed his eyes, resting his head against the seatback. And it wasn't long before – through the peculiar power of surrender – he joined Nettie in the dreaming of dreams.

* * *

Chauncy woke up when the carriage jerked to a halt. He opened his eyes, blinking rapidly...and felt a hard elbow strike his ribs.

"Oof," he grunted.

"Wake up," Nettie prompted, quite unnecessarily. "Time to spar, kid."

"Ow," he complained, rubbing his ribs. But he did as he was told, following her out of the carriage. Harry had parked it in a large meadow, with tall grass that rippled in the wind and beautiful wildflowers of every imaginable color. It occurred to him then that *all* flowers were wildflowers until tamed. Until people took the wild out of them by putting them in neat rows just so, removing any neighbors that didn't look like them. Everything alike together.

It reminded him suddenly of what The Dark One had told him, when they'd all visited the man at the lowest depths of his dark temple. That people were obsessed with categorization, putting everything in their proper boxes...both literal and psychic.

Perhaps The Wilds were magic because they were allowed to be themselves.

Chauncy considered this sudden revelation...and then considered the suddenness of the revelation itself. For he was struck with the realization that all of his revelations had come to him just like this. Out of the blue, without any effort at all. Revelation, it seemed, was a wild thing itself. Not sought for, but received. And perhaps that was why it felt so magical...a gift out of nowhere, given to those who had the courage to stop putting out and start taking in.

"Well I'll be," he breathed.

He blinked, returning to his usual state of being, and saw that absolutely no one was paying him any mind. Even Nettie, who'd moments earlier had prompted him to spar. He cleared his throat, and Nettie turned to him, a twinkle in her eyes.

"Got that feeling again eh?" she said.

"Sure did," he replied with a smile.

"Come outta nowhere, don't they?" she told him. Harry nodded.

"Funny thing 'bout nowhere is it's everywhere," he mused rather philosophically. "Gonna take a leak," he added less philosophically, turning about and going around the carriage to shield the others from seeing his undercarriage.

"Alright kid, let's do this," Nettie said. She led him far away from the carriage, and Harry and Valtora stood on the sidelines near the carriage to watch.

"I believe in you babe!" Valtora shouted. Chauncy smiled, waving at her.

"Ready?" Nettie inquired...and shot a jet of water at his face before he could answer. His head snapped back as the jet struck him, and he fell onto his back, sputtering and coughing.

"No," he gasped. Nettie chuckled, and Chauncy got to his feet. He gripped his staff tightly, then nodded. "Okay," he told her. "Now I..."

And swung his staff at her, just as hard as he could.

Nettie squeezed her Wetstone just in time, shooting up on a geyser of water. Chauncy's wind smashed into the bottom of the geyser, blasting it to mist. Which did nothing at all to Nettie, of course.

"Ha!" she jeered from a good sixty feet up.

"Ha ha!" he countered, swinging his staff wildly at her. Mad swings, over and over. Not just at Nettie, but all around her...so that wherever she went, one of his attacks was bound to strike true.

She made a sphere of water all around her just as they struck, and the sphere was blasted violently apart. Nettie was only partially spared, hurtling backward through the air...sixty feet above the ground.

"Crap!" Chauncy blurted out. For if she fell, she would most certainly die. But Nettie merely created another water sphere around her, falling to the ground within it. It landed with a splash...leaving her utterly intact. She sucked the water back into the Wetstone, smirking at Chauncy.

"Ha ha ha!" she retorted.

"Oh ho!" Chauncy shot back, getting into it now. "Blast attack!" he cried...and wound up to swing his staff. Nettie created a water shield ahead of her, but instead of swinging, he thrust the butt of his staff down and to the left, blasting himself upward and to the right. He hurtled a good twenty feet into the air, swinging his staff down at her exposed flank.

And with her water shield rippling in front of her, he bet she couldn't really see him.

But Nettie turned to face the blast just in time, her water shield flash-freezing to ice. The blast knocked her back a few steps, but left her unharmed. Her shield, however, was not so lucky, shattering to pieces.

"You're a ho!" Nettie trash-talked.

"I never asked for money!" Valtora interjected, clearly under the impression that Nettie had been talking to her. Nettie turned to stare at Valtora, then buried her head in her hands.

Chauncy saw his chance and by golly he took it.

Still in mid-air, he thrust the butt of his staff at her, and an air-missile struck her in the belly, knocking her right onto her butt. He fell to the ground, thrusting his staff downward to slow his fall, landing with rather impressive grace.

"Admit defeat, villain!" he cried with gusto, striking a heroic pose. Nettie got up with some difficulty, brushing off her clothes, then giving Chauncy a grudging nod.

"Not bad kid," she conceded.

"Feelin' his oats now," Harry noted.

"Makes *me* want to feel them," Valtora admitted.

"Right, anyway," Nettie grumbled. "Looks like you're ready to spar Harry."

Chauncy deflated, glancing at the old man.

"Oh," he mumbled. His shoulders slumped into a decidedly unheroic position. "Um…now?"

"Yes now," Nettie said. She turned to Harry, who was already limping toward them. The old man stopped a few yards away, giving Chauncy a grin he normally would have found reassuring.

"This is gonna be fun," Harry said.

"Be easy on me?" Chauncy requested.

"Yeah," Harry replied with a twinkle in his eye. "Sure."

Chauncy's face fell to match his shoulders, and he resigned himself to the inevitable. While Nettie was a formidable opponent – and had clearly been going easy on him – Harry was in a league of his own. And while wind could blast water away, it would prove far less effective against stone.

"Don't kill me," he pleaded.

"Yeah, sure," Harry repeated. In an equally unconvincing tone.

"Might wanna drain some life from some plants," Nettie told Rooter. "Chauncy's gonna need it." And then she cackled.

Harry took a few steps back, and Chauncy took the opportunity to take a few of his own, creating as much distance from the old man as he thought he could get away with.

"Ready?" Harry asked, slipping his shoes off to reveal bare feet.

"No."

"Probably gonna get hurt then," Harry said, wiggling a big toe into the ground. Chauncy grimaced.

"Lucky me."

"Might change your mind soon," Harry warned.

"You know what? I think I have," Chauncy decided. "I'm not doing this."

Right as a pebble shot up from the ground, smacking him in the family jewels.

Chauncy doubled over instantly, covering his battered boys, while making a sound that defied description. Much like the awful pain in his groin.

"More comin'," Harry warned.

"Not for a few days, I'd wager," Nettie countered from the sidelines. With a cackle.

"…wait…" Chauncy gasped, holding out a hand to stop Harry.

Another pebble shot up from the ground right under Chauncy, clocking him in the chin. His head snapped back, his teeth clanging together painfully.

"Ow!" he blurted out, stumbling backward. "I said wait!"

A third pebble shot up from behind, stinging his left butt cheek.

"Better get magickin'," Nettie warned. "'Cause once Harry gets goin', he don't stop."

Another pebble stung his right butt cheek. And, realizing that Nettie was right, Chauncy finally fought back. He swung his staff at the old man, whipping it extra hard. A blast of wind struck Harry...and did absolutely nothing. The grass around him blew backward impressively, whipping the old man's clothes about. But Chauncy might as well have farted on a statue.

"Well crap," Chauncy muttered.

He thrust the butt of his staff at the ground, shooting up a good twenty feet into the air. But more pebbles popped up from the ground like popcorn below him, striking the bottom of his shoes and pelting his body. One struck him right between the eyes, but not too hard. Still, it smarted something fierce...and distracted him enough that he forgot all about attacking, focusing on getting away instead. He swung his staff before him, shooting himself backward. Falling downward and backward, he slowed his descent with another downward thrust, landing a good fifty feet away from Harry.

"All right," he told himself. "Time to..."

A pebble shot up between his legs, striking his bruised balls a second time.

"Mmmpphhhuuuuuck!" he shouted. And promptly collapsed into the fetal position on the ground. His staff fell from his hands, lying uselessly on the ground next to him.

"Chauncy!" he heard Valtora cry.

"Good shot honey," he heard Nettie yell.

"Fuck," Chauncy repeated, gritting his teeth at the waves of pain bursting from his battered ballsack. "Fuckity fuck fuck *fuck*."

Valtora ran up to him, kneeling at his side. She put a hand on his shoulder.

"Are you okay?" she asked worriedly.

"Fuck," he answered. More footsteps approached, and Chauncy looked up to see Harry limping toward him with a big grin.

"Bet that hurt," the old man mused.

"Let me see," Valtora demanded, reaching for the hem of Chauncy's robe.

"No!" he shouted, batting her hands away. Or at least he tried to. For while her regular hand was easily batted, her diamond one was not. She used it to overpower him, lifting his robe and peering into the depths beyond. Her eyebrows shot up.

"Oh," she blurted out, putting her other hand to her mouth.

"Is it bad?" Chauncy asked.

She just stared.

"Is it *bad*," Chauncy repeated. She nodded mutely.

"Probably matches yer robe," Harry guessed.

"I'll get Rooter," Valtora declared.

And with that, she got up and did just that, so that the little stone golem could heal Chauncy's mangled groin. But Chauncy strongly suspected that, even after his flesh was mended, that his pride would remain as maimed as it was now. For it was clear to him that he was absolutely no match for Harry, not even close.

And if he couldn't beat Harry, what chance did he stand against The Dark One?

Chapter 18

Cumulus was the capitol city of the Kingdom of Pravus, and as such, was by necessity the most impressive of all of the kingdom's cities. And not just because of the castle and royal grounds in the center of the city, which were jaw-dropping in their own right. For the city was chock-full of other, smaller castles and estates, the homes of the Lords of Pravus, third only in power to the king himself. Second in power were the Lords' wives, naturally…though theirs was a power not ordained by the law. It hardly needed to be, for human nature was a more powerful law than anything written by the human hand.

Surrounding Cumulus was a great wall not unlike the Great Wall surrounding the vast kingdom itself. A wall built to protect the city not from outsiders, but the most dangerous insider of all: The Dark One, personification of all the evils of Man's nature, the enemy of Good. A magical wall, one nigh-indestructible.

But the problem with walls was that they were scalable, or easily dug under, or flown over. A fact that, on this particular night, was keeping King Pravus wide awake in his bed. He sighed, staring up at the ridiculously high and vaulted ceiling of his royal bedchamber, feeling his latest lover's shoulder pressing against his. A fantastically fit fellow from the gym, one he'd been eyeing for a while. Stoking up a good flame for, for a good month now. They'd just engaged in a bit of vigorous stress relief, but – having been relieved not once, but thrice – Pravus found himself irritatingly irritated. For instead of drifting off to sleep in the customary fashion, his thoughts and fears had conspired to keep him wide awake.

"Leave me," he ordered. And being king, his companion did just that.

Pravus watched him go, then sighed, rolling onto his side. Irritating, to be conscious after all that. Honestly, he'd pulled the trigger on pulling the trigger with the man mostly out of desperation. For, plagued by the most recent news regarding The Dark One's armies, Pravus had known damn well that tonight would be a sleepless one. The prospect of remaining awake contemplating his kingdom's impending doom, then having to deal with all the nonsense of governing the next day, had been downright soul-sucking. And sucking, it'd turned out, hadn't prevented this unfortunate fate.

"Well," he muttered, turning onto his back to stare up at the ornately sculpted ceiling, wrought of gold and silver and obsidian and other gorgeous nonsense. "I'm screwed."

The ceiling ignored this bit of history, having witnessed it only moments ago.

"What now?" he wondered aloud. Which was a bad sign. For Pravus had cultivated a habit of keeping his thinking between his ears, where other ears couldn't hear them. He was clearly out of sorts. Hardly surprising, given the news he'd received earlier that day. The Dark One's minions had razed two more cities, a mere thirty miles from Cumulus. The message was clear.

The Dark One was closing in...and fast.

"And still no *fricking* word on those Chosen Ones," he told the ceiling, glaring at it.

They'd vanished after being spotted beyond the Wall. Which meant that they'd either been massacred by The Dark One, in which case the kingdom was doomed...or they'd reneged on their duties, to a similar end. Or perhaps they'd simply avoided detection somehow. A cheery thought, but unlikely. For Pravus knew that people were creatures of habit, and the habit of these particular Chosen Ones had been to run away from their destinies rather than toward them.

"Sigh," he sighed.

He supposed he could do a bit of a workout in his personal gym within the castle, but he really didn't have the urge to. It was far away for one, and honestly, he was just too stressed out. He couldn't very well justify indulging in bicep curls when the kingdom was being ritually massacred by the personification of evil. It would be ridiculously inappropriate. He had responsibilities, after all. Millions of innocent – and not-so-innocent, but far more interesting – lives were at stake.

The Dark One's army was closing in, only a few days from here now. There was a very good chance that, despite his best efforts, Pravus would be the first king of his great country to fail in his sacred task to protect his people. And in dooming the kingdom that bore his name, he would be dooming the world. For The Dark One would not stop at conquering the magical kingdom of Pravus. No, he would only be emboldened by his victory, and pass through the Gate to the world beyond.

Until all of humanity was destroyed…or enslaved to darkness forever.

Chapter 19

Chauncy was depressed.

He came to this conclusion whilst seated in his usual position in the carriage, his head resting against the side window. Watching the scenery go by, an hours-long parade of trees and bushes and long grass, he found himself ruminating about the literal ball-busting he'd gotten from Harry that morning. While Rooter had healed his body, his mind was another story. For his battle with Harry had proven that he was inadequate to the task he'd been given. That he was, in short, an incompetent wizard at best…and utterly unprepared to deal with the likes of The Dark One.

It was a fall from grace indeed. For Chauncy had spent the last six months believing that he'd met his destiny and slain his metaphorical dragon. That he'd reached the pinnacle of his powers, becoming a wizard of some renown. As it turned out, he'd been fooling himself. For he was precisely what he'd been before battling Marie Merrick at the Great Wood. A bumbling idiot incapable of doing anything on his own.

Nettie and Harry beat Marie, he told himself. *You didn't do a damn thing.*

He sighed, lifting his head from the window, then letting it fall back onto it with a *thump*. Then he did it again. And again. Gently enough so Nettie wouldn't notice, but firmly enough to hurt a little. In a nice, steady rhythm.

Thump. Thump. Thump.

Eventually Nettie stirred, glancing at him. Chauncy stopped *thumping*, resting his head against the window, ignoring her gaze as best he could.

"What's eating you?" she asked.

"Tired," he replied.

"You're not tired," she retorted. "You're depressed."

He didn't say anything.

"Well snap out of it," she told him, punching him in the shoulder. Which hurt quite a bit, surprisingly. "If ya got the blues, you can't see any other colors."

Chauncy frowned, turning to face her.

"Excuse me?" he asked.

"If ya got the blues, everything looks blue," she clarified. "No room for reds or greens or yellows or nothing." She scoffed. "Terrible way to see if you ask me."

"That rhymed," he noted, smiling a little despite himself.

"There it is," she declared with a smile of her own. "Finally got some sunshine outta ya. You been moping ever since Harry busted your balls."

Chauncy grimaced at the double-meaning.

"Your balls lookin' blue ain't depression," she continued. "That's their real color now."

"Ha ha."

"Taint the end of the world," she continued. "Rooter healed you up good, right?"

"My balls are swell, thank you," Chauncy grumbled. She smirked.

"Bet they are."

"Can we change the subject?" he pleaded.

"Sore subject, eh?"

"Enough already!" he retorted.

"Now now, don't get yer undies in a twist," Nettie said. "If you can't have fun losing, you'll barely have any fun at all."

"Why, because I'm a loser?"

"Everyone is," Nettie replied evenly. "We all lose sometimes. Just gotta lose enough times until you win, that's all."

"Or until you die horribly," Chauncy countered. "Like I'm going to do when we reach The Dark One."

"Could be," she conceded. He blinked.

"Excuse me?"

"You might die," she told him. "And horribly, too. But it's not like you have a choice. If you don't go to The Dark One, he'll come for you. After all, you're the guy who's porking his wife."

Chauncy blushed.

"You and Harry sure have a way with words," he grumbled.

"So does your girlfriend," Nettie reminded him. Which was undeniably true. "Difference is, we know when we're doing it."

"I just think...I'm not ready," he confessed.

"Sure aren't," she agreed.

"Wait, I'm not?"

"Nope," she confirmed. "You're way outta your league, kid. Not ready at all. And at this rate," she added, "...you'll never be."

He just stared at her.

"Problem is, your heart's not in it," Nettie told him. "You don't wanna be here, and you don't wanna fight The Dark One...just like the last time."

"What are you talking about?" he retorted. "I was going to fight The Dark One, but he ended up being our ally! At the time!"

"But you didn't want to," Nettie insisted. "Your heart wasn't in it, Chauncy. That's why you wouldn't have won then. And why you won't win now, if you keep it up. Or don't start keeping up, that is."

"What?" he asked, utterly confused.

"You've got magic Chauncy," Nettie admitted. "Powerful magic, when you let it out. Problem is, it only comes out when you let it in."

"Uh..."

"Shut up," she interjected. "Point is, you got a lot of potential," she continued. "But you're not using it."

Chauncy sighed.

"I know, I know," he muttered. "I should do better."

"Should shmood," Nettie retorted. "Nobody ever did anything good on should."

"Another rhyme," he noted.

"Well this one's true," she replied. "Forget should, Chauncy. If you don't wanna do something, you'll hate doin' it. And there's no magic in that."

"I *don't* want to be here doing this," Chauncy confessed. "I don't want to kill The Dark One. I just want to go home and enjoy my life with Valtora."

"Well tough shit," Nettie replied. "You can't. So if you can't do whatcha wanna do, you gotta figure out how to like what you don't wanna do."

"Or what?"

"Roll over and die," she answered.

"Ah," he mumbled. "How...do I figure out how to like what I don't want to do?"

"Do it on your terms," she answered. "*Your* way."

"Huh."

Nettie turned away from him, clearly indicating that their conversation was over. Chauncy turned to look out of his own window at the passing scenery, picking at his lower lip absently.

Do it your way.

He frowned, feeling the book in his pocket pressing quite strongly against his left thigh. He pulled it out, feeling it trying to fall rightward instead of downward. Opening it to page six, he found the illustration he'd seen earlier, of the gluttonous vampire.

The Vampire Shuud.

Then he turned to page sixty-nine, smiling at the giggle this would've gotten out of Valtora. He re-read the poem there, with some difficulty.

To Before and After it
Will never bow,
For The Magic of Magic is
Here and Now.

"Here and now," he murmured to himself.

He pondered this for a while, but while it seemed like a pithy and true-ish saying, it wasn't much help for his current predicament. For The Dark One wasn't here or now, he was there and then. In the wrong place and the wrong when.

He shut the book, putting it in his right robe pocket. But it fell rightward within, making the pocket bulge. So he switched it to the left pocket, which was the right one, instead of the right one, which was the wrong one.

He sighed, realizing that, despite having been on the road for a few days, he still hadn't come up with any magical items that'd help him defeat The Dark One. By this point the last time, he'd made the Staff of Wind and the Wetstone.

Some wizard I am, he thought.

But at the moment, no ideas came to him. So, with nothing else to do but wait, Chauncy rested his head against his side window, closing his eyes. For, quite contrary to his magic book, Here and Now was just an intermission between his past and his future. So, with nothing to do in the moment, he decided to sleep this particular intermission away, so as to meet his future a bit sooner…and get it over with already.

* * *

When Chauncy opened his eyes, it was to more intermission. Specifically, an end-of-day carriage stop. They were, Harry notified them, about halfway to Mount Thrall. They were making excellent time, unfortunately. But while Chauncy was nervously preoccupied with the upcoming battle to the death, everyone else seemed blissfully unaware of their likely impending doom. A fact that Chauncy found rather irritating.

"Don't you realize we're all going to die?" he asked them as they stood around the campfire Harry was busy nurturing.

"Not us," Nettie countered, patting Harry on the lower back, which was about as high as she could reach. "We're immortal, remember?"

"What?" Chauncy replied.

"Immortal," Nettie repeated. "All the wizards in the Order of Mundus are immortal."

"So you can't die?"

"Not unless we're killed," she replied.

"Right," Chauncy stated. "I'm sure The Dark One will be happy to do the honors."

"You got me there kid," she agreed.

"Isn't anyone concerned?" he pressed, looking around the growing campfire. Harry threw another log into the flames, and Valtora stood by Peter, stroking his mane lovingly. Rocky sat down before the fire, Rooter perched on one blocky shoulder, as usual. Nettie looked at them, then at Chauncy.

"Nope," she replied.

"Well you *should* be," he insisted, crossing his arms over his chest. Nettie's eyebrows went up.

"Should, eh?" she replied. "Now what'd I tell you about that word?"

"Nothing good ever came from should," Chauncy recited. Reluctantly.

"Damn right," Nettie agreed.

"Wise words," Harry mused, throwing another log in, then easing himself down to sit next to Rocky, with considerable difficulty.

"Of course they are," Nettie replied. "I said 'em, didn't I?"

"He did," Harry pointed out, pointing to Chauncy.

"Well I said 'em first!" Nettie shot back.

"Touchy, ain't she?" Harry told Chauncy, his eyes twinkling.

"I'll touch you all right," Nettie replied, making a fist at Harry rather threateningly.

"Oh boy," Harry said, grinning from ear-to-ear.

"Not that way, ya perve!"

"Oh darn," Harry corrected, his smiling fading.

"So what, we just ignore our impending dooms and live like it's not going to happen?" Chauncy blurted out.

"Well sure," Harry replied evenly. "That's what you've been doing yer whole life, ain't it?"

Chauncy blinked, taken aback.

"Huh?" he asked.

"You've been going to die your whole life," Harry explained.

Chauncy frowned, processing this. He supposed it was impossible to argue with Harry; *everyone* was going to die eventually, himself included. And in the meantime, he'd gone about living as if it would never happen...precisely as everyone was doing right now.

"Oh," he mumbled. Harry waggled his eyebrows at Nettie.

"Guess yer not the only one with wise words," he told her.

"Shut up, wise guy," she retorted. Then they both burst out laughing. Chauncy sighed, realizing he wasn't going to be able to strike fear into the hearts of anyone present. He didn't even bother with Valtora, knowing that she was utterly incapable of being afraid of anything. She rarely thought of the future, mostly because she was a terrible procrastinator. She always put off worrying until she had to, because it was far too much work...and unpleasant work to boot.

"Fine," he muttered, crossing his arms over his chest and sitting down. He glared at everyone present, though he felt like he was the only one *not* present. For everyone else seemed to be enjoying themselves right now, while he was suffering from the future. He sighed, staring at the flames of the campfire and settling in do to some quality moping. But Valtora sat down next to him, draping an arm around his shoulders and leaning her head against his.

"Hi baby," she greeted.

"Eh," he replied. He spotted a few strands of rainbow-colored hair on her cheek, and brushed them away irritatedly. But her shoulders and chest were covered in rainbow dandruff, a constant reminder of her constant affection toward Peter. And a reminder of Peter's brand-new rainbow-colored peter.

"About Peter," he stated, leaning a bit away from her.

"Huh?"

"His…peter," he stated. "Did you…bedazzle it?"

"Of course," she replied, her eyes lighting up. "He's beautiful, isn't he?"

"Yes," he admitted. Irritatedly. "But his…thingy," he pressed. "You bedazzled that too."

"Sure did," she agreed. With a big smile. She turned to gaze at her work. "It's just *gorgeous*, isn't it? My finest handiwork."

Chauncy grimaced at the word choice.

"That's my question," he told her. "Did it take a…handy…to work?"

"Huh?"

"Did you, you know…touch it?"

"Huh?"

"You know what I mean," he pressed. She just stared at him blankly. "Come on," he pressed. "Just tell me!"

She blinked, staring at him. Then blinked again.

"Huh?"

"That's it," he declared, standing up. "I'm going to bed."

"Haven't pitched a tent yet," Harry noted.

Chauncy stomped off to the carriage, pulling his tent out of one of the packs and unfolding it. He got to work setting it up, but found it far harder – and less enjoyable – to pitch a tent all by himself than to do it with some help. Eventually he got it up, and crawled inside, sitting alone inside of it. He even shut the tent door so he wouldn't have to look at the others enjoying themselves.

"This sucks," he declared, crossing his arms over his chest and pouting. His stomach growled, and he ignored it…and the scent of soup and roasting bread coming from outside. He was far too irritated to eat, and far too hungry to be anything but irritated. So he just sat there, fuming. While fantasizing about a rematch between him and Harry. It didn't take long for that fantasy to get pretty dark, and he soon found himself smiling grimly at the grisly images his mind had conjured. Ones involving testicles smashed beyond all repair…and not his. Eventually his imagination had gone a bit too far, such that even he found himself recoiling from his own ghastly fantasies. It was then that the door flap to his tent opened up, and Valtora came inside. With a steaming cup of soup and some bread, no less.

"Here you go," she said, giving him both. "Little punk-ass bitch," she added non-constructively.

"Whatever," he grumbled. But he devoured the soup and the bread, burning his mouth a little in the process. Still, by the time he finished the food, he was feeling quite a bit better, and even smiled reluctantly at Valtora. "Sorry," he told her.

"Apology accepted," she replied, beaming a smile at him. "You're the sweetest guy I know, except when you're hungry."

"True."

"Then you're a fucking asshole," she added, unnecessarily.

"I get it," he replied.

"I mean, a *real*..."

"I get it!" he interjected.

"Nettie told me to tell you to take a walk after you ate," she relayed. "She said not to come back until you felt some magic."

He sighed.

"Fine," he replied.

"Would it help if I made some magic with you first?" she offered. He broke out into a big smile, which was answer enough. Still, for clarity's sake, his body answered in other ways, making it quite clear that he was up for it.

So it was that, while Chauncy missed out on Valtora helping him pitch his tent, she more than made up for it by helping him take it down. All while bedazzling him, not with her magic, but through more mundane, if not exactly conventional – or even strictly legal – means. Still, for those meant for each other, there was magic *in* the mundane, and in the process of being bedazzled, Chauncy couldn't tell the difference between the two.

Then, feeling much, much better, Chauncy left the love of his life behind, so that he could search for an altogether different kind of magic. One that might – just might – offer him a long lifetime to enjoy the magic he felt with Valtora.

Chapter 20

To Chauncy, there was something profound about nighttime. Ever since he was a boy, he'd occasionally been struck by the sudden feeling that the starlit world was somehow more…real. The movement of things was smoother, the smells crisper. Perhaps the fact that much of the world was hidden in darkness made a mystery of each shadowy abyss. Or maybe it was because at night, most of the world was asleep. And in the relative quiet, no longer distracted by the obligations of dealing with others and one's responsibilities, Chauncy could just…be.

A good half-hour's stroll from camp, along the narrow path that wound through the woods, Chauncy was struck again by this very feeling. Moonlight kissed the branches overhead with the subtlest silver, stars playing peek-a-boo between the leaves. A warm breeze caressed him, swirling about and bringing with it the scent of wildflowers and earth. He smiled, taking a deep breath in while he strolled, knowing well enough to enjoy this feeling while it lasted. For as Nettie had told him more than once, nothing lasted forever.

"What a nice night," he mused. And then fell silent, because when it came to a night like this, his voice could only ruin it. Words were clumsy things, and were utterly inadequate in describing the experience of life. Perhaps that's what the Cave of Wonder was trying to show him when it made him quite literally trip over the word "word." A mistake he wouldn't fall for this time.

Instead, Chauncy strolled in silence, hands stuffed in his robe-pockets, taking it all in. With no destination in mind, his mind was freed from considering what was to come, and instead focused on what was already here.

That, of course, was him, the world, and everything. Just as it was. And though Chauncy had been tasked with making something magical, the night as it was…well, was plenty magical by itself. To the point where found himself not particularly compelled to do anything at all, other than enjoy it.

So he did.

But as nothing lasted forever, after a few minutes, the sensation faded. And its magic faded with it.

"Huh," Chauncy murmured to himself. For it was clear to him that magic had always been like this for him. A feeling, fleeting but powerful, of connection with things. Or rather, with things in a particular moment. He'd always assumed that wizards would be able to feel magic all the time, but perhaps this wasn't the case. After all, if he could feel the magic of everything all the time, it wouldn't feel magical at all, he supposed. It'd just be…ordinary.

Magic, it appeared, was only magical in that it was momentary.

"Well I'll be," he said. If that were the case, he hardly needed to feel so inadequate because he felt magic intermittently. And perhaps that was the problem. He was so focused on the fact that he wasn't good enough that he remained not good enough.

The solution to the problem is the problem itself, he recalled from the Cave of Wonder. And in recalling it, he felt a chill, and a sense of wonder. Which promptly faded. But this time, he didn't mind.

"I need to stop worrying about being a wizard and just be a damn wizard," he realized. For the worry was the reason he wasn't being a wizard…and therefore the worry was the reason for the worry.

The solution to the problem is the problem itself.

With that, Chauncy turned about, trotting with renewed vigor toward the camp. For while he hadn't created a magical trinket to aid him in his predestined battle with The Dark One, he believed he'd come up with something far more valuable.

A frame of mind…one that would allow him to become the wizard he'd been born to be.

* * *

"You were supposed to make a thing!" Nettie complained as soon as Chauncy returned to the camp empty-handed. But not empty-minded, or empty-hearted for that matter. Still, revealing his revelation hadn't impressed Nettie one bit, much to Chauncy's consternation. Harry, for his part, seemed more intrigued.

"Not everything needs to be a thing," the old man counseled. Nettie glared at him.

"Everything has *every* and *thing* in it," she retorted. "Idiot," she added, in case it wasn't obvious from her tone.

"I have something more important than a thing," Chauncy insisted. "I have a…um…"

"A think?" Nettie replied, arching an eyebrow. Chauncy nodded. "Right."

"How about you go spar Harry then with that 'think,'" she grumbled. "Go on, see where it gets you!"

Chauncy hesitated, glancing at Harry. And then remembering the battering his balls had borne. Still, he stood firm.

"Good idea," he replied. "You up for it Harry?"

"Well sure," Harry answered. "Why not?"

With that, Chauncy got his staff, and he and Harry walked a good distance from the campfire, until they were facing each other on the narrow dirt path, a good twenty feet away from each other.

"Ready?" Harry asked, digging a bare toe into the dirt. Chauncy gazed past the old man, at the path winding into the darkness, and the countless stars twinkling in the night sky above. He felt the warm air, just as he had on his walk. And, in that moment, he was *in* the moment.

"Am now," he replied.

A huge rock hand burst out of the path from directly below Chauncy, huge earthen fingers closing in to grab his legs in a stony grip. But to his surprise, he felt no surprise at all…or fear, for that matter. He merely reacted, shoving the butt of his staff downward to strike the ground at his feet. And in response, he launched upward into the sky, far above the grasping hand.

"Whoopee!" he cried, feeling a burst of elation. "I'm *flying!*"

"Gone lost his mind," Nettie muttered, shaking her head. Not that Chauncy noticed.

Chauncy giggled, shoving his staff downward again, and launching himself further upward. Now he was easily seventy feet high, far too far up for Harry's hand to grasp. So the hand sank into the earth, melding with, and becoming, the path once again.

"I prefer the hands-off approach!" Chauncy declared, whipping his staff at Harry. But the resultant blast of wind barely budged the guy, seeing as he was part stone himself. Still, the staff's swing launched Chauncy backward, and he enjoyed his impromptu flight, rather than feeling the fear he would've normally felt. And as he fell toward the path below, he thrust his staff downward, slowing his descent to touch down gently on the ground.

Then he got *serious*.

Chauncy crouched down, scowling furiously at Harry and thrusting his free hand outward.

"Fireball!" he cried menacingly. "Electric zap!"

"Here we go again," Nettie groaned from the sidelines.

"Don't interrupt," Valtora scolded.

Chauncy cackled, then spun in a circle while standing up, swinging his staff as he did so. This created a whirlwind around him, pulling small rocks and dirt from the path in a spiral upward. He thrust the staff at Harry then...and the rocks and dirt shot outward at the old man, pelting him rather viciously in the face.

"Ka-pow!" Chauncy exclaimed. "Swallow my stones, villain!"

"Rather not," Harry replied, even as the stones *dinged* off of him. With his rock-hard skin, he was hardly fazed by the attack. Still, as far as Chauncy was concerned, he was just getting started.

"You'll swallow what I give you to swallow!" he cried, really getting into it. A rock shot upward from between his legs, but Chauncy expected it, and smacked it with the butt of his staff...sending it hurtling toward Harry's head. It bounced off the old man's lips with a *ding*, making Chauncy chuckle.

"Pretty good aim," Nettie conceded.

"Pretty good *pow!*" Chauncy declared, thrusting the butt of his staff forward and downward at the path ahead of him. It struck, shooting him backward and upward...and sending a spray of pebbles and dirt fanning outward at Harry. All of which did nothing to the old man, of course, but it was fun to watch.

"Trash-talking is garbage though," Valtora told Nettie. Which Chauncy could hear, because whispering was not one of Valtora's strengths. Chauncy landed a good sixty feet away from Harry, posing rather heroically.

"It really stinks," Nettie agreed.

"Come on old fart," Chauncy taunted. "Show me whatcha got!"

"All right," Harry agreed. But before the old man could show him, Chauncy drew out the Sunstone from his pocket. And, seeing as how it absorbed light around it when prompted to do so, it effectively enveloped him in a large sphere of inky-black darkness.

Which, at nighttime, made him awfully hard to see.

"Well where'n the hell he go?" Nettie wondered.

"Beats me," Harry replied. Still, to be careful, he shot out a few stones from the path where Chauncy had been standing a moment ago, perfectly aimed to bust his balls. But Chauncy wasn't there for the busting. For he'd sidestepped in advance, Harry's rocks popping off harmlessly to Chauncy's right. Not that Chauncy could see them, seeing as how he was immersed in darkness. He launched himself into the air again, knowing full well that, against the night sky, he would be practically invisible. Which meant that he could reign terror from above.

"I am the night!" he cried as he arced downward toward where he knew Harry was, readying his staff for a good chopping. And immediately regretted it. For in issuing forth his battle cry, he'd revealed his position.

If Chauncy could've seen through the darkness, he would've beheld a rocky hand shooting up from the path in front of Harry to grab Chauncy. As it was, he only realized what was happening when he felt its stony fingers close on him, holding him fast.

"Crap," he blurted out. The Sunstone fell from his hand with the sudden stop, landing between his legs just below him. And promptly shot upward, smacking him right in the nuts.

Chauncy shrieked.

"Good shot hon!" Nettie exclaimed.

"Come on Chauncy," Valtora urged. "Get up and avenge your balls!"

"Mrrrrmmphhh," Chauncy moaned.

"Go on Rooter," Nettie prompted. "Chauncy's nuts need you."

The stony hand holding Chauncy let him go, and he landed on his side, curling up into the fetal position. The pain was extraordinary, pulsing between his legs like a second heart.

"Fuuuuu-"

"Come on Chauncy," Nettie told him. "Walk it off."

Chauncy ignored the advice, moaning while Valtora escorted Rooter to some nearby trees to suck the life out of. Then Rooter returned, putting a hand on Chauncy's shoulder. The little golem's head began to glow, and that light went up the roots of the plant atop Rooter's head to its stem and leaves, which glowed bright green. The pain in Chauncy's groin abated, until it was completely gone.

"Oh thank heaven," Chauncy gushed. "Thank you thank you thank you."

Rooter's stony crack for a mouth turned upward in a stiff, but ridiculously cute, smile.

"Aww," Valtora said. "So darn *coot*."

"You're the night, huh?" Harry asked, limping up to Chauncy and offering a hand. Chauncy took it, and Harry hauled him to his feet.

"He's an idiot," Nettie corrected. "Now why the hell would you give yourself away like that?"

"I was excited," Chauncy answered rather defensively.

"Well get less excited," Nettie grumbled.

"Nothin' wrong with gettin' excited," Harry countered, patting Chauncy on the shoulder. "Just gotta do it quietly."

"Should've gotten loads of practice doing that," Nettie said, eyeing Chauncy with a smirk. "Living all those years with your grandma."

Chauncy blushed.

"Come on you two," Valtora chided. "He did better."

"True," Nettie conceded. "Looked like you were having a ball, until...you know."

Chauncy rolled his eyes.

"It's late, and I'm going to bed," he informed them. And promptly went to his tent. Valtora came with him, going inside and closing the door behind her. Chauncy sighed, lifting his robe to check on his parts. And grimaced at the underwear he was wearing. For it was, like all the other pairs Valtora had packed for him, something he wouldn't be caught dead wearing in public.

"Here, let me check," Valtora offered. And promptly began a thorough inspection.

"Oh," he blurted out.

"Does it hurt?" she asked, continuing onto the hydraulic lift portion of the inspection.

"Nope."

"How about this?" she pressed, putting him through more rigorous testing.

"Not at all."

"Better be sure," she decided. "We need to do a full inspection, to make sure Rooter doesn't need to do more healing."

"Okay," Chauncy agreed. Which was really the only right answer.

So, while Chauncy's evening had seen its ups and downs, and ended with more of the same, he fell asleep content. For, while he still hadn't beaten Harry, he felt that he'd gotten a little closer to becoming the wizard he was meant to be. And, with the realization that magic was momentary, he was able to fully enjoy his night with Valtora. For life, like magic, was also momentary, doomed to end in the...well, the end. But while he lived, Chauncy would enjoy his life to the fullest.

And that meant spending as much of it as possible with Valtora, Harry, and Nettie...the people he loved.

Chapter 21

After reaching the Gates of Pravus and using Skibbard to unlock the giant silver doors into the magical kingdom, Gavin decided to make good on his promise to the strange little wizard. An uncharacteristic decision, to allow a valuable wizard to go free, especially one who knew Gavin had entered the kingdom against King Pravus's wishes. But uncharacteristic was precisely how Gavin had been feeling since Marie's death, and without her, his character was unmoored.

While his Shadowsteed's main magic was in its ability to bind its shadow to a location and zoom back to it with enormous speed, it was fantastically fast in its own right. Many times faster, in fact, that an ordinary horse. In a single day, it brought Skibbard not to the Great Wood where Gavin had expected the man to want to live, but to a much smaller forest many miles away from it.

"Why here?" Gavin asked as the carriage rolled to a stop at the tree line of the small forest.

"Why not?" Skibbard retorted.

"It's…small," Gavin explained. "The bigger Wilds have more magic."

"I prefer my world small," Skibbard explained tersely. "In a little world, I matter big. In a big one, I matter little."

Gavin didn't reply.

"When it comes to magic," the wizard added, "…I've quite enough. And enough is more than you'll ever have."

With that, Skibbard hopped down from the carriage, striding quickly into the woods. Gavin watched the man go, feeling numb.

Enough is more than you'll ever have.

He dismissed the thought immediately, writing the wizard off in his mind. Skibbard was just a strange little man, a sad hermit living alone in the woods. Probably eating crickets and mice, and shitting in a hole. Perhaps the poor man would feel content living in squalor, holed up in some mud hut in the woods. But that was hardly the kind of life Gavin – or anyone else in their right mind – would want.

"Fool," he muttered, tearing his eyes away from Skibbard. He turned to the front window, rapping his knuckles on it. The Shadowsteed knew their next destination, having already been told of it. An incredibly intelligent animal...nearly as smart as some men, or so Gavin had been told.

The carriage took off, gaining speed rapidly. Gavin sighed, leaning back in his seat. He reached into his pants pocket, retrieving a silver ring he always kept there. The ring that had saved him from King Pravus that fateful day, when the idiot king had gotten lucky during their fight. As Pravus had tried to strangle him, Gavin had reached inside his pants pocket for this very ring, activating it with a thought. It had transported him back to Borrin, through an identical ring there. And through its magic, it could do the opposite.

Gavin pictured the king seated smugly on his throne, with that maddening smirk on his lips. Gavin smiled grimly himself, knowing full well that it wouldn't be long before he would get the chance to wipe the monarch's smile off his face.

Permanently.

* * *

King Pravus frowned.

He was perched atop a massive fire dragon standing in the center of Rivercrest, a picturesque little town only a hundred miles from Cumulus. Or rather, formerly picturesque. For now it was the picture of devastation, both structural and human. The town was in utter shambles, buildings shattered and charred, a nearby lake piled with bloated, floating bodies and blackened debris. Not a single soul had survived the attack.

Not one.

Pravus slid off the saddle, levitating gently down to the street far below. An enormous number of his royal guards surrounded him, quiet unnecessarily. For if the fire dragon couldn't have protected Pravus, his guards wouldn't have stood a chance either.

He stared at the ruins of the town, turning in a slow circle to take it all in. A town that had been *his* responsibility. Such that its destruction was his failure. As was every life lost, in this town and in the many others that The Dark One had razed.

I failed, he thought.

And he realized at that moment, with sudden, absolute clarity, that he didn't want to be king. Not for a single second longer.

His father had never failed like this. Nor his grandfather. The people of Pravus had trusted them, and they'd earned that trust. Made good on the promise to protect and provide. Yes, The Dark One had attacked during their reigns, but the damage had been slight in comparison. Forgivable.

This…this was not.

Pravus's heart sank as he took in the full reality of his failure, his shoulders slumping. There was nothing to say…and nothing to do. What was done was done…and would almost certainly be done again. For The Dark One would not stop, he knew. And without the Chosen Ones, King Pravus could not defeat him.

I failed, he repeated, kicking himself. He should've demanded that those Chosen Ones defeat The Dark One right away, after meeting them near the Great Wood. He never should have let them "rest" and "recover." Sure, he'd never heard of Chosen Ones abandoning their destinies, but still. It'd been the better part of a year, and he hadn't really pushed them. In fact, he'd only starting searching for them *after* The Dark One had starting attacking.

That was his failure. And innocent men and women, and even dear, sweet children, had paid the price for it.

Pravus closed his eyes, feeling utterly defeated.

"Sire?" he heard someone ask. He opened his eyes, seeing one of his guards looking at him. A man whose name he couldn't remember, but was high-ranking.

"What?" Pravus snapped.

"Your orders?" the man asked. Pravus blinked.

"Orders?"

"Yes, orders," the man confirmed. Pravus frowned, gazing at the ruins.

"Clean it up," he answered at last. "Rebuild. Offer survivors from other cities and towns a life here." He paused. "Give them houses of similar value to the ones they lost. At no cost to them," he added. "Ensure they have adequate provisions for the winter. And no taxes levied for a full year."

"Yes sire," the man replied.

Pravus paused.

"Your name?" he asked.

"Esrick," the man answered.

"Esrick," Pravus repeated, vowing to remember it. "Thank you." The man bowed.

"My pleasure to serve you, my liege," Esrick replied.

"Is it?" Pravus asked. The man blinked.

"Sire?"

"Never mind," Pravus muttered. He turned about, levitating up toward the dragon's saddle far above. Through the many powers of his monarchal uniform, of course. He reached the saddle on the dragon's back, then sighed.

"Home," he ordered.

And with that, the dragon spread its massive wings, casting a great shadow over Rivercrest. But not nearly as dark or great as the shadow The Dark One had cast over the town. And as the fire dragon took Pravus upward toward the heavens, and back to the relative safety of Cumulus, Pravus found himself gazing back at the ruins of Rivercrest, imagining The Dark One's shadow spreading over the land, destroying everything in its path. Until the great legacy that Pravus's forebearers had created, never once faltering in their war with evil, ended due to a king who – no matter the size of his muscles – couldn't measure up.

Chapter 22

The next morning, Chauncy found himself back in the carriage with Nettie, Harry in the driver's seat and Valtora riding Peter, as usual. The secret path they'd taken through the woods eventually merged with a larger road, one that wound through a rather familiar rocky plain. Wildflowers blossomed amidst rocks and boulders, the sun bringing out brilliant colors in each flower.

"This is the road we took the last time," Nettie explained. She pointed out the window. "You got Rooter and that Sunstone around here somewhere."

"I remember," he replied with a smile, gazing at the scenery. It was simply lovely, and put him in the same mindset as he'd been the last time he'd been here. Peaceful. Willing to just…receive.

"And that's still all you got," Nettie continued less pleasantly, "…other than yer fartstick."

"Staff of the Wind," he corrected.

"Staff of Breaking Wind," she shot back. "Sorry to burst your bubble, kid. But farts ain't gonna do shit against The Dark One."

"I know," he admitted.

"Well we're gettin' closer," she warned.

"I know," he repeated a bit more irritably.

"Why don'tcha take another one of your walks?" she proposed. He sighed, gazing out of the window, then nodded.

"All right," he agreed.

Nettie told Harry to stop the carriage, and Chauncy got out, strolling away aimlessly off into the rocky plains. A strong wind whipped through his hair and robe, making his staff practically *hum* in his hand as it absorbed the wind's power.

"Fartstick, huh?" he muttered. Nettie always did have a way with words. And that way was seldom flattering. He sighed, trudging along. But with the sun gently baking his skin and the wind in his hair, it was hard for Chauncy to be upset for long. Nature had a way of settling his mind, and as he ventured further into it – and away from other people – he found himself feeling quite content to be doing so. So he transitioned from trudging to strolling, and from having a bad time to have a good one. And as often happened when he was having a good time, time itself seemed to lose its meaning, and he found himself – sometime later – nearing a forest ahead. Quite a small one, compared to those he'd visited before. And, on a whim, he decided right then and there to pay it a visit. Because why not?

So, wanting to, he did.

Chauncy reached the forest, passing under the magnificent canopy. Each tree's branches intertwined with each other high above, working together to build an unbroken ceiling of fluttering leaves. Without a thought, they'd come together to make something beautiful, without anyone telling them to.

"I wonder if people could do the same," Chauncy mused. For the very concept of authority was strange within The Wilds. No creature or plant was told what to do, after all. Yet in acting in accordance with their natures, they created an order far more complicated and beautiful than any built by human hands. All arising without a single plan.

Huh.

Deeper into the woods Chauncy wandered, and surrounded by its charms, he forgot the purpose of his walk. And what wondrous charms they were!

Little mushrooms clinging to tree trunks, of all sorts of colors and shapes! And lichen and moss, yellow and green, and bushes and vines of all kinds. Life upon life upon life, each a home to the other, or food for the other.

"Wow," he breathed, looking at it all as if for the first time. For while he'd seen such things countless times before, he'd never really paid attention. Or rather, in *not* trying to pay attention, or focus on any one thing, the full majesty of the forest became clear to him.

At precisely the moment that an army of black-skinned goblins became visible far ahead, charging around the trees toward him!

"Oh!" Chauncy gasped, freezing in place.

The mass of goblins – hundreds of them – rushed toward him in a mad frenzy, identical to the goblins who'd attacked Borrin over half a year ago. Their hide was plated with obsidian armor, their only weapons their long, razor-sharp claws. They weaved around the trees like a goblin tidal wave, coming right at him.

So, seized with sudden terror, Chauncy ran.

He sprinted back the way he'd come, dodging tree trunks as he dashed madly away from the goblins. They cheered with horrible, sadistic glee, crashing loudly through the underbrush after him. Chauncy pushed himself harder, running as fast as his legs would take him.

But it wasn't nearly fast enough.

He heard the goblins gaining on them, their high-pitched whoops and wild screeches getting louder as they gained on him. Glancing back, he saw the first line of them only fifty feet away now, and closing fast.

Crap!

Chauncy spotted the end of the forest ahead, and barreled toward it, pushing his body to the very limit. His lungs burned, his heart hammering in his chest until he felt it would burst out of it. The goblins closed in, only thirty feet away now.

Twenty.

Ten.

He cried out in horror as one of the goblins reached for him, its sharp claws closing on his right shoulder. He yanked it away, holding his staff in front of him.

Staff!

Chauncy thrust the butt of his staff at the goblin's head, connecting with a *whump*…and watched the goblin's head blast right off its neck in a spray of blood, smashing into its fellows and knocking a dozen of them over.

He gawked at the sight, then at the butt of his staff, hardly believing his eyes.

But the remaining goblin army merely surged around and over the fallen goblins, charging at him with psychotic abandon. Far too fast for him to run away from, especially considering the carriage – and Harry and Nettie – were still far, far away. So Chauncy did the only thing he could.

He gripped his staff, and skid to a halt, turning and swinging it as hard as he could at the goblin horde.

A blast of wind struck the front line of goblins like a brick wall, and they shot backward, smashing into their brethren behind them. The front lines tumbled to the forest floor in a pile of writhing bodies, while the goblins behind them trampled right over their fallen fellows, ignoring their comrades' screams as they did so.

Chauncy swung again, blasting this second wave, which tumbled atop the first. A third wave came, lunging at him with claws bared.

But instead of being filled with terror, Chauncy found himself being filled with an entirely different kind of emotion.

"Oh *yeah* baby," he cried, getting a nice grip on his staff, then swinging it a third time. Goblins scattered like leaves in a powerful gust, and he couldn't help but cackle. "Eat my fartstick, gob-bitches!"

The first and second waves scrambled to their feet, rushing at him. But Chauncy merely swung again and again, sending them right back onto their backs.

"Oh, you've done it now," he warned, stopping for a good shoulder-stretch. He wiggled the fingers of his free hand. "You got Chauncy feeling *frisky!*"

A goblin tried flanking him, attacking from the left. Chauncy scoffed, shoving the butt of his staff at its face...and sending it flying backward as if struck by an invisible arrow.

"Boom!" he cried. "Eat my thrust!"

More goblins rushed at him from the front, stupidly. Chauncy rolled his eyes, letting them get real close. Then he smirked, thrusting his staff into the ground. He shot upward, sailing high above them as they passed by underneath...and then felt his head smack into a tree branch above.

Then the world went black, and he felt himself falling, before feeling nothing at all.

* * *

Chauncy woke up to find himself lying on his back on the forest floor, with a man kneeling over him. A man who looked to have fewer years left than he'd already lived, with tanned skin lined with wrinkles. Most of them frown-wrinkles. And the man had long, curly black hair and a long black beard, and wore a robe made entirely of animal skins and furs.

Chauncy gasped, reaching out blindly for his staff, but found himself empty-handed, his staff nowhere in sight.

"Relax," the man grumbled in a gravelly voice. Chauncy hesitated, then did so.

"Okay," he agreed. Then he frowned, sitting up and rubbing his aching head. He had a lump atop it, and it took him a moment to remember what'd happened. "The goblins!" he gasped, jumping to his feet. And promptly felt so lightheaded he sat down rather violently, bruising his buttocks.

"Relax," the man repeated. "They're dead."

"Dead?"

"Killed dead," the man clarified. Sort of.

"Who killed them?"

"My friend," the man answered. And pointed behind Chauncy. Chauncy turned, then shrieked. For there, not ten feet away, was a truly massive…thing. A plant with a stalk twenty feet tall and wider around than he was, topped with a truly enormous flower-head that looked rather like a flytrap-plant. Complete with long, sharp teeth that, it should be noted, were dripping with fresh blood. Surrounding the plant were various goblin body parts, none of which seemed to go with each other.

Chauncy stumbled backward…right into the man.

"Oh," he blurted out, spinning around. "Sorry."

"Eh," the man replied.

"What is that thing?" Chauncy asked, eyeing the plant warily. And half-expecting it to lunge at him.

"A Giant Carnivorous Clawtrap," the little man answered. For, now that Chauncy was standing up, it was clear that the guy was barely five feet tall.

"And it's your friend?" he pressed.

"It's a plant," the guy replied, as if that explained it.

"Thanks for saving me," Chauncy offered, rubbing the bump on his head gingerly. "I'm Chauncy, by the way."

"Skibbard."

"Nice to meet you," Chauncy said. "Awfully nice, given the circumstances."

"Would've let you die if you hadn't been a wizard," Skibbard offered rather disturbingly. Chauncy blinked, taken aback.

"How'd you know I was a wizard?" he asked. Skibbard raised an eyebrow, eyeing Chauncy as if he were a complete idiot. So Chauncy looked down. At his fabulous, glittery, silky smooth wizard's robe. "Oh," he mumbled.

"One of two possibilities," Skibbard told him.

"Got it," Chauncy replied. "So…why save a wizard?"

"Wizards stick together," Skibbard answered. "Except liches. *FUCK* liches!" he added with sudden, startling ferocity. So much so that he spit whilst saying it. Chauncy flinched, partially because of the spit, which had landed on his face.

"Yeah," he mumbled, wiping it off. "Fuck 'em all, you know?"

"Goblins of Thrall don't do forests," Skibbard noted. "Why were they after you?"

"Well, um," Chauncy replied. "Kind of a Chosen One, actually. On a quest to kill The Dark One."

Skibbard's eyebrows went up.

"Really?" he replied, eyeing Chauncy critically. "You?"

"Yes me," Chauncy confirmed, squirming a bit. "There's others," he added. "I'm with them."

"Better be better than you," Skibbard grumbled. "Watch where you're going next time," he added.

"I got a bit carried away," Chauncy countered rather defensively. "I could've beaten them."

Skibbard, to Chauncy's irritation, didn't reply. They stood there awkwardly for a moment, and then Skibbard turned about.

"Well bye," the man said, walking away from Chauncy.

"Wait!" Chauncy blurted out. Skibbard stopped, turning to glare at him. "Um, you're a wizard, right?"

"And?"

"We could use another wizard on our team," Chauncy told him. "To fight The Dark One."

"Clearly."

Chauncy grimaced.

"What do you say?" he pressed.

"No."

Chauncy blinked again.

"What?" he asked.

"No," Skibbard repeated. "Not interested. "Staying in my forest."

"But…The Dark One will destroy your forest if we don't destroy him first," he pointed out. He paused, then decided to take one for the team. "And as you said, we're clearly not good enough to beat him without you."

"*You're* not good enough," Skibbard corrected. "Haven't met the others."

"Right, fine," Chauncy muttered. "Anyway, without your help, your forest will be…" He clapped his palms together, then made smooshing motions, then pretended to sprinkle the results of this devastation on the forest floor. And then stomped on them for good measure, rotating his heel on the bits to really drive the point home.

Skibbard watched this display without a single change in his dour expression.

"We might kill some liches?" Chauncy offered. "The Dark One has liches, right?"

That did the trick.

"I'll get my seeds," Skibbard declared.

Chapter 23

Upon returning to the carriage, introductions were made, after which Chauncy told the harrowing tale of his near-death by The Dark One's evil minions. He was forced to admit the reason for Skibbard's having to rescue him, after which Nettie dropped her head in her hands and Harry just chuckled. Rooter healed Chauncy's head without asking, and without any sort of negative commentary, for which Chauncy was grateful. Of course, Rooter owed his entire existence to Chauncy's magic. But still, it was nice to have someone in his corner.

"So what the hell kinda wizard are you?" Nettie demanded, eyeing Skibbard suspiciously. Skibbard said not a word, but took a seed from one of the enormous number of hidden pockets in his robe, dropping it on the ground and shoving a bare toe into the ground atop it. Within moments, a seedling sprouted from the ground, growing rapidly upward. Spiraling up Skibbard's leg, in fact, all the way to his groin. From there, a few white flowers bloomed before their eyes, and promptly grew beans. String beans, Chauncy noted.

"Ooo," Valtora said, reaching down between Skibbard's legs and plucking a long bean that happened to be hanging in a rather suggestive position. She plopped it in her mouth, chewing vigorously. "Mmm," she exclaimed. "It's so sweet!"

"Hrmph," Skibbard harrumphed. Valtora plucked a second bean, with a similar lack of consent, munching on it happily.

"Beans ain't gonna beat The Dark One," Nettie noted. "We got enough food."

"He grew a plant that killed like, tons of goblins," Chauncy offered.

"Giant Carnivorous Clawtrap," Skibbard explained. Harry's eyebrows rose.

"Heard of 'em," the old man said.

"Me too," Nettie admitted. "You're on the team."

"Hrmph," Skibbard repeated.

With that, they all prepared for their journey to Mount Thrall, with Skibbard choosing to ride Rocky along with Rooter, and everyone else taking their usual positions. Nettie eyed Chauncy as the carriage started forward, the *clip-clop* of Peter's hooves picking up pace.

"Well?" she asked.

"Well what?" Chauncy replied.

"Did you make some magic during yer walk?"

"Um…no," he confessed. "But I did find a wizard," he pointed out. She gave him a look, crossing her arms over her chest.

"Chauncy!" she complained. "When're you gonna be a wizard and make some magic already?"

"I…I don't know," he confessed, shrugging his shoulders helplessly. "I mean, I've felt magical a few times during the trip, but it didn't make anything this time."

"You sure?" she pressed.

"Pretty sure."

Nettie sighed, shaking her head. She didn't say anything, but in not saying anything, she said quite enough. Chauncy echoed that sigh, slumping back into his seat and staring out of the window at the passing scenery, mostly to avoid her disappointed expression. He felt his magic book pressing against his left thigh, and took it out of his pocket. But he forgot that it fell to the right instead of down, and the book slipped out of his fingers, "falling" to smack Nettie on the side of the head.

"Ow!" she blurted out, even as the book tumbled to strike her window. It rested there, still closed. "What the hell?"

"Oh! Sorry," Chauncy apologized, reaching over her for the book. She batted him away, rubbing the side of her head.

"What's this?" she demanded, grabbing the book. And promptly dropped it, not expecting it to fall rightward. She blinked, then retrieved it again, this time handling it more carefully. "The Magic of Magic," she read.

"It's a book from the Cave of Wonder," Chauncy told her.

"You've had a magic book from the Cave of Wonder all this time, and you didn't tell us?" she asked incredulously.

"Well, I don't know if it's *magic*," he countered.

"It falls to the right!" she shot back.

"Well yes," he conceded. "But other than that, it's mostly just a book. I think."

"You think!" she retorted, cracking the book open. "That's the problem," she added, shaking her head. "Too much thinking!"

With that, she began to read, doing so far more carefully than Chauncy had. For while he'd sort of skipped from page to page, Nettie started at the beginning and made her way forward from there. He watched her read, feeling rather stupid that he hadn't done so in the same way. For in skipping over things, it was very likely he'd skipped over something important.

"Huh," Nettie mumbled after a good ten minutes.

"What?" Chauncy inquired.

"This book," she stated. "It's ridiculous."

"What do you mean?"

"It doesn't make any damn sense," she explained. "It's bat-shit crazy. Lunatic. A psychotic fever-dream. Like Valtora," she added.

"Well that's what *I* thought," Chauncy replied, feeling rather vindicated. "It's why I didn't tell you about it earlier."

"Got a headache," Nettie said. "Can't tell if it's from reading it or getting smacked upside the head with it." She handed it back to him, with extreme care. "Knock yourself out this time," she added.

Chauncy took the book back, and was about to put it back in his robe-pocket when he found himself eyeing the cover. Specifically, the golden, glittery amethyst-like crystals that served as its background. They were identical of course to his robe, which he'd noted before. But now that he *really* looked at them, he found they were also identical to the floor of the Cave of Wonder. For, like the magical cave, he found that the deeper he looked into those crystals, the deeper he could see. That, in fact, they *had* depth. He furrowed his brow, holding the book closer to his face and staring into it.

And as deep as he looked, he saw more depth.

"Wow," he murmured.

You'll only see as deep as you see, he thought. *The deeper you look, the deeper you'll be.*

"What?" Nettie grumbled, breaking him from his instant reverie. Chauncy blinked, turning to look at her.

"It *does* make sense," Chauncy said.

"What?"

"The book," he clarified. "It's ridiculous on purpose," he realized. "Because *magic* is ridiculous. Bat-shit crazy. Lunatic," he added. "A psychotic fever-dream." He turned to look through the front window of the carriage, looking past Harry to see Valtora riding Peter blissfully. He broke out into a smile. "Like Valtora."

Nettie smiled, patting him on the shoulder.

"Now that's the smartest thing you've said since the last smart thing you said," she told him. "And that was a long time ago."

"Thanks," he replied, choosing to ignore the second half of her statement. He put the book back in his left pocket, feeling its weight pressing against his hip. He found this familiar and reassuring. In fact, the fact that it fell right *felt* right.

"But you still haven't figured out how to beat The Dark One," she chided.

"To be fair, we were going to fight him a half-year ago," Chauncy countered. "And I was less experienced then."

"We fully expected to die," Nettie confessed. "But we had to try."

"You didn't tell me that," Chauncy accused.

"Yes I did," she shot back. "I told you we'd probably die, but at least you'll have died having lived a bit."

Chauncy realized with dismay that she was right.

"Well, why do *I* have to be the one to beat him?" he pressed. "I'm not the only Chosen One, you know."

"Yeah, but you're the most powerful of us," she retorted. He blinked.

"What?"

"Your magic," she clarified. "It's more powerful than mine or Harry's."

"But…"

"We're better at using ours," she interrupted. "But if you ever got to really figuring your magic out, you'd be more powerful."

"You think so?"

"I know so," Nettie confirmed. "Thing is, you're so far up yer own ass you can't see past the shit wizard you think you are," she added. "You think you stink, so you stink."

He frowned, lowering his gaze to his lap.

The solution to the problem is the problem itself.

Maybe Nettie was right. Maybe the problem with him was that he *thought* there was a problem with him. And the solution to that would be believing that there wasn't.

That he was enough. Just as he was, here and now.

He retrieved The Magic of Magic from his pocket, opening it to page sixty-nine and reading the awfully ornate poem there:

To Before and After it

Will never bow,
For The Magic of Magic is
Here and Now.

Chauncy closed the book, staring at the cover without seeing it. And in that moment, utterly without warning, revelation came to him.

Ever since being forced to go on this trip, he'd believed that he'd only be happy afterward. That he couldn't enjoy Valtora until she and The Dark One were divorced. But before realizing she was married, Chauncy had enjoyed her without reservation. In casting his happiness into the future rather than the present, he'd taken the happiness *out* of the present.

"I need to be happy here and now," he realized. "That's where my magic is."

Nettie patted his knee, smiling proudly at him.

"Damn right kid," she agreed. "But you better find your happy place quick," she added. "Gonna need it real soon."

Chauncy frowned.

"Why?" he asked. She pointed out of her window, and Chauncy stared out of it. His eyes widened, a sensation very much different than happiness coming over him.

For there, miles in the distance, was a black, dead landscape with pools of glowing lava, covered in an awful pall of choking gray smoke and gray ash. And beyond that, standing tall amidst the devastation, stood the giant volcano that was Mount Thrall.

* * *

The road ended less than a mile from the charred landscape of Thrall, forcing everyone to abandon the carriage. And Peter, much to Valtora's dismay. She spent a rather long and tender moment embracing the bedazzled unicorn, and was even a bit teary-eyed when she separated from him at last. To Chauncy's surprise, Peter was a bit teary-eyed too, rainbow-colored tears dripping down his cheeks. It appeared that all of the unicorn's fluids were rainbow-colored now, as a brief spurt of urination earlier had proven.

"All right, break it up," Nettie grumbled.

"I'll be back soon," Valtora vowed. She turned to Chauncy, hooking her elbow in his. "Let's go baby."

"Okay poopy-dooz," he agreed.

"Ohhh kaaaah," Rocky concurred, Rooter smiling happily from his perennial perch on the stone giant's shoulder. With that, Skibbard, Rocky, Rooter, Chauncy, Valtora, Nettie, and Harry all started forward to the ash-covered obsidian landscape ahead, each a Chosen One or someone chosen by a Chosen One to help the Chosen Ones. Chauncy heard a neigh behind him, and heard the *clippity-clop* of hooves catching up to them. He turned, seeing Peter there.

"Peter, what are you doing?" Valtora asked. The unicorn snorted, slowing to a trot beside her. "You can't come," she told him. "The mountain's too steep. You could break a leg you know."

Peter snorted, whipping his mane about with sickening handsomeness. Then he pointed his rainbow horn at Rooter.

"I guess you're right," Valtora said. "Rooter could heal you."

Peter neighed.

"What do you think guys?" Valtora asked the others. "Can Peter come?"

Harry chuckled, and Nettie elbowed the old man, then winced, rubbing her elbow.

"You're so damn hard all the time," she grumbled.

"So's Peter," Harry replied. Which prompted everyone to see if Harry was right. Which, to Chauncy's dismay, he was. He stared, then glanced at Valtora, who was also staring.

Nettie gave a low whistle.

"Guess he's gonna come whether we want him to or not," Harry said. And chuckled again.

"For the love of Pete!" Nettie complained.

Everyone shared a laugh, except for Skibbard. The curmudgeonly wizard seemed even more subdued than normal, eyeing Peter with what could only be described as utter depression.

"What's the plan, Chauncy?" Valtora asked. Chauncy considered this, then shrugged.

"Wing it," he answered.

"Good enough for me!" Valtora proclaimed.

"We're gonna die," Nettie stated.

"Eventually," Harry agreed.

"Sooner rather than later," she countered.

"Hope you go first," Harry said, wrapping a long arm around her shoulders and giving her a kiss on the top of her head. She frowned up at him.

"Now why would you say that ya big oaf?" she demanded.

"Well, it wouldn't be heaven without my angel there," he replied. She broke out into a smile, her eyes growing moist.

"Shut up Harry," she muttered. But for once, she clearly didn't mean it. Still, Harry, ever the good husband, happily obeyed.

"I hope you die first too," Valtora told Chauncy. He blinked...and found it rather disturbing that Peter seemed to snort in agreement.

"Why?" he asked.

"So I can bedazzle your corpse," she answered. "I'd make it the best frickin' corpse *ever*," she added zestily. "People would like, talk about it forever."

"Gee, thanks."

"And if I bedazzled it, it wouldn't decompose," she continued. "It'd have to stay beautiful forever. So I could keep it in the house, and talk to it and stuff. I'd probably just pretend like you took a vow of silence. It'd be almost like you were still alive, you know?"

"Uh...no?"

"But if *I* died first," she continued, "...my corpse would just pus up and bloat and blast nasty gasses and shit, and that'd be that." She sighed, looking down at her left hand. "All that'd be left is my left hand."

"You've really thought about this," Chauncy realized.

"*Oh* yeah," she agreed. "I bedazzled some flowers back home after killing them, like *months* ago. Still haven't decomposed."

"I don't wanna talk about this anymore," he stated, feeling rather disturbed at the thought of her keeping his bedazzled body around. Valtora shrugged, and they continued forward in silence.

"You people are crazy," Skibbard spoke up.

"We are a little nuts," Valtora agreed.

"Nuts make sense," Skibbard countered. "You guys don't."

"What's the point in making sense?" Valtora countered, clearly sensing an opportunity for an argument.

"It makes sense to make sense," Skibbard answered. "It doesn't make sense to not make sense."

"Gotta admit, that makes sense," Harry conceded.

"Shut up Harry!" Nettie shot back.

"No it doesn't," Valtora argued.

"How could making sense not make sense?" Skibbard retorted.

"Sometimes it makes sense to not make sense," Valtora reasoned. "And sometimes you can sense that the most sensible thing doesn't make sense in the moment. Right Chauncy?"

"Right," Chauncy agreed. He'd learned as much from Grandma Little. The most sensible thing – working at the shop, making a reasonable living, staying completely, boringly safe – had nearly killed him, after all. Only by doing something insensible – something utterly *ridiculous* – had he found true happiness. In Valtora, magic, and everything else.

Skibbard looked at Valtora, then at Chauncy. Then rubbed his forehead wearily.

"Don't say anything," Nettie warned. "She loves to argue."

"No I don't," Valtora retorted.

"Yes you…" Nettie began, then stopped herself, her jaw snapping shut. And said nothing more.

"Aww," Valtora said, pouting prettily.

"So let me get this straight," Nettie stated. "We're going to scale Mount Thrall, defeat The Dark One's armies, reach the summit, destroy The Dark One…"

"And kill liches," Skibbard interjected.

"And maybe kill some liches," Nettie added, "…and our master plan is to…wing it?"

Chauncy glanced at Valtora, then at Harry, who smiled encouragingly.

"Right," he agreed.

"Right," Nettie muttered.

"That's ridiculous!" Skibbard proclaimed.

"I agree," Chauncy replied. "But maybe that's the point," he added. "Is Valtora's magical bedazzling appropriate in battle? Is Nettie's water magic great against lava? Or is my staff of wind? Or a pocket full of seeds?"

"No," Skibbard admitted.

"Pravus has plenty of magic, and armies," Chauncy continued, really feeling himself now. "But do they stand a chance against The Dark One?"

"Nope," Nettie answered. "Need Chosen Ones for that."

"Right!" Chauncy agreed. "See, the last time we saved the world, it took a whole lot of inappropriate magic to do it. And by golly it worked. This time," he added, "…inappropriate magic might not be enough. If we're going to beat The Dark One, we're going to need *ridiculously* inappropriate magic to do it!"

Chapter 24

By the time King Pravus returned to Cumulus, an enormous amount of paperwork – and an even more enormous backlog of meetings – greeted him. Paperwork regarding the liquidation and distribution of cash reserves for rebuilding cities and towns, and for paying overtime for soldiers. And sick pay for those injured in battle, and funerals for those injured quite literally gravely. Not to mention the levying of additional taxes on the rich to support such efforts, which promised to generate more meetings with those so affected. Mountains of paperwork and blabbing to endure, with no end in sight.

It was, as Pravus realized whilst sitting in his oversized chair in his oversized office, staring at oversized stacks of paperwork on his oversized desk, a problem so oversized that he was simply overwhelmed at the thought of solving it.

So he slumped in his chair, staring at it glumly, feeling utterly defeated.

Then came a knock on his door.

"Go away," he ordered. "No," he added hastily. "Kill me first, then go away."

A moment passed, and the door opened. And while Pravus half-hoped it would be an executioner, it was perhaps the only other soul who could lift his spirit. But while the executioner would have lifted his spirit *from* his body, this particular visitor lifted his spirit without such separation.

"Templeton!" he cried, bolting upright from his chair. And getting on his tippy-toes to make eye contact with his cousin over the tall stacks of paperwork. "Thank god you're here. I'm afraid I'm dying."

"Dying?" Templeton asked, his expression immediately aghast.

"Inside," Pravus clarified, to Templeton's obvious relief. He gestured at the mounds of work before him. "I can't do this," he confessed, feeling a sudden, unfamiliar sensation build up within him. His eyes blurred, and tears – actual tears! – welled up in his eyes, threatening to spill over onto his royal cheeks.

"Cousin!" Templeton gasped, rushing to Pravus's side and putting a hand on his shoulder. Templeton knelt down before Pravus, gazing up at him with heroic resolve. "If your load is too great, let me have it, my liege!"

Pravus broke out into a smile, touched by Templeton's offer. And, given the position Templeton had placed himself in, wished quite fervently that Templeton's offer had involved touching. For Pravus's load *was* great. And letting Templeton have it would have brightened his mood considerably. But alas, he merely touched Templeton's shoulder, giving the man his affection rather than his erection.

"Thank you, dearest cousin," he replied. "I do think I need help," he confessed. And it was a most unusual thing for him to say. For he'd spent his life much like his time in the gym, always able to lift the weight no one else could. And never taking more than was safe to handle.

But the crown, while so light on his head at first, had proven far heavier than any weight he'd chosen to bear. Mostly because he *hadn't* chosen it. It had chosen him…and for the mere fact that it held no magic for him, it'd become impossibly heavy.

"Ask and you shall receive," Templeton declared at once, standing up.

"This paperwork," Pravus stated, gesturing at it again. "And all these meetings. I simply can't get through it all, not while coordinating our defenses and trying to hunt down those Chosen Ones!"

"I shall enlist the help of your lawyers to tackle the paperwork," Templeton stated at once, with his usual charmingly cheerful vigor. "And as to the meetings, the Lords can manage the less important ones and report to you their findings."

"But who will delegate it all?" Pravus inquired. "Even you can't do all of those things in a night!"

There was another knock on the door, and both men turned to it.

"Come in," they said in unison.

There was a moment of hesitation, and the door cracked open, a single eyeball peering through. Then the door opened all the way, revealing none other than Desmond. The old-ish man glanced at Pravus, then at Templeton.

"I heard dramatic speech," he noted.
"These are dramatic times," Pravus replied.
"Have you been…crying, my liege?" Desmond inquired, eyeing Pravus with considerably less compassion than such a statement should merit.
"Nearly," Pravus confessed.
"I see," the old man stated. And just stared at him.
"What are you still doing here, Desmond?" Pravus snapped grumpily. "Weren't you supposed to be home hours ago?"
"Finishing up work," Desmond answered.
"What work?" Pravus retorted.
"Anything I can find."
Pravus frowned.
"Why?" he pressed.
"I'd hoped that things wouldn't get worse at home," Desmond explained.
"And?"
"My hopes were dashed," Desmond answered.
"Go home Desmond," Pravus said with a sigh, rubbing his forehead wearily. "We have a lot of things to do, and honestly, dealing with your awful marriage isn't one of them."
"I agree," Desmond agreed. "Which is why I'd like to be included in that 'we.'"
"Ah," Pravus murmured. "I see."
"We could use the extra help," Templeton reasoned. "Desmond can help delegate tasks to your lawyers while I organize the lords. We'll act as your metaphorical shields, taking the blows that would maim you, so that your royal sword can be turned against our enemy in service to the kingdom!"
Pravus practically beamed at the two men.
"Why, I think I love you," he declared. "Both," he added, as he'd been gazing at Templeton when he said it.
"And I you, my liege," Templeton replied. Pravus eyed Desmond, who looked rather uncomfortable all of a sudden.
"Desmond?" he prodded.
"Fond of you, sire," Desmond replied at last.
"Irritatingly?" Pravus pressed.
"Regrettably."
"Good enough," Pravus declared. "Very well. I appreciate you both, and together we will lift a weight that neither of us could lift separately!"

"Your royal spotters!" Templeton declared. After which he got a familiar twinkle in his eye. "Speaking of which, I do believe it's been some time since we last went to the gym."

"Too long," Pravus agreed.

"Care for a bit of worship at the old temple?" Templeton inquired.

"That would be downright heavenly," Pravus replied. "But we've so much work to do," he added, eyeing the stacks of paperwork yet to be read with a sigh. "I'm afraid I can't justify it."

"Of course you can," Desmond replied. "You're king."

"But…" Pravus began.

"You can't attend to others without first attending to yourself," the servant insisted. "That leads to utter misery. A life you'll regret."

"Are you speaking from experience, Desmond?" Pravus inquired.

"I regret so," Desmond confirmed.

"But I really should focus on the kingdom," Pravus insisted.

"Doing what you love will give you the strength to do what you don't," Desmond declared. "And we need our king to be as strong as possible to carry his kingdom and his people safely into the future."

Templeton arched an eyebrow at the servant, then turned to Pravus.

"I see now why you made Desmond your advisor," he said.

"Yes, well, I've often considered myself an excellent judge of character," Pravus agreed.

"I've been working for you since you were born, sire," Desmond pointed out.

"To the gym!" Pravus cried, ignoring the impudent servant/advisor. "And after a good pump, I shall unsheathe my royal sword, and thrust it deep into The Dark One, ending his tyranny once and for all!"

Chapter 25

The blasted, awful, ash-covered lands of Thrall extended for over a mile around the perimeter of The Dark One's massive volcano, its streams and pools of lava never seeming to cool. This, Valtora explained as they walked ever-closer to the base of the mountain, was because of the fire elementals that lived within such pools. Chauncy nodded, exchanging glances with Nettie and Harry. For they'd battled a fire elemental that'd popped out of just such a pool, burning poor Rocky badly. Rocky grunted, clearly recalling the incident, and Rooter patted the giant's cheek with one tiny golem-hand.

"God, I didn't miss this place," Valtora mused, shaking her head at the bleak devastation all around them. "Can't *believe* I spent most of my life here."

"With no ill effects whatsoever," Nettie quipped.

"Surprisingly," Valtora agreed obliviously. Then she frowned. "Looks awfully deserted."

"Did last time too," Nettie noted. "Until that Rock Dervish and the lava elemental pounced on us."

"And Magmara," Harry added.

"Don't gotta remind me," Nettie grumbled.

"That's because we didn't *actually* want to beat you," Valtora pointed out. "Believe me, if The Dark One wanted to crush us all, he would. His armies are frickin' *ginormous*."

"Like his…" Harry began, but Nettie elbowed him.

"Shut up Harry."

"So…why hasn't he?" Chauncy asked. "Crushed us all, I mean."

"That's not his style," Valtora answered. "He likes a challenge. More dramatic, you know?"

"So The Dark One's a drama queen?" Nettie asked.

"Drama *king*," Valtora corrected. "He's lived like, forever and shit. At least as long as humans have. Gets boring after a while. Drama's all he's got at this point."

"Understandable," Chauncy conceded. He couldn't imagine how boring living forever would be. Especially in a volcano.

"I think that's why he married me," Valtora mused, gazing off into the distance. "After millennia of black and white, all he wanted was a little color."

Chauncy nodded, glancing down at her diamond-hand. Even in the relative darkness of the ashen clouds that blanketed the sky, it glittered with all the colors of the rainbow. As if it were a window into her colorful kaleidoscope of a soul. It reminded him of his first trial in the Cave of Wonder, where he'd nearly succumbed to a world of black, white, and gray. Only the color within him had saved him.

"Maybe he wants magic," he theorized, staring up at the volcano.

"He's got plenty of magic," Nettie retorted. "Dragons and goblins and dervishes and ogres and harpies."

"And liches," Skibbard added.

"They're magical creatures," Chauncy conceded. "But does The Dark One have magic of his own?"

"Black magic," Valtora replied. "He's evil incarnate."

"So what can he…do?" Chauncy asked. Which was a good question. After all, if they were going to beat The Dark One, they needed to know what he was capable of.

"Fog armor, for one," Valtora answered.

"And?" Nettie pressed.

"No idea," Valtora admitted. "He never really talked about it. Or showed me anything."

"Except Gigantor," Harry pointed out.

"*Any*way," Chauncy interjected before Valtora could answer, "…that means we're going in blind. We'll have to wing it."

"Which was your plan in the first place," Valtora agreed.

"Which is a terrible plan," Skibbard grumbled.

"It's not a plan at all," Nettie argued.

"Yes it is," Valtora retorted, her eyes lighting up. But Nettie knew better than to be baited into another argument. "Hag," she added hopefully, to no avail. Valtora pouted, kicking a black pebble into a lava pool. It sputtered and hissed, melting slowly into the pool to become lava itself.

"Anyone got a better idea?" Chauncy inquired.

No one did.

"All right then," he declared.

With that, everyone fell silent, in a morbid, resigned kind of way. Except for Harry and Valtora, who were seemingly incapable of sour moods. Chauncy found himself eyeing Skibbard as they began the march up the slopes of Mount Thrall. Sour moods appeared to be the strange little man's baseline.

"What's your story?" Chauncy asked him.

"Eh," Skibbard replied.

"I grew up in Borrin," Chauncy told him. "Worked in a magic shop selling useless trinkets most of my life. My grandmother told me that was all there was to life. That magic wasn't real. After twenty-five years of working for imaginary numbers, I was ready to end it." He smiled, glancing at Harry and Nettie. "Then magic saved me."

"I was president of a bank," Skibbard revealed. "I made imaginary numbers making imaginary numbers from imaginary numbers, and loaning those imaginary numbers to other people to make more imaginary numbers from them."

"Ouch," Chauncy replied.

"One day I realized my life was no life at all, and I quit," Skibbard continued. "Went off into the woods to kill myself."

"What happened?"

"I found myself instead," Skibbard answered.

Chauncy considered this.

"Maybe that's how it is," he mused. "We're all born into this stupid imaginary game, and we have to kill the imaginary person we were pretending to be to find the *real* person we were *meant* to be."

"Which was who we were all along," Skibbard agreed. "But were told we couldn't be."

"Huh," Chauncy murmured. He stared at his feet for a while, then eyed Skibbard sidelong. "I think we could be friends."

"Eh," Skibbard replied. But not quite as dismissively as before.

"I might grow on you," Chauncy quipped.

"You're not a plant," Skibbard retorted.

The man fell silent then, making it quite clear without saying so that the conversation was over, and that further attempts at conversing would be most unwelcome. Chauncy took the hint, falling into a comfortable silence. For, while silence had once given him the irresistible compulsion to fill it, now the silence filled *him*. It was a space between conversations…and like the space between the sun and the earth, it was as important as the things it separated. Silence offered a time to take in rather than put out. For most conversations were a mutual putting out, a dance of talking, then pretending to listen while impatiently waiting for the moment to speak again.

Perhaps that was why Skibbard disliked talking, Chauncy theorized. After decades of being alone, the odd little wizard almost certainly saw conversations for what they were. And that mere words could never properly describe the depth of experience, the magic of each moment. Chauncy smiled, thinking back to when he was a boy, and Grandma Little's books described wizards incanting spells with odd languages. In reality, magic was wordless, a spell cast by connection, not conversation.

Unless there was a wizard who thought words themselves were magic, he supposed.

"Keep an eye out now," Nettie warned everyone.

Her words tore Chauncy from his pleasant contemplations, and up the mountain they went, eyes peeled for goblins, dervishes, elementals, giants, harpies, and such. But nothing whatsoever came to stop them.

"This is weird," Nettie muttered. "Something's not right."

"He's *got* to be screwing with us," Valtora stated. "The Dark One loves to build up some good terror right before he strikes. He thinks it's boring just to kill people outright."

"No drama in it?" Harry inquired.

"Right," she agreed. "Much more fun to watch them scream and piss themselves and beg for their lives and stuff." She smiled at the thought, which made Chauncy frown.

"That's terrible," he pointed out.

"Nah, it's frickin' hilarious," she countered. His eyebrows rose. "I mean, you wouldn't think so, but you really have to see it to appreciate it," she added with a disturbing gleam in her eyes.

"See, a hero wouldn't say that," Chauncy pointed out.

"Anyway, the point is, don't be scared," she advised. "If we don't give him what he wants, it'll really frustrate him. Believe me, I've been doing it for three years."

"Poor Gigantor," Harry piped in.

"Pfft," Valtora replied. "He's got hundreds of Succubi. And Incubi, for that matter. Gigantor is well taken care of, believe me."

"Incubi?" Chauncy asked.

"Male versions of succubi," Valtora explained. "All they do is seduce people and have tons of sex with them. Half of 'em are gay."

"Oh."

"I like succubi," Harry said.

"You never had one," Nettie retorted. "So how the hell would you know?"

"Guess I better figure it out," Harry said.

"My ass," Nettie countered.

"Already figured that out."

"Well you're not figuring out any damn succubus," Nettie argued. "Unless I get me an incubus."

Harry rubbed his chin thoughtfully.

"Shut up Harry," Nettie grumbled.

"But I didn't say anything."

"You did in your head!" she retorted. He grinned at her, putting a hand around her shoulders. And then sliding it down to her butt and giving it a squeeze. Chauncy closed his eyes, willing away the visions that always seemed to accompany their conversations. Visions that, not to be too graphic, were far too graphic for him. For while his mind could censor most things, his mind's eye was not one of them.

Onward and upward they went, minutes dribbling on into hours, the clouds of ash over their heads growing thicker and darker, and falling like snowflakes on their heads. The stench of sulfur violated Chauncy's nostrils, threatening to choke the air out of his lungs. Indeed, the falling ash became so dense that they could barely see more than a few yards ahead of them. He felt a sudden anxiety grip him, a squirmy feeling in the pit of his stomach. He peered through the ash around them, gripping Valtora's hand tightly.

"What's wrong?" she asked.

"I don't know," he confessed.

"I do," Nettie said. "This was the place where Magmara attacked us last time." She reached out, holding Harry's hand. "And where my heart broke."

"Turned out alright," Harry said, smiling down at her and squeezing her hand. She smiled back.

"Just like you always say it will," she agreed. Harry pushed his glasses a bit up his nose, grinning at her impishly.

"Guess that makes me a genius."

"Genius my ass," she retorted, pulling her hand away.

"Genius for marrying yours," he countered.

"Well that's true."

And that, dear reader, was when Magmara struck.

Chapter 26

The Shadowsteed brought Gavin's carriage near the enormous wall surrounding Cumulus, capitol of the magical kingdom of Pravus. The huge silver gates guarding the entrance to the fabled city were almost identical to those at the Wall in Southwick, making it impossible to see the city – or Pravus's castle – until one had passed beyond. Which, given that the gates were currently closed, was not a possibility at this time.

So, Gavin waited, a half-mile outside the city.

And waited.

But the gates didn't open. Which was quite unusual, because when Gavin had been here last – and indeed, every time he'd been here – the gates had been wide open. The fact that they weren't could mean several things, none of which were particularly pleasant for Gavin. For either Pravus somehow knew that he was coming…or the gates were closed off to someone else. Gavin immediately rejected the former, knowing that it was unlikely that Pravus would have discovered Gavin's ploy. Which meant the latter had to be true.

The Dark One.

It made perfect sense, of course. The Dark One – some villain that periodically attacked the kingdom, for some reason – had been threatening Pravus six months ago. At around the same time as Marie had been murdered, and Gavin had barely escaped Pravus's quite literal clutches alive. Pravus had offered to let Gavin read up on The Dark One, but at the time, Gavin had declined.

In retrospect, he wished he hadn't.

Still, if the gates were closed, that meant that Cumulus was unavailable to him now. Which meant his quest for vengeance was in jeopardy. There was no way for him to open them himself, which meant that he'd just have to wait. And there was no telling just how long it would take for them to open again.

Damn it.

He should've kept Skibbard around for this contingency. Assuming that this gate was like the one in Southwick, and could be opened by a wizard.

Idiot, he chastised himself. But he didn't have to self-flagellate for long. For without warning, there was a loud *thunk* that echoed across the land, and before his eyes, the doors swung slowly open. Almost immediately, a procession of troops marched out, complete with infantry, numerous armored carriages pulled by huge magical beasts Gavin didn't recognize, an enormous number of cavalry, and even a black dragon-like creature with no arms called a wyvern. The procession made its way down the main road, which luckily Gavin was nowhere near. For he'd parked the carriage quite a ways off-road.

Still, he felt a twinge of anxiety as the procession made its way down the road toward him. But it ignored him completely, passing by without so much as noticing him. He waited for the army to pass, nervous that the gates might close behind the tail of the procession. But to his relief, it didn't.

Yet.

Gavin prompted the Shadowsteed forward, and it brought him on a smooth ride back to the road, the carriage's magical wheels evening out the bumps in the terrain. Then he followed the road all the way to the open gates, where a few guards had been posted to check passers-by. He slouched back a bit in his seat to look as casual as possible, affecting a practiced boredom, as if everything that were going on were beneath him. Which it usually was. He stopped the carriage at the gate, rolling down his side-window and turning to face one of the guards there, as if it annoyed the hell out of him to do so.

"Yes?" he inquired impatiently.

"Name and reason for entry," the guard prompted.

"Gavin Merrick," he answered. "Assassination of King Pravus."

The guard blinked.

"Um," the man blubbered. To which Gavin reached into his pocket, retrieving a golden coin. He flicked it at the man, striking the guard in the chest...and turning him instantly to gold.

"Hey!" another guard protested, rushing toward the carriage and drawing his sword. He brushed against the golden guard's shoulder in the process, and froze, becoming a golden statue much like the first guard.

Gavin snapped his fingers, summoning the coin back into his hand.

"Holy…!" one of the three remaining guards exclaimed. Gavin tossed the coin again and again, turning them all to pure gold. Then he placed the coin back in his pocket, getting out of the carriage and turning to the Shadowsteed.

"Go home," he ordered it. And – its shadow still anchored in Borrin – the magical horse zoomed away, dashing over the land so fast it was impossible to follow. Gavin strode into Cumulus, past the golden guards…and the many more in the wide courtyard ahead that had been alerted to the goings-on. These guards rushed toward him, clad in gold and black armor, the official colors of Pravus.

"Stop!" one of them cried, stopping a few yards from Gavin and unsheathing their sword. A few more did the same, one of them readying a crossbow and aiming it at Gavin. But Gavin didn't stop. "Stop or we *will* kill you!"

"I doubt it," Gavin replied calmly. The crossbowman shot at him, the crossbow bolt zipping through the air toward him. It struck his magical golden tie, bouncing off harmlessly. As would any nonmagical – and most magical – weapons.

The guards gawked, backing up a few steps as Gavin continued toward them. Gavin did stop then, reaching into his pocket to retrieve his silver ring. He drew it out, tossing it on the ground before him. If he'd put it on his finger, it would've transported him back to Borrin. Instead, he did an incantation.

"Portus," he declared.

The ring rotated so that it stood up, then expanded, forming a silver portal. And through that portal, a veritable army of his finest soldiers came from Borrin into Cumulus. A very large army, equipped with the finest magical weapons that the Evermore Trading Company had to offer. And, to make it absolutely clear who was behind the attack, they wore fine green suits with golden ties. Not nearly as magical as Gavin's, but effective armor nonetheless. Pravus's guards backpedaled frantically as Gavin's private army filled the courtyard.

"My turn," Gavin told them. He lifted his fist into the air. "Attack!" he commanded.

Chapter 27

Magmara, the dreaded guardian of Mount Thrall, an enormous dragon wrought of obsidian and lava – and according to some reports, bound together with pure evil – was something out of Chauncy's worst nightmares. A being so large she defied description, with glowing red eyes that, with a single look, could strike dread in those unlucky enough to be beheld by her. An awful monster – or monstress, more accurately – that had killed more Chosen Ones than history could count. And quite horribly, to boot.

So when Magmara's massive head burst from the haze of falling ash ahead of them, crimson eyes locked on Chauncy and the others, Chauncy did what anyone would do in that situation.

He peed himself. Just a little. But enough to be messy.

Huge black wings spread outward, their movement sweeping the ash clear from the surrounding area, revealing Magmara in all her horrible splendor.

She opened her great maw, and *roared*.

"Elementals!" Nettie cried, grabbing the Wetstone and squeezing it. She created her water elemental, and Harry created his earth elemental, and they fused it together into one. An earth elemental with a watery outer flesh, which Nettie flash-froze into thick plates of ice armor. At the same time, she extended watery tentacles out to Valtora, Rocky, and even Peter and Skibbard, hauling them to safety within the elemental's hollow chest-chamber. Soon they were all floating chest-deep within it, looking through a thick windshield of ice out at the lava dragon, while Chauncy stood at the elemental's feet.

"Hey! What about me?" he blurted out.

"You gotta fight her!" Nettie yelled from above.

Chauncy peed a bit more.

"Maggie!" Valtora cried, waving wildly at the dragon from within the elemental. "Hi!"

Magmara's mouth closed, and she cocked her head to the side, turning one baleful eye on Valtora. Then she snorted, smoke shooting from her nostrils.

"I'm gonna drown this bitch," Nettie vowed, extending one of the water elemental's hands to do just that. But Valtora stopped her.

"If you get her wet, it'll just get steamy," she warned. "Remember the plan!"

"What plan?" Nettie retorted. Valtora smiled, putting her diamond hand on Nettie's heart.

"Kindness," she replied.

"Get your hand off my jugs!" Nettie retorted, slapping Valtora's hand away. Or at least she tried to. For Valtora's hand, being made of diamond, was even harder than Harry. "Ow!" Nettie complained, shaking her hand out.

"Um, guys," Chauncy warned from below, pointing beyond the ice-windshield. Magmara had turned her terrible head to face them, and her maw was opening, revealing her long throat. An orange-red glow shone from deep within, lava no doubt rising within her to blast them!

But instead, Magmara emitted a sound that, well, sounded for all the world like a happy squeal. A very shrill, ear-splitting, bone-rattling squeal. But happy. Probably.

"Maggie!" Valtora gushed, removing her diamond hand from Nettie's bust and putting it on her own. "Ohmygod I *missed* you babygirl!"

Chauncy blinked.

"Let me *out* already," Valtora ordered Nettie, wading up to the windshield.

"Your funeral," Nettie grumbled. But she complied, liquifying the windshield and extending a watery tentacle to let Valtora all the way down to the ground beside Chauncy. Valtora ran right at Magmara, who lowered her giant dragon-head toward Valtora, opening her maw to swallow Valtora whole!

Except she didn't. She let out another squeak instead, and lowered her nose to Valtora, who rubbed it with her diamond-hand.

"How's my sweet widdle cootsie wootsie dwagon?" Valtora cooed.

Magmara snorted, smoke shooting up around Valtora.

"Aww," Valtora said, pouting a bit. "Is my idiot husband still being mean to you?"

Another snort.

"Men," Valtora said, putting her hands on her hips and shaking her head. "*God* they're so stupid. Idiots, every last one of 'em."

Magmara nodded, and Chauncy frowned, feeling rather put out.

"I mean, she has a point," Nettie said. Harry ignored her.

"I mean, they're practically *useless*," Valtora continued. "Dicks with dicks, y'know? Hey, where is The Dark Dick anyway?"

Magmara made some sounds that, to Chauncy's ears, were a series of awful, bone-rumbling roars. For quite a while, in fact. He covered his ears, but Valtora only nodded sagely as Magmara continued, until at last the dragon finished.

"Got it," she said. "Let me talk to the others." She turned to Chauncy. "Come with me," she told him.

And with that, Valtora and Chauncy went into the elemental, Nettie extending a water tentacle to bring them into the elemental's chest-cavity. Valtora turned to Chauncy as they floated within, smiling happily. He crossed his arms over his chest, glaring at her.

"So we're all idiots, huh?" he accused. "Practically useless?"

"Oh, that's just girl talk," Valtora replied, waving his concerns away. "It's all just hating men and shit. Gotta play the game, right?"

"Um…right," Chauncy replied, though it didn't seem at all right to him.

"Anyway, The Dark One's where he was the last time we met him," she continued. "Come on, let's go."

"Wait," Nettie interjected. "So…that's it?"

"Well yeah," Valtora replied. "Duh," she added, unhelpfully.

"What about the damn dragon?" Nettie pressed, gesturing at Magmara.

"Oh, Maggie-poo'll take us there," Valtora replied. Nettie stared at her for a while, then rubbed her forehead vigorously, until it turned bright red.

"She's supposed to try to kill us!" Nettie complained.

"Nah," Valtora replied happily. "Like I said, we're *tight*."

Harry patted Chauncy on the shoulder.

"You're a lucky man, Chauncy," he told him.

"Shut up Harry!" Nettie barked.

"See, no one likes loose lips," Harry quipped. Nettie wound up to punch him in the shoulder, then paused, turning to Valtora.

"Punch him for me," she requested.

"Okay!" Valtora replied, always up for a bit of violence. She punched Harry in the shoulder with her diamond hand. Hard.

"Ow!" Harry complained, rubbing his shoulder. Nettie cackled, and Valtora joined her.

"Can we focus please?" Chauncy pleaded. "What the hell's going on?"

"The Dark One's waiting for us," she told him. "Maggie says to ride her to his temple and meet him there."

"Right, so she can just drop us in the lava on the way?" Nettie shot back, folding her arms over her chest. "Do I look like an idiot to you?"

Valtora eyed Nettie, considering her answer.

"No," she decided reluctantly. "But if she tries, Chauncy can just tornado us to safety or something. Right Chauncy?"

"Um, sure?" Chauncy replied.

"Let's go," Valtora prompted.

Nettie glanced at Harry, who shrugged, and then sighed. She let everyone out of the elemental on watery tentacles, after which she sucked her part of the elemental back into her Wetstone, and Harry sucked the life out of his earth elemental. They all got onto Magmara's back, except for Peter and Rocky, of course. Magmara's back was quite warm, naturally. To the point of being uncomfortable. But it quickly dried Chauncy's pee-soaked robe and underwear, which was worth the price of baked buns.

"What's that smell?" Nettie said from her seat behind him.

"Smells like popcorn," Harry ventured. Chauncy grimaced, hunching down and squeezing his thighs as hard as he could around Magmara, to create a better odor seal.

"Bye Peter!" Valtora called out, waving to the unicorn. "Bye shmookie tookums, bye Rootie-poo!"

And with that, Magmara spread her wings, taking them up, up, and away, to the summit of Mount Thrall.

* * *

In the center of the massive, lava-filled crater of Mount Thrall was a small island, upon which a huge obsidian temple stood. A temple right out of Chauncy's nightmares, complete with horrifying gargoyles leering at them as if posed to strike, bloodstained spikes jutting from the earth in random clusters, and innumerable skeletons littering the ground leading up to the temple entrance. Human skeletons, Chauncy noted. Many clad in armor and lying next to swords and other such weapons. Legions of men, and probably women, because to exclude the possibility was to be accused of being irredeemably prejudicial. Although the alternative explanation was that women were in fact too smart to rush up active volcanos and cross lakes of lava to fight pure evil that would eventually just resurrect itself anyway.

In any case, there they were, and Chauncy was once again struck with the horrible realization that he would soon be joining them.

He forced himself to look away from these former would-be heroes, gazing up at the many black chimneys rising from the roof of the temple. These were the source of the endless ash falling from the sky, pumping the stuff high into the atmosphere in a never-ending geyser. Turning the whole world gray, choking the life and color from the land.

Everything black as obsidian, or white as ash. And nothing else.

Chauncy looked down, seeing his purple, silky, sparkly robe, just *bursting* with color against this dull canvas. And Valtora's diamond fist, turning black and white into every color of the rainbow. Even Harry's brown and Skibbard's green, and Nettie's blue cut through the bleakness, as if to be a Chosen One was to tell the world that there was more to life than black and white. More than good and evil, right and wrong. Another dimension to life altogether, beyond the endless game of trying in vain to win.

Because in the end, win or lose, they'd all end up like these skeletons on the ground, Chauncy realized. The end was assured, though when and where were perhaps negotiable. So in the end, the end didn't matter.

But Chauncy wasn't at the end. He was here and now. And that, according to The Magic of Magic, was where magic lived.

"Let's do this," he declared, setting his staff before him rather grandly, whilst striking a heroic, wizardly pose. Valtora beamed at him, clutching onto his arm adoringly.

"My hero!" she gushed, jumping into his arms.

"Mmmf!" he grunted as she assaulted him, kissing him passionately. He kissed her back, which only got her going. To the point where it was abundantly clear that she'd forgotten that anyone else was there.

"Break it up!" Nettie ordered, grabbing Valtora and yanking her off of Chauncy.

"I'm not finished!" Valtora retorted, resisting mightily.

"Finish later," Nettie shot back, throwing her bodily away, then blocking Valtora's path back to Chauncy. "You gotta divorce your husband, remember?"

"Oh, right," Valtora replied.

"Don't want your child to be a bastard," Harry noted.

"Marriage doesn't guarantee that," Skibbard groused. "Believe me."

"Let's go," Chauncy grumbled, smoothing out his wizard's robe. Which sent out a fresh waft of odor.

"I smell popcorn too," Valtora said, sniffing the air.

Chauncy ignored her, marching through the gigantic, terrifying front doorway of the temple, inscribed as it was with awfully graphic depictions of murder and other nonconsensual acts. Into the temple they went, traversing its familiar long, dark, narrow hallways, shrinking from hideous shadows cast by far too few flickering torches bolted to the walls. Valtora quickly took the lead, cheerily guiding them down hallway after hallway and down stairwell after stairwell, pointing out all sorts of traps that would have certainly killed them. Eventually they reached the final stone staircase leading deep into the bowels of the earth, the one that would bring them to the very bottom of the temple. It spiraled down into the darkness in tight circles, lit rather ineffectively by black stone statues inset into the walls every few feet, with eyes and gaping mouths that glowed very faint red. Statues of various demonic entities, male and female, and rather distractingly nude. And even more distractingly endowed. For the males carried formidable staffs, though not in their hands, and the women had curves that rivaled the staircase itself.

"I remember this," Harry said, eyeing the latter. Nettie rolled her eyes.

"You would, ya horn-dog," she grumbled.

"You said it," he agreed. They started down the stairs, going two-by-two. "Gonna have to help me later," he added. "All this pent-up energy."

"Uh huh," Nettie muttered.

"Can't leave a man hanging," Harry insisted. "A man is liable to stray."

"If you're hanging when I leave you, you won't stray," Nettie noted. She chuckled then, and so did Harry. Chauncy smiled, glancing at Valtora, who grabbed his hand and squeezed it. They traded a quick kiss, not needing to say a thing. For they both loved Nettie and Harry, even if Nettie hated Valtora. Then again, considering Nettie insulted Harry even more than she insulted Valtora, perhaps Nettie didn't hate Valtora so much after all.

They continued down the spiraling stairs, and Chauncy found himself eyeing the sheer drop down the center of it.

"You think they'd have installed a guard rail," he grumbled, staying close to the wall. And brushing up against a few...staves in the process.

"Not very safe," Harry agreed.

After several nervous minutes, they finally reached the bottom of the staircase, to Chauncy's relief. A familiar long hallway with magma waterfalls flowing down the walls on either side greeted them, ending at a normal-sized black stone door at the other end of it. They walked toward the door, wincing at the dry heat from the magma. Valtora led the way, stopping at the door.

"Ready?" Valtora asked, eyeing the others. Nettie nodded, Harry winked, and Chauncy swallowed. Skibbard – who Chauncy had forgotten was even there – just stared. Valtora turned to face the door. "Knock knock!" she shouted at the top of her lungs.

A moment passed.

"**Who dares venture into the domicile of the dark one?**" a deep, bone-chilling voice boomed from all around them. It gave Chauncy the creeps, just as it had the last time.

"Me, idiot!" Valtora yelled back. "Now let me in!"

"**Only if the favor is returned**," the creepy voice replied. Creepily.

"Blow yourself," Valtora shot back.

"**It is within my power.**"

"Just open up, asshole!" Valtora snapped. "Shut up!" she added before The Dark One could reply. A moment later, there was a loud *thunk*, and the door creaked open. Beyond the door, Chauncy saw a well-lit living room. It was comfortable but contemporary, with two U-shaped couches facing each other in the middle of the room.

And on one of the couches sat an old man.

He was tall and slender, and appeared to be a very fit eighty-year-old. Despite this, his hair was pure black, and sprung in wild curls from his head. He sported an equally impressive mustache and curly black beard, and wore a black shirt and pants. But his feet were bare, his skin as pale as an albino's. Indeed, the only color he possessed was in his eyes, for they glowed with an awful red light. One that, as soon as Chauncy beheld them, made him feel like peeing himself yet again. But to his relief, he didn't relieve himself.

"Fuck you," Valtora greeted, stepping through the doorway and crossing her arms over her chest. The Dark One smirked, rising to his feet to face her.

"If you're offering," he replied, using a slightly-more-mortal voice. One that still sent shivers down Chauncy's spine.

"I'm not," she retorted. "I want a divorce."

"I'm aware," The Dark One admitted. He turned to Chauncy then, which made Chauncy squirm. "So you're leaving me for…this?"

"Hell yeah," Valtora confirmed. "I'd leave you for *nothing*."

"I imagine that makes you feel special," The Dark One told Chauncy, a little smirk curling his lips. Chauncy grimaced, avoiding his gaze by pretending that he had a spot on his purple robe. Which, despite his recent incontinence, he didn't. Such was its magic, although his underwear – what little of it there was, thanks to Valtora – wasn't so lucky.

"I definitely smell popcorn," Nettie grumbled, shoving past Chauncy and making her way into the living room. "All right dipshit," she declared, eyeing The Dark One. "We gonna fight or what?"

The Dark One's eyebrows rose.

"Fight?" he inquired. "Whatever for?"

"We're Chosen Ones," she answered. "You're The Dark One. You rose to conquer Pravus, so now we've come to beat you."

The Dark One frowned at her, then sighed, sitting back down on the couch and gesturing at the couch opposite him.

"Have a seat," he requested. "Coffee anyone?"

"No," everyone replied.

"I'm not going to poison you," The Dark One insisted, with a smirk that said he totally would.

"Enough bullshit," Valtora said, holding out her diamond hand. "Divorce papers!"

The Dark One eyed her hand, then raised an eyebrow.

"Did you draft them?" he inquired. She blinked.

"Huh?"

"You came to get a divorce but you didn't bring anything for me to sign?" he pressed. "Did you hire a lawyer?"

"Huh?"

"So you came all this way empty-handed?" The Dark One inquired. "Not very prepared."

"She came to *end* you," Nettie retorted. "And so did we." He smirked at her.

"Not very prepared for that either."

"Yeah, well we wouldn't've come at all if you hadn't forced us!" Valtora accused. "You're the one who sent all those minions to kill us!"

"To kill you?" The Dark One scoffed. "Hardly. I sent them for precisely this," he added, gesturing at Valtora. She frowned.

"Huh?"

"I knew you'd merely hide away in Borrin, pretending our marriage never existed," The Dark One explained. "Lying to poor Chauncy here day after day."

"He knows," Valtora retorted.

"Who told him?" The Dark One inquired. Valtora grimaced, and Chauncy did too. For Valtora had lied to him right up until Nettie had told the truth.

"I was trying to spare his feelings!" Valtora shot back.

"You were trying to spare your own," The Dark One countered calmly. "You were afraid he'd be mad or even leave you, so you hid it. For your own selfish ends."

"Bullshit!" Valtora retorted.

"I am the incarnation of evil," The Dark One replied. "Who understands human motivations better than I?"

"Not all motivations are evil," Nettie countered.

"But they *are* selfish," The Dark One pointed out. "We love because it makes us feel good. We hate for the same reasons. Everything is for ourselves, because our *selves* are the only thing we can truly know or care about."

"Speak for yourself," Nettie grumbled.

"I am," The Dark One replied with a smirk. "And as evil, I speak for all humanity." He sat back down on the couch. "Please," he insisted. "Sit."

"Why should we?" Nettie asked.

"Violence is a standing activity," The Dark One explained. "Sitting is nonviolent. When you're sitting, and become enraged, what do you do?"

"Stand up," Harry answered. Nettie elbowed him.

"Shut up Harry."

"Correct," The Dark One replied. "I have no intention toward violence with any of you, so I would prefer that we sit and talk like civilized beings."

"Civilized my ass," Valtora argued. Still, she sighed, walking up to the couch opposite him and sitting down. While pulling Chauncy along to do the same. Nettie and Harry followed suit, while Skibbard stood by the door. Everyone ignored the little wizard, not out of spite, but because honestly, they forgot he was there.

"As I was saying, I knew you'd hide in Borrin forever if I didn't intervene," The Dark One stated. "So I sent my minions to attack Pravus, knowing that it would prompt them to send for the Chosen Ones to save the land from my evil."

"Wait," Nettie interrupted. "You sent armies to kill innocent people just to force your wife to come back to you?"

"Correct," he confirmed.

"That's fucked up," Valtora argued.

"Agreed," he...well, agreed. "As the incarnation of evil, I'm naturally emotionally abusive and manipulative, and put my selfish desires above any consideration of others."

"Well at least he knows it," Harry said. Nettie glared at him.

"Now didn't I tell you to shut up?" she shot back.

"Got to give him credit," Harry pressed.

"We ain't got to give him shit," Nettie replied.

"Actually, that's all you've been giving me so far," The Dark One interjected.

No one could argue with that.

"So why'd you send that damn ogre after us?" Nettie demanded. "And those harpies, and the goblins?"

"To keep you motivated," The Dark One replied. "And honestly, for fun."

"Strange definition of fun," Nettie muttered.

"I *am* a sadist."

"And I was a masochist, staying with you for all those years," Valtora grumbled. He grinned at her.

"Actually, I seem to recall you enjoying both roles," he replied. He turned to Chauncy. "You wouldn't *believe* what we did together, Chauncy. Over and over and over…"

"Shut up," Valtora interjected. "I was young and stupid."

"And prolific," The Dark One added. His grin broadened. "And not just with me," he added. "Did she mention her stint with the incubi?" he asked Chauncy.

"Uh…" Chauncy said.

"That's it," Valtora exclaimed, standing up from the couch suddenly. "Enough talk. Divorce or death asshole. Choose!"

The Dark One completely ignored her.

"I believe it was after she caught me having a dalliance with a few succubi," he recalled, steepling his fingertips together. "Valtora *loves* an argument, you see. And in this case, she was...shall we say...quite determined to win."

"Right. Death it is," Valtora decided. She lunged at The Dark One, swinging her diamond fist at his head. But he merely caught it by the wrist, putting his other hand on the back of her head and pulling her downward. She landed with her head in his lap.

"This is how I usually won our arguments," The Dark One explained to Chauncy.

Valtora struggled, thrashing her arms and trying to pull away. At length, The Dark One let her go, and she stumbled backward, landing beside Chauncy on the opposite couch, looking dazed.

"After my dalliance, she decided to one-up me, so to speak," The Dark One continued, as if nothing had happened. "So she went to the incubi and copulated with them."

"Oh," Chauncy replied, taken aback.

"Half of them," The Dark One added. Chauncy frowned, glancing at Valtora, whose cheeks were flushing madly.

"How...many of them are there?" Chauncy asked. And immediately regretted it. For Valtora shot him a glare so deadly that frankly, he was surprised he didn't die on the spot.

"One thousand total," The Dark One replied. "Half of whom were interested in her gender."

Chauncy paled.

"Oh," he mumbled.

"Oh," Harry said, adjusting his glasses.

"Oh," Nettie exclaimed, covering her mouth with her hand.

"Quite a week, wasn't it my dear?" The Dark One mused.

"Five hundred in a week?" Nettie blurted out. "How in hell did she manage that?"

"Certainly not one at a time," The Dark One replied. Chauncy paled even further, staring at Valtora in horror. She refused to meet his gaze, slouching into the couch and staring at her lap. A lap that, Chauncy realized, had been far more adventurous than he'd ever imagined.

"Even two at a time'd be tough," Harry said with a frown, rubbing his chin thoughtfully. "Five hundred divided by seven's oh, about seventy-one a day. You'd need at least five at a time to make it work."

"Shut up Harry!" Nettie and Valtora snapped in unison.

"As I said," The Dark One replied. "Efficient."

Valtora glared at him, crossing her arms over her chest.

"Don't even *try* to slut-shame me, asshole," she retorted. "Anything I did you did ten times worse!"

"Ten times better," The Dark One corrected.

"Everything I did was because I was unhappy," Valtora argued. "Chauncy makes me five *hundred* times happier than you or any incubus, which is why I only need *one* of him!"

Chauncy blinked, then broke out into a broad smile.

"You really mean it?" he asked her. She smiled back, grabbing his hand in both of hers.

"I do," she confirmed.

"That was a good line," Harry admitted. Nettie went to elbow him in the ribs reflexively, but stopped herself.

"You're right, it was," she agreed.

"Aww," Valtora replied. "Thanks Nettie!"

"Enough already!" a gruff voice said. Everyone turned, realizing it was Skibbard, still standing by the doorway. The wizard's arms were crossed over his chest, and he was glaring at all of them. He turned to Chauncy, pointing one stubby finger at him. "YOU promised me I'd get to kill some liches. So where are they?"

Chauncy blinked, finding himself a bit at a loss for words. He *had* promised Skibbard that.

"Um..." he began.

"I believe I can help with that," The Dark One told Skibbard. "In fact, I know *exactly* where you can find a lich."

"Great. Where?" Skibbard asked.

"Right..." The Dark One replied, extending his hand and pointing at the far corner of the room. He swung it around the room in a slow half-circle...until it was pointing at something.

And that something was Chauncy.

"...there," The Dark One concluded.

Chauncy blinked, pointing at himself even as The Dark One pointed at him.

"Me?" he blurted out. "I'm not a lich!"

"Indeed," The Dark One agreed. "You're barely even a wizard."

Chauncy blushed.

"But you have a man inside of you, don't you, Chauncy?" The Dark One continued.

"Huh?" Chauncy asked. For he was quite sure he'd never had a man inside of him in his life.

"Right now?" Valtora asked, looking at Chauncy with sudden alarm.

"Right now," The Dark One confirmed. "In fact, it's how I've been able to track your precise location all this time. And see – and hear – everything you've been doing for the past six months."

Chauncy paled even further, feeling quite dizzy all of a sudden. He glanced at Valtora, who looked to be in a similar state.

"Everything?" Chauncy squeaked, recalling everything they'd done together. The Dark One gave the most wickedly satisfied smile Chauncy had ever seen.

"Everything," he confirmed.

"Now what the hell are you talking about?" Nettie interjected.

"Come out Zarzibar," The Dark One prompted, gesturing with one hand.

Chauncy felt a *pulling* sensation within him, and suddenly a ghostly, translucent skeletal being shot out of his body, levitating between him and The Dark One. It glowed pale white, with eyes that burned with a horrid red fire, similar to The Dark One's eyes. It had black bracers on its arms and legs, each with a few links of chain attached to them.

Chains that had once bound it to a certain carriage owned by a certain Marie Merrick.

Chapter 28

Everyone stared at the lich levitating before Chauncy, their eyes wide and mouths slack.

"Oh," Chauncy blurted out. For he'd utterly forgotten about the lich after defeating Marie. The lich he'd freed from bondage, by allowing it to use his body as a home.

"Holy crap," Nettie blurted out. "Chauncy, you've had that guy inside you this whole time?"

"Sort of?" Chauncy admitted, wincing at the word choice.

"What the hell!" Skibbard blurted out, reaching into one of his pockets for a seed. "You're the lich that destroyed my home!"

"Indeed," The Dark One confirmed. "One of the many acts that Zarzibar was forced to carry out by the Evermore Trading Company."

"Die lich!" Skibbard exclaimed, throwing a seed at the lich. But it merely passed through the lich's body, and turned black instantly. Dead.

"Liches are wizards," The Dark One explained. "Ones who find death and decay as magical as Nettie finds water, or Valtora finds superficial beauty. We call those wizards necromancers…and necromancers that decide to gain immortality by making a pact with evil itself are known as liches. And Zarzibar, well, he was *quite* the necromancer. Weren't you, Zarzibar?"

Zarzibar said nothing, his red, evil eyes boring into Chauncy's soul.

"And since I'm evil incarnate, making a pact with evil means making a pact with *me*," The Dark One concluded. "So everything Zarzibar senses, I can sense. Wherever he is, I will know his precise location."

"Well shit," Nettie swore. "Great job, Chauncy."

"I didn't mean to," Chauncy protested.

"You're an idiot," Nettie added.

"I forgot!"

"Idiot!" Nettie insisted.

"To be fair, we all forgot," Harry pointed out. Nettie shot him a deadly glare.

"Shut up Harry!"

"So we're all idiots," Harry added. "Myself included," he added to his addition, which mollified Nettie a smidge.

"Well I coulda told you that," she grumbled.

"You do," Harry replied. "Every day."

"Well that's true," she agreed. To which they both chuckled.

"You promised to help me kill liches," Skibbard accused, glaring at all of them...especially Chauncy. "You didn't tell me you were harboring one!"

"I forgot," Chauncy repeated, even more pathetically than the first time.

"Right," Skibbard shot back. "Asshole!" he added.

"I'm not," Chauncy insisted.

"He really isn't," Valtora agreed.

"I have to agree," The Dark One piped in reluctantly. "Though he technically cheated with my wife, he had no idea he was doing it. Until after he *did* know," he added. "And did it anyway." He paused. "I suppose he *is* an asshole. But then again, everyone is."

"Not everyone," Valtora argued.

"Everyone," The Dark One insisted. "Evil is in all mankind, darling. There is no shadow without light. And as long as light exists, shadow must too."

"Unless we kill you," Valtora argued.

"I'm the personification of evil," The Dark One reminded her. "As long as evil exists, I exist. And since every human has evil within them..."

"Wait," Nettie interjected, folding her arms over her chest. "You're saying we can't kill you?"

"Naturally," The Dark One confirmed. "Why do you think I always rise again, no matter how many times I've fallen?" He smirked, eyeing Valtora. "I seem to remember you being amazed at my ability to rise so quickly after...felling me."

"Die," Valtora shot back.

"So you see darling, you can't kill me. And if I don't agree to this divorce, you can't force me to nullify it."

"Bull," Valtora argued.

"We signed the marriage certificate in blood," he reminded her. "And I gave you a hint of my dark essence. The 'badass fog armor,' as you call it."

"So?" she pressed.

"As long as you carry it within you, you're my wife," he explained. "It binds us, more completely than any legal contract. Or that diamond engagement hand of yours."

Chauncy frowned, eyeing Valtora's glittering fist.

"He gave that to you instead of an engagement ring?" he asked her.

"No," she retorted. "I did it to myself." She turned to The Dark One. "So take your fog armor back," she ordered him.

He leaned back on the couch, steepling his fingertips together.

"No," he replied.

"Why not?" she pressed. "I don't wanna be married to you anymore!"

"That makes it sweeter."

"That it's nonconsensual?" she asked.

"As you should be well aware," he replied with a smirk. "Which brings me to my offer."

Valtora frowned, eyeing him suspiciously.

"What offer?" she demanded.

"I'll agree to a divorce," he told her. "But at a price."

"What price?"

"A child," he answered. She blinked, staring at him blankly.

"A what?" she asked.

"A child," The Dark One repeated. "More specifically, I request that you bear mine."

She bolted up from the couch.

"Hell no!" she yelled.

"Then the marriage stands," he replied evenly. Valtora cocked her fist back, ready to lunge at him again, but Chauncy leapt between them, holding her back.

"Honey, wait," he told her.

"Why d'ya want a kid with her anyway?" Nettie asked.

"I am evil incarnate," The Dark One answered. "All dark and no light. I am defined by my opposite, as all categories are separated into what belongs and what does not."

"And?" she pressed.

"The border between what belongs and what does not is what separates them," he explained. "But it is also what connects them." He gestured at Valtora. "Your very desire to be separated from me necessarily connects you to me."

"Huh?" Valtora said.

"If you did not desire to be separate, I would have no connection to you," he reasoned. "I have power over you only inasmuch as you allow."

"Unless you kill me," Valtora argued, her eyes lighting up. For it was clear she was in an argument now.

"In which case I eliminate my power over you," he pointed out. "If my only power is to eliminate my power, that's hardly power at all."

"But if I want to live, it's still power over me," she shot back.

"Your desire to exist gives those who can eliminate your existence power over you," he replied. "The concept holds."

Chauncy frowned, thinking back to the Cave of Wonder. *The solution to the problem is the problem itself.*

Which meant, of course, that if they didn't see their problem as a problem, they wouldn't need a solution to it.

"But why do you want a child with..." Valtora continued, when Chauncy stood from the couch suddenly.

"Right," he stated abruptly, inclining his head at The Dark One. "Thank you for your hospitality," he stated. "Come on guys, let's go."

And with that, he strode toward the door.

"Where the hell do you think you're going?" Nettie inquired, standing up as well. Harry stood with her, taking a bit longer to do so.

"I don't care if Valtora is married," Chauncy explained, smiling at her. "I just care that she doesn't want to be with him, and wants to be with me."

"Well duh," Valtora stated, smiling back. "That's what I told you in the first place. Idiot."

"You did," he conceded, rubbing the back of his head and blushing a bit. "I should've listened."

"Typical man," Valtora grumbled, rolling her eyes at half of humanity. But given that she disrespected both genders equally, Chauncy hardly took offense.

"Come on guys," he repeated, grabbing the doorknob and twisting it. But to his surprise, it didn't budge. He tried again, but it was no use. It was clearly locked. He turned to face The Dark One, who was smirking.

"Well done Chauncy," The Dark One declared, standing up and facing Chauncy. "There's more to you than the typical Chosen One.

So much unmet potential," he mused with a *tsk*. "But I'm afraid that, as right as you are, I've changed my mind. I'm going to kill you."

"Wait, what?" Chauncy blurted out. "Why?"

"You took my wife from me," he answered.

"But she didn't want you," Chauncy pointed out.

"That may be," The Dark One agreed. "But I'm the epitome of all of mankind's undesirable traits," he added. "Like petty jealousy...and vengeance."

"Oh," Chauncy replied. Because he honestly couldn't think of anything else to say. The Dark One smiled at all of them...even as the rest of the Chosen Ones joined Chauncy by the door.

"It *does* smell like popcorn," Skibbard noted, wrinkling his nose. The Dark One grinned at Chauncy, his glowing red eyes flashing evilly.

"I know that smell," he purred. Then he cracked his knuckles. "Shall we?"

Chapter 29

There was a place for everyone, a location – both mentally and physically – that felt like home. A place where one felt grounded. Secure. Centered. A *me* place, where one was most purely themselves. A magical place.

And for King Pravus, that place was the gym.

He took off his crown, all-too-happy to set its awful weight on the floor beside him. Then he stepped up to the squat rack, where a barbell had been placed, level with his shoulders. He grabbed it, lifting it and stepping back precisely two steps.

"Right behind you sire," Templeton declared, from right behind him. Pravus hoisted the bar up above his head easily, then brought it back down to his upper chest. A warm-up set, with only forty-five pounds, the weight of the bar. But he never skipped the warm-up set, knowing that it would prepare him for much greater loads to come. Preparation was key to lifting heavy weights, after all. The mind and body required a bit of centering of their own before attempting great things.

He brought it up again, then down, then up, performing no less than twenty repetitions. A ritual of his, and like most rituals, it was terribly important. For rituals themselves allowed one to become centered. They were a way of ordering one's day. The dose made the poison, of course. Too much ritual and one's day was too rigid. Too little, and one's day was chaotic. Thus the warm-up set. A ritual at the beginning, then freedom thereafter.

Pravus finished the set, feeling a mild, pleasing burn in his shoulders. He set the bar down, feeling positively *marvelous*.

"Why Templeton," he declared, allowing his cousin to take a turn. "I believe I needed this."

"Indeed," Templeton agreed, lifting the bar up above his head. The military press, one of Pravus's favorite exercises. Literally and figuratively one of his most uplifting techniques. He watched his cousin, noting Templeton's pert buttocks, clenched quite appropriately to maintain the proper upright position. And beholding them threatened to provide Pravus with an upright position of his own.

"Exquisite," he declared, eyeing said anatomy. Templeton – sweet, oblivious Templeton! – took this to mean his form, to which the man smiled, even while completing his set.

"I learned from the best," his cousin replied.

"Indeed," Pravus agreed. And oh, there was so much more he could teach Templeton, if only his cousin were willing to receive such instruction! For the sheer variety of acts that they could engage in far exceeded the opportunities afforded a mere conventional pairing. And it was Pravus's desperate desire to guide his cousin lovingly through each. But alas, it was not to be so, and so Pravus had to settle for enjoying Templeton in the manner he would consent to.

"You're up, my liege," Templeton stated, stepping back from the bar. Pravus blinked, then glanced down at himself. But to his relief, it was clear Templeton was referring to the next set. He loaded the bar for a total of two hundred and twenty-five pounds, then set up for his next set. This he did with precisely the same form as his warm-up, refusing to sacrifice safety to the bloody alter of accomplishment.

"Well done," Templeton breathed, regarding Pravus with a mixture of pride and awe. "It looks for all the world like you're lifting balloons!"

"Perfect effort seems effortless," Pravus replied, finishing his set and setting the bar down. And while he could've performed two to three more reps, he never did. For to risk injury was to risk days – or weeks! – of not being able to work out. A risk Pravus simply refused to take. For self-improvement was found in regular, incremental improvement, not the ghastly all-day marathons of bodily destruction beginners inevitably championed. And in trusting this gentler process, and never competing with his peers, Pravus had exceeded all of them. Without having to suffer the awful anxiety of compulsive comparison.

"It's good to see your smile again," Templeton said, going in for his next set. Pravus realized he *was* smiling. From ear-to-ear, actually. He felt better than he had in…why, since The Dark One's armies had pillaged his provinces.

In fact, in having lifted weights, experiencing what was magic to him, Pravus felt perfectly capable of carry the weight of his royal duties again.

"I never should have denied myself the gym," he realized. For in denying himself what was magical to him, his life had become mundane. And a mundane life, in his experience, was hardly one worth living.

"Indeed," Templeton agreed, finishing his set.

"From now on I shall first care for myself," Pravus declared, putting even more weight on, then performing his next set. "So that I...might better care for...others!"

"Wisdom to live by," Templeton concurred.

"And live by it...we shall!" Pravus exclaimed. And, having finished his set, he set the bar back on the rack, feeling a pleasant burning sensation in his shoulders, triceps, and upper back. And the very beginnings of that simply marvelous sensation:

The *pump*.

His muscles seemed to expand, stretching his skin to its limit, veins filled practically to bursting in his arms.

Why, it was practically orgiastic, this feeling. And to think he'd denied himself for so long!

"If I ever fail to go to the gym like this again," he told Templeton, "...tie me up and force the pump on me, dearest cousin."

"With pleasure," Templeton replied zestfully. But had he been aware of the awful images such instructions had conjured in Pravus's mind, surely Templeton would have had less zest at Pravus's bawdy behest!

"Barbell curls?" Pravus inquired arching an eyebrow and flashing his cousin a grin. Templeton beamed back at him.

"Why, you've read my mind!"

"Men of like mind don't need to read minds," Pravus pointed out. He grabbed a barbell, lifting it with perfect back-sparing form, then executing precisely twenty warm-up repetitions. Then he put it down, stepping back for Templeton to take a turn.

"Exquisite form as always," Templeton opined. Then he bent over to lift the barbell just as Pravus had, tightening his pert posterior in preparation for the task at hand. They'd chosen to lift where there were no mirrors, which allowed Pravus to leer with nary a consequence. Consequently, leer he did, admiring Templeton's form in a far different manner than Templeton had admired his.

Mmm mmm *mmm*. Simply *scrumptious*.

"I could do this all day," Pravus mused. But as it turned out, he didn't get a chance. For at that very moment, a group of his personal guards rushed into the gym and toward him, looking positively spooked.

"Your Highness!" one of them cried, skidding to a halt before Pravus and bowing deeply. "The kingdom…it's under attack!"

Pravus frowned, putting his hands on his hips and striking a most heroic pose. One that came naturally after experiencing the pump.

"Explain at once," he commanded. Heroically.

"An army is swarming the city," the guard informed. "Men in green suits, your Highness. They're headed for the castle!"

"And wearing golden ties, no doubt," Pravus replied. The guard nodded, surprised at Pravus's apparent prescience. "Templeton, it appears that that scoundrel Gavin Merrick is bent on penetrating my defenses," he declared. "Without my consent, villain that he is."

And with that, he picked his crown up from the floor, putting it atop his head. With a thought – and the presence of his magical crown atop his head – his kingly uniform appeared instantly upon his body. And, through pantomiming the unsheathing of a sword, a sword appeared in his hand, out of thin air. A golden sword, quite broad and intimidatingly long. One might accuse a person possessed of such a sword of overcompensating, but in Pravus's case, it was merely honest advertising.

"To the castle, at once!" he declared valiantly, holding the sword up high above his head. "We shall rebuff the Evermore Trading Company's advances, and I shall thrust my sword through the heartless chest of Gavin Merrick. And by the hand of King Pravus the Eighth, Evermore will be nevermore!"

Chapter 30

"Zarzibar," The Dark One prompted, still grinning evilly at Chauncy. "Kindly murder these Chosen Ones."

The lich turned his head to face Chauncy, red eyes glowing with a light eerily similar to The Dark One's.

"Don't do it," Chauncy pleaded.

"Beg all you want," The Dark One said. "The lich owes his immortality to evil magic. As a being infused with evil, he knows that I will always know where he is. If he disobeys me, I shall hunt him down and destroy the vessel that contains his soul...destroying *him*."

"Well, that's the thing," Chauncy replied. "*I'm* the vessel that contains his soul. So..."

He shrugged, allowing The Dark One to come to the obvious conclusion himself.

"Ah," The Dark One replied. "I see."

"Ha!" Nettie declared. "He's got ya there, dipshit!"

"Indeed," The Dark One agreed. "Very well," he decided with a sigh. "I'll do it myself."

And then black fog enveloped him, forming evil fog-armor identical to that which Valtora had worn when Chauncy first met her. But in addition, a black fog-sword with a cruel edge that glowed with a devastatingly badass red light.

"Oh shit," Chauncy blurted out.

"Everyone, do something!" Nettie cried. Which was a terrible plan, all things considered. But to Chauncy, doing something – *anything*, in fact – was precisely what he needed to do.

So he did.

"Wind blast!" he cried, swinging his Staff of Wind at The Dark One. A blast of wind smashed through the living room, shoving the couches backward and tearing paintings from the walls. It blasted the fog-armor right off of the Dark One, and made him stumble backward a bit. And to Chauncy's surprise, the fog-sword suffered a similar fate, dissolving in the wind.

"Stop telegraphing your moves, idiot!" Nettie reminded him.

"Right, sorry," he replied.

Harry kicked off a shoe, planting his bare foot on the stone floor. Upon which the floor split open like the fault line in an earthquake...right between The Dark One's legs. The Dark One's fog-armor reappeared around him, including his badass sword. He stepped to one side of the expanding fissure, his red eyes flashing.

"Nice try," he stated...and then a big rock shot upward from the floor, striking him right between the legs with a *clang*. He grunted, but stood his ground. "You'll have to do better than..."

And then a huge rock fist shot up from the floor, uppercutting him in the same spot. And lifting him right up to the ceiling, smashing him against it.

"Ooo," Chauncy said, wincing a bit.

"Nice shot Harry!" Valtora exclaimed.

"Taint nothing," Harry replied.

"Not anymore," Nettie quipped with a cackle.

The stony fist retracted into the floor, and The Dark One floated downward, levitating a few feet above it.

"**Your puny attacks cannot defeat me**," the Dark One declared in his creepiest voice. One that sent chills down Chauncy's spine.

"You can talk as creepy as you want," Chauncy replied rather dramatically, holding his staff before him and striking a defiant pose. "I might be afraid, but that means I'm still alive. And while that's the case, I can fight!"

"**Badly**," The Dark One added. Chauncy scoffed.

"Not badly," he retorted. "Boldly!"

Then he lifted the butt of his staff, jabbing it in The Dark One's direction.

"Air spear!" he cried.

"For cripe's sake, stop telegraphing!" Nettie exclaimed.

The air spear only blew The Dark One away literally, in that it dissipated his fog somewhat. But Nettie shot a spear of her own at the man. A water spear that quickly flash-froze into an ice spear. And, with The Dark One's armor temporarily dissipated, the spear speared him right through the chest.

The Dark One grunted, stumbling back a few steps, the ice spear jutting out of him.

"That was cool," Harry quipped.

"Shut up Harry," Nettie grumbled.

"Finishing blast!" Chauncy cried, bringing a leg up as he wound his staff up for a good swinging. And swing he did, sending a blast of wind at The Dark One to finish him off. The Dark One flew backward, slamming into the far wall, the icicle in his chest pinning him to it.

Chauncy leaned on his staff, smirking at his enemy.

"Guess a little Chauncy Little was a little too much for him," he quipped, feeling positively badass.

"Fuckin' *badass*," Valtora confirmed, beaming at him.

Everyone stared at The Dark One, pinned to the wall. Hanging a few feet from the ground, Chauncy noted. The man just hung there, red eyes glowing vacantly. And then, as they watched, the glow faded.

"Huh," Nettie said.

Everyone stood there for a bit longer.

"That's it?" Harry asked.

"I dunno," Valtora replied. "Better make sure." She turned to Nettie. "Could I have another icicle?" Nettie nodded, fashioning one for her. Then Valtora turned to The Dark One, hoisting her icicle-spear over her shoulder.

And promptly charged across the room, leaping into the air and thrusting the icicle into The Dark One. Such that he was pinned to the wall via an entirely different portion of his anatomy, whose nature was suggested by the very long icicle protruding from said anatomy.

"Ooo," Skibbard blurted out, involuntarily covering his own anatomy. Indeed, every man in the room – lich included – did a male version of a curtsy at the sight, whilst grimacing empathetically.

"Dick move," Harry mused.

"Shut up Harry!" Nettie shot back. Then chuckled, elbowing him in the ribs. He grinned at her. "Be nice to her, Chauncy," she warned. Chauncy smiled at Valtora.

"God I love you," he told her. She walked back to him, tossing her hair back with a casual flick. And making all the men's eyes widen and jaws go slack. For when Valtora did her hair toss, it was truly epic…as if time itself slowed down a bit to enjoy it.

"Damn," Skibbard breathed, having never seen it before.

"Let's go," Valtora prompted.

"What about your fog armor?" Chauncy asked. "If you still have it, it means you're not divorced."

"Eh, don't give a shit," Valtora replied with a shrug.

And with that, black fog burst from her body, forming fog-armor around her...and then promptly flowing backward across the room into The Dark One's body.

"Oh," Chauncy blurted out.

"Huh," Valtora said. She did a cute frowny-face, scrunching her eyebrows together and clenching her fists.

"You takin' a dump?" Nettie inquired.

"Maybe she needs shit to bedazzle," Harry ventured. Valtora relaxed her face, shooting them both a glare.

"*No*," she retorted. "I was trying to summon the fog-armor. I can't do it."

"Well good," Nettie replied. "Guess you got your divorce after all."

"It was like he said," Chauncy mused. "The fact that you desperately wanted to be apart from him tied him to you." He smiled then.

The solution to the problem is the problem itself.

He looked down at his purple, sparkly robe, patting his pocket.

"Thanks, Magic of Magic," he said. And then he sighed. "Ready?" he asked everyone.

"Ready," everyone agreed.

"What about the lich?" Skibbard demanded, glaring at Zarzibar. Who'd watched everything silently.

"Hmm," Chauncy murmured, rubbing his chin. "What would *you* like to do, Zar?" Which was the nickname he just came up with for the lich.

Zarzibar shot back into Chauncy, and in doing so, Chauncy knew the lich's mind. Without knowing how, which was proof that it was magic.

"He wants to stay with us," Chauncy informed everyone. He broke out into a smile. "He says he likes us." Then he frowned. "Because we're idiots, but entertaining."

"Well that's true," Harry replied.

"Speak for yourself, boulder-brains," Nettie grumbled.

"That's it?" Skibbard said, glaring at Chauncy. "You're going to let the lich live?"

"Yep," Chauncy confirmed.

"He murdered my forest!" Skibbard protested. "And helped...injure me!"

Chauncy, frowned, and through his bond with Zarzibar, he instantly knew what Skibbard was talking about. His gaze dropped to Skibbard's groin, his eyes widening.

"Oh," he mumbled, putting a hand to his mouth. "Um...Zarzibar didn't want to," he added. "Marie made him do it. She threatened to destroy him if he didn't obey."

"I don't care," Skibbard shot back.

"He says he'll make it up to you," Chauncy pressed.

"By letting me destroy him?"

"Um...no," Chauncy replied.

"Then not good enough."

"We killed Marie," Chauncy argued.

"*I* killed Marie," Valtora corrected proudly. "Smashed her twisted little skull in with this," she added, making a fist with her diamond hand.

"Oh," Skibbard replied. "Thanks."

"We can help you with your...uh...shortcoming," Chauncy offered, glancing at Skibbard's lap again.

"What happened to him?" Nettie asked.

"They, ah," Chauncy stammered, scratching his head. "Pruned him."

"Oh," Nettie murmured, her gaze following Chauncy's.

"Gives new meaning to 'stump sprouting,'" Valtora quipped. To which Skibbard shot her a glare so deadly that she grimaced. But Nettie burst out laughing, and soon Valtora did too. And so did everyone else, except of course for Skibbard.

"You shouldn't make fun of me," Skibbard complained. "It's inappropriate!"

"Ridiculously inappropriate," Chauncy agreed, doing his best to stop laughing. Which at length he did.

"We can heal him with Rooter!" Valtora exclaimed.

"My thought exactly," Chauncy agreed. "Rooter can heal almost any wound," he explained to Skibbard.

"That golem with the plant on its head?" Skibbard asked.

"Right," Chauncy confirmed.

"Deal," the little wizard agreed.

"Does this mean you forgive Zarzibar?" Chauncy asked. Skibbard grimaced.

"Fine," he grumbled. "But he still owes me."

"Fair enough," Chauncy replied.

They all turned to look at The Dark One, still pinned to the wall. The icicles were slowly melting, making a puddle on the floor below him.

"Well, guess that's it," Nettie stated.

"Come on Chauncy," Valtora prompted, grabbing his hand and hauling him toward the door. "Let's make a *baby!*"

* * *

Making a baby with Valtora was a marvelous plan, at least to attempt. And Chauncy found himself rather eagerly anticipating the various logistics of executing it. But when Valtora gripped the doorknob to open the door, it didn't budge. Because it was still locked, because no one had unlocked it since the last time they'd tried it.

"Shit," Valtora swore, trying harder. Then she tried with her diamond hand, with no success.

"Don't tell me it's locked!" Nettie complained.

"It's locked," Valtora told her, clearly enjoying doing what she'd been told not to do.

"Well shit," Nettie blurted out.

"That's what I said," Valtora agreed.

"Well ain't there a key or something?" Nettie asked. Valtora glared at her, putting her hands on her hips.

"How should I know?"

"You lived here for twenty-five damn years!" Nettie pointed out.

"Never gave me a key," Valtora replied evenly.

"Wow," Chauncy said. "I would've given you a key."

"You did," Valtora said with a smile. "On the first day."

Nettie raised her eyebrows at Chauncy, who blushed.

"When you know, you know," he stated. "You know?"

"Nope," Nettie replied.

"Not usually," Harry agreed.

"Everyone says that until they get divorced," Skibbard grumbled. And it was clear from his expression that he'd suffered this precise fate. Chauncy grimaced, but Valtora only grabbed his hand, squeezing it and smiling radiantly at him.

"We'll show them," she promised.

"By making a baby?" Nettie inquired. Harry's eyebrows went up, his blue eyes twinkling.

"Could use some popcorn for that show," he mused. Then he sniffed the air. "Only got the smell though."

"Shut up and open that door already," Nettie ordered her husband. He chuckled, then limped up to the door, putting a hand on it. And lo and behold, the door swung open.

"How…?" Chauncy blurted out.

"Made of stone," Harry replied, waggling his eyebrows. "After you, angel," he added, gesturing for Nettie to go through. So she did, and then Valtora, and then everyone else. They closed the door behind them, finally leaving The Dark One – and Valtora's past – behind. And in closing the door on Valtora's past, Chauncy was free to realize that the door to a future with her had been present all along. Quite literally present in the present, in fact.

To Before and After it
Will never bow,
For The Magic of Magic is
Here and Now.

He'd had Valtora all along, of course. He'd just put off the idea of happiness with her to the future, until after she got divorced. And in casting his happiness into the future, it'd quite naturally left the present.

"Still up for making a baby?" he inquired, waggling his eyebrows at Valtora. She grinned, grabbing his hand and squeezing it as they strolled across the dark, hot, magma-lit hallway beyond.

"If you're up for it," she replied.

"Kinda have to be," he quipped.

"And you complain about *us*," Nettie grumbled, shaking her head at them and shoving past them. Harry chuckled, limping a bit faster to catch up with her. While giving Chauncy a nudge and a wink as he passed by. Chauncy smiled, knowing exactly what Harry meant by that. For as Harry had mentioned several times before, Valtora was more like Nettie than Nettie cared to admit. Brash, inappropriate, colorful, and capable of extreme violence.

Chauncy recalled having wished for a relationship like Harry and Nettie's during their first adventure. Something so wrong it was right. And as luck would have it – indeed, as destiny had preordained – through the magic of magic, his wish had come true.

Chapter 31

Evermore's green and gold army tore through Pravus's outer security forces with ease, aided by the element of surprise. And the fact that a large portion of Pravus's military had either just left Cumulus, or was already involved in battles with The Dark One's forces far, far away. Gavin watched with grim satisfaction as his men slaughtered Pravus's, as his plan for vengeance was executed with admirable efficiency. He'd paid a small fortune for the best men that Borrin had to offer; a price that, for Marie, he'd been more than happy to pay.

But he wouldn't be truly satisfied until the one paying the price was King Pravus himself. Until the upstart, effete monarch was executed, by none other than Gavin himself.

He smiled at the thought of the king lying on the ground with Gavin atop him. Of wrapping his hands around the man's throat and squeezing until the veins on the idiot's head popped out. Until his eyeballs bulged out of their sockets, his face turning red, then purple.

Until the light faded from his eyes at last, and the last person he saw was his sworn enemy smirking down at him.

Gavin realized he was clenching his fists, as if his hands really *were* around Pravus's throat, and forced them to relax. He watched the carnage from the wide main street leading from the outer wall of Cumulus toward the inner wall surrounding the castle, a street over a mile long. A contingent of personal guards surrounded him in a loose ring, which was entirely unnecessary. For with Gavin's magical suit protecting him, none of the enemy guards could have harmed him. It was the same suit worn by his legendary grandfather, Archibald Merrick. Made back when the world was wilder…and magic was more powerful.

Wild, like Marie. And so unlike Gavin.

"Forward!" his men shouted as they cut down the last of the guards barring their way further into the city. Gavin followed behind them as they charged down the street, watching as bystanders fled into the various shops and other buildings flanking the street.

"Let them be," Gavin reminded them. "Guards only." The citizens of Cumulus should not suffer the sins of their king, after all. They were innocent bystanders...innocent of the crime of killing Gavin's wife, at least. His men obeyed, of course. They were professionals, the best of the best. Some of them were the few surviving veterans of Marie's raiding teams, and had a personal stake in seeing her murderer brought to bloody justice. But none more personal than Gavin's.

Gavin ignored the citizens fleeing his army. He tried to ignore the enemy soldiers ahead rushing to intercept them...and their screams as they were slaughtered. It gave him no joy whatsoever to kill Pravus's men. They were merely pawns of the king, men with wives and children, hopes and dreams. And now they were dead, paying for the crimes of the man they'd been taught to worship and obey.

He'd been the cause of many deaths in his long life, but had only rarely been present to witness them firsthand. That had been Marie's joy, the thrill of combat. Gavin had much preferred combat with paper and ink, the weapons of business.

Or as Skibbard had called them, symbols.

As Gavin watched his men gleefully murdering other men, the weird little wizard's words came to him.

You live a life of symbols.

Gavin grimaced, focusing on the gigantic wall in the distance, the inner wall protecting Pravus's castle. But the screams of dying men grated on his nerves, tearing at them until he felt *un*-nerved.

Transactional relationships with compulsion to profit from them.

He stared at his men, the men he'd hired to carry out this raid. They of course would never have agreed to work for him if they hadn't been paid handsomely. His relationship with them *was* transactional. And his profit was revenge.

Always doing to profit from the doing, never for the doing itself.

Gavin stared at Pravus's guards as their throats were slashed. As they were stabbed, cut, impaled. Bashed, strangled, and broken. And while Marie had enjoyed such things, and his men clearly did as well, Gavin only felt a sudden nausea overcome him. An emptiness, and a sudden *I don't want to do this* feeling. For there was no pleasure in doing this. He was – once again – doing this for the profit of it, not for the thing itself.

His jawline rippled, and he took a deep breath in, marching forward…and shoving Skibbard's words aside. For while he found no joy in murdering innocents, he *would* enjoy murdering the guilty. And unfortunately, there was no other way to get to Pravus than this.

Stay the course, he told himself. *Stay strong.*

Skibbard had weaseled his way into Gavin's mind somehow, inserting doubt where none had been before. A conniving little wizard, Skibbard. Manipulating Gavin as revenge for having imprisoned him for so long. Gavin couldn't allow that to affect him. Couldn't let it derail his focus.

King Pravus was responsible for Marie's death, and for Gavin, that was the death of magic. And for that crime, Pravus had to die.

He focused ahead, at the giant wall with its silver double doors. Those doors were closed, and nigh-impenetrable. In attacking now, Gavin had undoubtedly already alerted the king. And the king would of course hide like a coward behind that wall, in his castle.

But Gavin had a plan. And while there was no profiting from a transaction that included a loss as enormous as his wife's death, at least Gavin would have his revenge.

Chapter 32

Chauncy, Valtora, Nettie, Harry, and Skibbard made their way down the long hallway leading away from The Dark One's den, the heat from the magma waterfalls on either side baking their skin. Nettie cooled things off with some ice-cold water sprayed above all of them, for which Chauncy was grateful. Eventually they made it to the end of the hallway, to the creepy stone staircase spiraling upward as far as the eye could see. Hundreds of faintly glowing red eyes and mouths greeted them, the minimalistic mood-lighting of the well-endowed demon-statues carved into the walls.

"Ladies first," Harry offered Nettie.

"Why, so you can ogle my rear?" Nettie inquired.

"Yup."

She took him up on the offer, and he gave her a little boost with a hand on her bottom. Chauncy offered for Valtora to go first, and she did so. But being chivalrous, he declined to boost in a similar fashion.

"Hey," she complained, turning to glare at him. "Touch my *butt*."

"Oh," he blurted out. And in a similar fashion, he boosted her. Skibbard lagged behind, clearly getting the least enjoyable of the views, given that his view was Chauncy. Thus they began the long journey up the stairs.

"Don't you think that was a little too easy?" Skibbard inquired.

"What?" Chauncy asked.

"Killing The Dark One," he clarified.

"Too easy?" Chauncy pressed.

"It *was* a bit easy," Nettie admitted.

"Not hard at all," Harry agreed. He glanced at one of the male demon statues. "This guy's harder than he was."

"Shut up Harry," Nettie grumbled. But it was clear that he had a point. "Think we should be worried?" she asked.

"Prepared," Harry replied. And that would have been nice. But by the time he said it, it was a bit too late.

One of the statues next to him came to life, leaping out at him and shoving him off the stairs into the center of the spiraling stairwell. Harry plummeted down the sheer drop, falling some fifty feet before slamming into the floor below with a *whump!*

"Harry!" Chauncy cried out in horror…even as the stone arms of another statue reached out from the wall, grabbing him from behind and pulling him back-first against it. The statue's grip was unbelievably strong, its flesh as hard as rock. And, somewhat relatedly, it was definitively male.

Chauncy gasped, that horrible grip squeezing the air right out of his lungs. He tried to take a breath in, but it was impossible. Almost immediately, black spots formed in his vision, and he felt himself fading away into unconsciousness.

It occurred to him right then and there that this was how death came, sudden and without fanfare, a slipping away, then nothing.

Valtora slammed her diamond fist in the statue's temple, making that temple cave in with a *crunch*. Its arms went lax, and Chauncy gasped for air, stumbling away from it. Which, unfortunately, was right off the edge of the stairwell. A fact his blackened vision hadn't warned him of until it was too late.

"Oh," was all he could manage before he plummeted.

But as soon as his drop began, water swallowed his body whole, and pulled him right back onto the stairs. He turned to see Nettie summoning more water from her Wetstone…water that engulfed Valtora and Skibbard and herself as well.

"Going up!" she exclaimed, even as the water surged up the middle of the stairwell. It carried everyone along with it, forcing Chauncy to hold his breath. But then he had a horrible thought.

Harry!

The old man had fallen all the way to the bottom of the stairs…and was still down there, assuming he was even alive. But Chauncy didn't have time to worry about it, for more of the demon-statues were leaping outward from the walls, diving at them!

But Nettie clearly anticipated this, and flash-froze the outer portion of the column of water sending them upward. This made a thick ice-wall to protect them as they rose, one the statues slammed into. The ice cracked with their impacts, but held true, and in moments they'd made it all the way to the top of the stairwell. Nettie deposited them there, leaving the water last and shoving the rest of them through the doorway beyond. Statues charged up the stairs after them, their eyes and open mouths glowing with blood-red light.

"But Harry!" Chauncy protested as he was shoved bodily into the dark hallway beyond.

"Go!" Nettie snapped.

Chauncy sprinted after Valtora and Skibbard, the demon-statues charging after them. The long, narrow hallway extended forward a hundred yards, and the statues were shockingly fast. It wouldn't be long before they caught up.

"Raging river!" Nettie cried, grabbing the Wetstone and squeezing. Water burst outward from it, and Nettie shaped it with her magic, creating a raging river that swept over Chauncy, Valtora, and Skibbard, sweeping them off their feet and carrying them forward rapidly. So rapidly, in fact, that they soon left the statues far behind.

"Go Nettie!" Valtora exclaimed exuberantly.

"Weee!" Skibbard cried.

They reached the end of the long hallway in moments, and Nettie slowed the river, then sucked the water back into the Wetstone. Everyone slid a little bit on the slick stone floor, then Chauncy helped Nettie to her feet, and they rushed through the doorway at the end of the hallway, reaching another stairwell leading upward. One without demon-statues on the walls, thank heaven. They made quick work of ascending this, navigating the series of dark, twisted hallways and more stairwells as quickly as possible. Without Valtora's expert navigation, they would've gotten horribly lost, but as it was she led them unerringly through the mazelike corridors, bringing them all the way back to the large, spooky lobby near the entrance. Chauncy spotted light peeking through the double-doors at the exit a hundred feet ahead, and rushed toward it eagerly.

"Almost there!" he exclaimed.

"No...shit!" Nettie gasped, struggling to keep up.

And then the floor ahead of them caved in, a gaping hole appearing in the center of it.

"Crap!" Chauncy blurted out, skidding to a halt. He waited for a writhing mass of nightmarish creatures to rise from the hole and massacre them. But instead, a man rose up through the hole on a small platform of stone. A tall man with a stooped back, wearing silver glasses.

"Hey hey," the man greeted.

"Harry!" Chauncy cried, filled to the brim with elation. He ran up to the man, giving him a big hug. "I thought you were a goner!"

"Nah," Harry replied. "I'm terrible at dying," he added with a twinkle in his eye. "Haven't practiced enough I guess."

"Well don't start," Nettie replied, wiping a few tears from her eyes and giving Harry a hug. After shoving Chauncy aside. "Don't scare me like that, you ol' fart," she added.

"You rhymed," Chauncy noted with a smile. Harry smiled back, giving his wife a squeeze.

"All good wizards do," he explained. "And angels too."

"I see what you did there," Valtora piped in.

"Let's get outta here," Nettie urged.

They did just that, hurrying as best they could to the double-doors. Valtora got there first, shoving one door open with her diamond hand, revealing the small obsidian island with its lake of lava beyond. Everyone spilled through the doorway, stepping out into the awful dry heat and stink of sulfur.

"We did it!" Valtora exclaimed, thrusting her diamond fist into the air in triumph.

And then the countless skeletons of the dead heroes littering the ground ahead of them rose up, their eye sockets glowing with an unholy red light.

"Well shit," Valtora exclaimed. And Chauncy didn't quite comply. But he did pee himself a bit, partly because he was scared stiff. Mostly because he hadn't had the opportunity to relieve himself for quite some time.

"Oh," was all he could say.

And the enemy attacked.

* * *

A literal army of skeletons came to un-life before Chauncy and the rest of the Chosen Ones, some wielding weapons, others armed only with their fists. Hundreds of them. *Thousands* of them. All glaring at Chauncy with awful, terror-inducing unholy red eyes. But to his surprise, Chauncy wasn't terrified. He wasn't even scared. He was just tired of it all.

"Right," he decided. "Guess I'm gonna have to kick me some bony dead *ass*."

And he wound up right then and there, swinging his Staff of Wind at the undead army with all of his might.

A blast of wind smashed into the enemy with the force of a hurricane, sending the skeletons flying backward in the air. Some landed on the blackened ground, while others were tossed right into the lava lake beyond. These melted before Chauncy's eyes, sinking slowly into the red-hot stuff.

"Oh," Valtora blurted out.

"Tornado of triumph!" Chauncy cried, spinning his staff like a top and sending it forward. It spun madly, creating the very tornado he'd warned about, sucking more undead into itself. These poor fellows flew upward spun about, tossed in all directions at the top of the tornado a good fifty feet up. The tornado continued forward, massacring the army directly ahead of Chauncy, sending bones flying everywhere.

"My *hero!*" Valtora gushed, clinging to his arm precisely in the way he'd always imagined a damsel would.

"Damn straight," he agreed. Epically. He extended a hand, and the Staff of Wind shot back into it with a satisfying *thunk*.

"Fuckin' *badass*," Valtora exclaimed.

"About that baby," he prompted. She stared up at him, her eyes wide with awe.

"Now?" she gasped, biting her lower lip.

"Wait for it," he replied badass-edly, to her obvious delight.

"Flood of Doom!" Nettie cried, gripping her Wetstone tight. A huge ring of water bust outward, expanding rapidly and carrying every last one of the undead soldiers away. All the way, in fact, to the lava, where they ignited instantly in a symphony of hissing and popping molten rock. With that, the undead army was defeated, leaving the Chosen Ones alone on the island.

"Well damn," Chauncy muttered. "I was going to do that."

"Take me!" Valtora pleaded, tugging on his shoulder. He gazed down at her.

"Wait for it," he replied. To slightly less effect than before. But still, she seemed satisfied with the response.

"Please," Skibbard pleaded, rubbing his eyes vigorously. "Stop."

"That's how you used to be," Nettie noted, grinning at Chauncy.

"I'm better now," Chauncy replied with a smile of his own. He wrapped an arm around his adoring Valtora. "I used to be the man others said I should be," he added. "Living my life appropriately."

"Not anymore," Valtora declared happily.

"That's right," Chauncy agreed. "No more 'should,'" he declared. "It's time I was me, without apology!"

"Well shit, that's two rhymes," Harry noted, nudging Nettie. "He's getting there."

"Won't be long before he's a full wizard," Nettie agreed.

"You're all insane," Skibbard declared. Then he gave a grudging smile. "Guess I got lucky."

"You did," Valtora agreed. "And you will again…once we get you to Rooter!"

"Maybe," Skibbard grumbled, blushing a bit.

"All right," Chauncy interjected, eyeing the lava lake ahead. "We're gonna cross this lava. You want to do it, or should I?" he asked Nettie.

"How 'bout we do it as a team?" she proposed. Chauncy smiled.

"Deal," he agreed.

"Go on hon," Nettie told Harry, who led them by limping up to the edge of the lava. He knelt down with some difficulty, putting his hand on one of the stones on his vest. His hand turned gray…and he plunged it right into the lava.

"What…!" Skibbard blurted out.

"Tungsten," Harry explained, grinning at them. "Highest melting point of any metal."

With that, the lava ahead rose upward in a huge lava-hand. Nettie had everyone stand back, then used the Wetstone to create a thick ice wall right behind Harry, but in front of everyone else. Then Nettie sprayed a fine mist upward and forward over this wall, sending it raining down on the lava-hand. It hissed and sputtered on impact, steam billowing from the hand's palm. But eventually the lava cooled, until the hand was red-hot no more. But its wrist and forearm remained lava.

"Send us up Chauncy," Nettie prompted, melting the ice wall and sucking it back into her Wetstone. Chauncy hesitated, eyeing the rocky hand. It was a good fifteen feet above the lava.

"Can't you just…uh, water us up to it?" he asked.

"Sure," Nettie replied. "Wouldn't be teamwork if you didn't do something though."

"Right," he agreed. He grabbed onto Valtora's waist, gripping his staff with his other hand. "Ready darling?" he inquired.

"Ready," she replied.

He slammed the butt of his staff down and a bit backward, sending them flying forward and upward into the air. They soared over the rock-palm…a little *too* far, to Chauncy's dismay. He swung his staff a bit, slowing their forward motion, and they landed right in the center of the palm. He leaned in for a kiss, then pulled away.

"I have to save the others," he declared in a rather masculine tone.

"Go," she urged, giving him doe-eyes.

He leapt down from the palm, using his staff to slow his fall. He landed on the shore, then repeated the journey with Harry, Nettie, and Skibbard. And with each successful attempt, Chauncy grew bolder. And in that boldness, he second-guessed himself less, and more importantly, corrected himself less. So instead of overthinking, or even thinking, he just *did*.

And in just doing, he found that he did just fine.

It occurred to him then and there that confidence was not so much earned but learned, and was less something added than something taken away. It was, in fact, a matter of not getting in one's own way. It didn't so much require believing in oneself as much as it required not *disbelieving*.

In not getting in his own way, he *got* his way.

"All right," he declared, posing with perfect, heroic posture. The kind of posture he imagined a powerful wizard might possess. And while he wasn't as powerful as he could be, by golly he would get there eventually. "Let's do this."

"Sexy as *fuck*," Valtora gushed, to his delight.

The rock-hand lifted upward and swam forward through the lava, making its way toward the opposite shore in the distance. The heat from the lava was downright awful, but Nettie's water-magic helped considerably, in the form of a continuous spray of sleet to counteract the heat. It wasn't long before Harry's helping hand reached their destination, lowering itself to deposit them on the rim of the volcano's giant crater. They started the long journey down the slope of Mount Thrall then, plunging into the thick clouds of falling ash once again. So thick that they couldn't see more than a few yards past their noses.

"Well, guess it's time to go home," Chauncy said. "That wasn't so bad after all."

"Yeah," Valtora agreed. "Not gonna lie, I thought it was going to be *so* much worse." She smiled at Nettie. "Thanks for killing my ex-husband."

"My pleasure," Nettie replied rather civilly. "Psycho," she added, less civilly. But Valtora didn't seem to mind the nickname. Psychotic people were those who saw reality differently, after all. And while that was unacceptable in a place like Borrin, amongst wizards it was precisely how one should be.

Valtora held Chauncy's arm quite contentedly as they made their way ever-downward, dodging pools of lava and boulders and such. Which was a bit difficult at times due to the falling snow-like ash. It became ever-more difficult as they went, as the ash grew thicker and thicker, until Chauncy could only see a few feet ahead.

"Don't remember it being this thick," Nettie said.

"Heard that before," Harry quipped.

But before Nettie could tell him to shut up, the thick ash all around them seemed to coalesce in front of them, forming a dense cloud as black as the obsidian at their feet. And to Chauncy's horror, twin red lights appeared within that fog, glowing eyes that pierced through the fog like twin suns, staring right into his soul.

Terror gripped him, and he froze, his heart leaping into his throat.

The dark cloud coalesced further, forming a figure in black plate-mail armor, holding a truly massive black fog-sword in one hand. A sword whose edge glowed with the same red fire as the figure's eyes.

"**My turn,**" The Dark One declared.

"Right," Valtora said. "Whelp, we're dead."

Chapter 33

King Pravus the Eighth was ready to kick some Borrin ass.
He strode out of the exit of his gigantic gymnasium, wielding his massive golden sword in both hands. It was quite heavy, his oversized weapon, which was just his style. For its formidable heft made it a joy to use. He'd never wielded it in the heat of battle, but had practiced extensively with his beloved father as a boy, as all princes should. His black and gold armored guards surrounded him as he walked, forming a formidable barrier to any enemy that might dare assault their king. Pravus tolerated this. For a few seconds.
"No," he decided, stopping in his tracks. Desmond, poor soul, nearly rammed into him from behind. Something neither of them would have enjoyed.
"No what?" his adviser/servant inquired.
"I take the lead," Pravus explained. "All you guards follow behind."
"But sire," Desmond protested.
"No buts."
"Sire, they're for your protection," Desmond insisted.
"I don't need protection," Pravus retorted rather irritably. "Takes all the danger out of it. No danger, no fun."
"It's not wise, sire."
"I have to agree," Templeton concurred apologetically. "I'd hate for something to happen to you."
"Poppycock!" Pravus cried. "Kings always lead their armies into battle!"
Desmond grimaced.
"In the stories," the man conceded.
"I rest my case," Pravus agreed.
"But might I point out that those stories were approved by the monarchs supposedly involved…after the fact?" Desmond pointed out. Pravus frowned.
"Oh," he mumbled, taken aback.
"Right," Desmond replied.

"Well," Pravus declared rather valiantly, if he did say so himself, "…the stories I approve about myself will be true!"

And with that, he set out to prove his point, striding toward the castle far in the distance. And looking every bit as muscly and heroic as the heroically muscular statues surrounding the gymnasium. Everyone else hurried to keep up with his formidable pace, Desmond having the worst time of it. Templeton, of course, kept up with him with relative ease.

"By god, dear cousin," Pravus proclaimed. "No more fables and tall tales. Today, we'll prove that heroes *can* wear the crown!"

"Right behind you," Templeton replied zestily. "Never fear an attack from behind, my liege. I've got your back!"

And while Pravus was anything but afraid of attacks from behind, he appreciated Templeton's sentiment. Indeed, with his small army of guards behind him, Pravus felt quite wonderfully supported.

"Where are the vagabonds?" Pravus inquired.

"At the inner gate," Desmond called out breathlessly from rather far behind.

"To the inner gate!" Pravus commanded lustily. And lustily he charged, on foot no less. Which was, he realized, hardly practical. But he could hardly stop and demand a carriage now; it would ruin their momentum. So charge he did, running with such speed and vigor that he soon left everyone else behind. Everyone except for Templeton, that was. His cousin was perhaps the only man in the kingdom that could keep up with Pravus, having worked so diligently on his conditioning.

"Thank goodness it wasn't leg day, eh cousin?" Templeton quipped.

"The day would've been surely lost," Pravus agreed. For on leg day – and for a day or two after – a single stair or street curb could prove an enemy too formidable to conquer, much less an army.

"Nice bit of cardio for a warm-up," Templeton mused, not even out of breath. They'd left the others quite far behind now. "What would you guess, three miles to the gate?"

"Just so," Pravus confirmed.

They ran with admirable speed and, to anyone watching, even more admirable form, the result of years of training. And while to others such strenuous exertion would be considered terribly uncomfortable – indeed, something to avoid – to Pravus, it was immensely pleasurable. For to delight in the use of one's body was magical indeed, to reach the very limits of one's capabilities. And in doing so, to grow them.

In this way, Pravus neared the inner gate at the inner wall of Cumulus, spotting a large army of green-suited men marching toward the silver double-doors there. Which were closed, thank goodness.

"We approach the enemy!" Templeton declared from behind. With eager anticipation, Pravus noted. "Shall we stop to strategize?"

"No," Pravus replied. "Let heroism be our strategy and unwavering resolve be our advantage!"

"Indeed!" Templeton cried with gusto.

"We shall tackle the enemy front together, cousin," Pravus declared. "They'll think twice before coming here again!"

And with that, instead of stopping, they went even faster, charging headlong at the enemy army, now only a hundred yards away. Had Pravus glanced back, he would've found that they'd left his guards – and poor, tottering Desmond – a good mile and a half behind. But he didn't look back. Instead, he looked forward...to punting Gavin's perky posterior out of Pravus.

"For the good citizens of Pravus!" King Pravus cried as they approached, holding his sword – and his head – high.

* * *

Gavin Merrick stared as two men charged his army, one dressed in the familiar gold and black uniform and holding a truly massive golden sword, the other a more slender man carrying a far more slender fencing sword. It was King Pravus himself, accompanied by a man Gavin had seen before, but couldn't place a name to.

"I don't believe it," he blurted out, watching as the two men charged toward the front lines of Gavin's huge army.

"Who're those idiots?" one of his men asked. It was his second-in-command for his army.

"One of those idiots is the king," Gavin answered.

"Which one?"

"The one wearing the crown," Gavin snapped, giving the soldier a look. "He has magic," he warned.

"So do we," the commander replied.

"Subdue the king," Gavin commanded. "Kill the other guy."

The commander relayed the order, and the rest of the men faced the coming king, readying their weapons. Gavin watched as King

Pravus – the blithering fool – approached, wielding that ridiculous sword. As if he knew how to use it. In contrast, his men had been in countless battles, and knew precisely how to use *their* weapons. So as the king finally reached the front line, crying out in apparent glee, his men did just that.

King Pravus swung his sword in a wild arc, and the first men in the line blocked it with their swords. Or rather, they tried to. For the sheer force of the blow knocked their blades right out of their hands, and sent them stumbling backward.

Pravus's next swing cut five people in half.

"Holy…!" the commander blurted out. "He's cutting through their suits!"

Gavin grit his teeth, watching as Pravus swung again, lopping off limbs and chopping right through swords and maces with ease. His golden sword glimmered in the sunlight, unstoppable in the king's hands. The man accompanying the king joined the fray, adopting a fencing technique. In and out he thrust his sword, expertly penetrating the soldiers' defenses and impaling them one-by-one.

And more irritating than anything, they both seemed to be thoroughly enjoying themselves. In contrast to Gavin.

"Surround them!" Gavin barked. "Attack from all sides, all at once!"

"Yes sir," the commander replied. He relayed the orders, and the army of green-suited men changed formation, forming a large ring around the two enemies. Then the ring contracted, closing in on King Pravus and his fellow-in-arms. Gavin smiled grimly, knowing that even with his magical sword and clothes and crown, King Pravus couldn't defeat an entire army on his own. The king's end was near…and Marie would at last have the vengeance she deserved.

* * *

King Pravus spun in a slow circle as Evermore's army of green and gold closed in on him and Templeton from all sides.

"A sphincter attack!" Pravus warned, staying close to Templeton's side. "Watch your rear, cousin!"

"Back-to-back?" Templeton proposed.

"Brilliant idea," Pravus replied. "For then we shall be an affront to our enemies!" They pressed their backs together, and their buns, he noted with delight. And in having a friend behind him, Pravus only had to concern himself with what was in front of him. And that, of course, was nothing but a bunch of Borrin bastards.

"Come at us!" Pravus cried. "If you're going to die, die valiantly, villains!"

So the villains came, brandishing their swords and various other weapons, charging all at once.

Four of them swung at Pravus at one time, and he lifted his huge sword to block all of them with a righteous *clang*. The sudden weight of their blows felt absolutely marvelous, and he reveled in resisting it, bending his legs a bit to absorb the blows, then thrusting upward in perfect squatting form, shoving upward with his sword at the same time. This threw them all backward quite vigorously, tossing them into their teammates and bowling them all over.

"Ha!" Pravus exclaimed, kicking a soldier that tried rushing at him from the side. He followed up with a thrust of his magical sword, impaling the poor man. Yanking his sword upward, he cut the man mostly in half, which was a bit too gruesome for Pravus's tastes. Still, war was war, and distasteful to any who had the misfortune to experience it.

He glanced back, seeing Templeton wielding his fencing sword expertly, felling soldier after soldier with rapid thrusts.

"Well done, cousin!" Pravus congratulated.

"A dance of death!" Templeton proclaimed. And it was a pleasure to witness. For while Pravus's oversized sword destroyed his enemies in sprays of various uncomfortably hot fluids, Templeton's weapon was far more subtle in its taking of life. A fact that hardly bothered Pravus, of course. His temperament favored far grander displays, and to be honest, subtlety simply wasn't in his nature.

More of the Borrin soldiers threw themselves at Pravus, and paid for it with their lives. For Pravus's sword was easily twice as long as theirs, allowing him to cut them down before they ever had a chance of reaching him. It's gloriously gilded edge was soon soaked in blood and intestinal expulsions. The latter of which Pravus hadn't considered as a reality of battle.

"The smell," he blurted out, wrinkling his nose.

"That's why I favor penetration to evisceration," Templeton told him. And what iron will it took for Pravus to hold his tongue! He focused on slashing and thrusting instead, penetrating a few of Gavin's cutthroats in a symphony of screams. Several blows got past his defenses, but his kingly uniform and crown had potent magic, protecting him from harm. A fact that the soldiers soon realized made Pravus practically invulnerable to their efforts.

Which made them far less eager to continue.

They backed away from him and Templeton, the enemy sphincter expanding around the two in hopes of preventing further bloodshed.

"Come on then," Pravus teased, throwing in a cocky smirk and a merry twinkle of the eye as he eyed them. "Don't be shy. It's your duty to fight and die!"

"Don't be cowards now," Templeton added for good measure.

The ring of soldiers parted, revealing none other than Gavin Merrick himself. The man was as dashing and handsome as ever, the kind of fellow that usually made Pravus delight in all manner of ghastly fantasies. But as gorgeous as his exterior was, inside he was hollow, a man whose only passion was in conquest. A man bamboozled by the idea that there was a purpose to life, rather than living being the purpose itself.

There was no point, of course. And that *was* the point. Something Gavin would never understand. Which was why the man could hoard all the money and magic in the world…and never be able to enjoy it.

Gavin strode toward Pravus and Templeton, his hands in his green pants pockets. All casual and cool, as if he wasn't at all concerned about the fact that his foes had just massacred much of his army.

"Who's the coward?" the man inquired. "The king who risks nothing clad in his magical uniform, or the men who risk everything in battling him?"

"I'd say the coward who sends his men to fight his battles for him," Pravus replied, with just the right amount of snark. Gavin smirked, extending his arms out to the sides.

"Yet here I am," he retorted.

"Indeed," Pravus agreed. "Which begs the question: why *are* you here? To penetrate my natural resources? Steal more magic?"

"No," Gavin replied. "There's no magic left."

"Oh *really*."

"You took it from me," Gavin said, pointing a finger at him. Which was rude. "You killed my wife!"

Pravus blinked.

"What?" he blurted out. "I did no such thing."

"You had her killed," Gavin corrected. "Your Chosen Ones murdered her by the Great Wood."

"First of all, they're not *my* Chosen Ones," Pravus corrected. "And honestly, I hadn't met them until *after* they killed your wife. Who was trying to fell the Great Wood at the time, might I remind you. And not consensually."

Gavin stared at him for a long moment, his jaw working.

"It's true," Templeton confirmed. "I was riding with my liege to the Great Wood to save it at the time. But when we arrived, the Chosen Ones had already vanquished your army. I recall seeing a beautiful woman's corpse on the ground nearby," he added apologetically. "While we may be enemies, I myself have a wife. I can only imagine the torture of losing her." He bowed his head solemnly. "My condolences."

Pravus smiled, his heart swelling with pride. It was just like sweet, dearest Templeton to give quarter even to his foe, and see the humanity in everyone.

"Save your pity," Gavin retorted.

"I don't pity you," Templeton countered earnestly. "I have empathy for you."

"What's the difference?" Gavin argued.

"The former means I'd feel sorry for you," Templeton replied. "The latter means I feel what I imagine you must feel."

"You'll never know how I feel."

"Without specific magic to help, no," Templeton agreed. "But in any case, we're not the proper object of your vengeance, Mr. Merrick."

Gavin took a deep breath in, letting it out slowly.

"Then who is?" he demanded.

"The Chosen Ones," Pravus declared. "As I said," he added, even though it felt petty to do so. But being a little petty could feel oh-so-good, as this particular moment proved to be true.

"Who are they…and where are they?" Gavin pressed.

"Well, we're not quite sure," Templeton confessed. "They were supposed to travel to Mount Thrall to defeat The Dark One, but it appears they entered the kingdom and vanished. No one knows quite where they are."

"I see," Gavin replied. He squared his shoulders then. "Give me their names and descriptions, and I'll find them," he vowed.

"And let you murder the only ones who can save my kingdom from certain destruction?" Pravus scoffed. "Please."

"I'll only kill the one who killed Marie," Gavin promised. "And I'll destroy The Dark One as well."

"Oh *really*," Pravus shot back. "Do you really think it's that easy? Just stroll on up to Mount Thrall and kill a demigod, just like that?"

"If I fail, I die," Gavin pointed out. "Either way, you win."

"So you're asking me to let you go after you barged into my city and slaughtered my guards?" Pravus pressed. "And betray the very heroes that are destined to save my people from utter destruction?"

Gavin paused.

"Yes," he answered. "Like I said, either way, you win."

"And that's the very reason I detest you," Pravus declared. "Always about the winning." He thrust his marvelously chiseled jaw out firmly. "I decline your offer, Mr. Merrick. If I'm going to win, it'll be on *my* terms."

"And if you don't win, you'll have failed your people," Gavin retorted.

Pravus grimaced. The wily bastard had clearly deduced where his weakness lay, and had targeted it expertly.

"If I betray my ideals and my heroes," he countered, "…I'll have failed far more. Once again, your offer is declined."

"Then you're standing in the way of my revenge," Gavin declared. "Which means I'll just have to kill you first."

Pravus was about to reply when a gasping, wheezing Desmond, accompanied by a small army of royal guards, finally caught up with them.

"They're…Chauncy," the old man blurted out, "…Valtora, Nettie…and…Harry."

Pravus blinked, taken quite aback.

"And they…they're making their way…to…" he gasped, bending over and clutching at his knees as he panted, sweat pouring from his forehead. "Mount Thrall!"

"Desmond!" Pravus scolded. "How could you!"

"Safety…of…people," Desmond replied. "The people come…first."

"Mount Thrall," Gavin stated. "That's the volcano where The Dark One lives, if I remember correctly."

Everyone nodded.

"Goodbye Pravus," Gavin said. "May we never meet again."

"Indeed," Pravus agreed.

And with that, Gavin left as abruptly as he'd come, pulling out of the city and exiting through its open gate. Having left a bit of a bloody mess behind, unfortunately. Pravus watched the man and his army go, then turned on Desmond, pointing his golden sword at the man rather menacingly.

"You!" he snapped. "Betrayer of heroes! Defier of kings! Give me one reason why I shouldn't separate your head from its shoulders right now!"

Desmond stood up as straight as he could, eyeing the sword rather hopefully.

"Because it'd hurt me more not to," he replied.

Pravus considered this, then lowered his blade.

"You really are a sad little sack, aren't you old man?" he mused.

"Indeed sire."

"Is it really that bad?" Pravus pressed.

"Worse."

Pravus sighed, shaking his head at his unruly servant.

"Why on earth did you do that, Desmond?" he inquired. "I assume you had some grand master plan in mind?"

"Naturally sire," Desmond confirmed. "We've been looking for the Chosen Ones for some time now, with no success."

"Indeed," Templeton agreed solemnly. "I blame myself, sire."

"Take heart, dearest cousin," Pravus comforted. "It's exceedingly rare that you fail to rise to the occasion when stimulated to do so."

"Fair point," Templeton conceded.

"We may not have found them, but Gavin could," Pravus warned. "He is likely possessed of particular magic that could locate them."

"My thought exactly," Desmond agreed.

"But if he does, he might kill them," Pravus pointed out. "And then we'll have betrayed them!"

"If the Chosen Ones are really Chosen Ones, Gavin won't stand a chance," Desmond reasoned. "And if we were to, say, *follow* him, and let him take us right to them..."

"We could locate the Chosen Ones, stop Gavin from harming them, and help them defeat The Dark One!" Pravus concluded. His eyebrows shot up, and he lunged forward, scooping Desmond up in a hearty embrace. While lifting him right off the ground. Desmond gasped, his eyes widening quite alarmingly, and he stiffened in Pravus's grasp.

"Your...sword," he gasped.

Pravus paused, realizing that he was still carrying his sword. And that its crossguard was pressing rather firmly into poor Desmond's back. He let the man down, releasing him and taking a step back.

"You've done it again, Desmond!" he proclaimed. "Why, I knew it was a stroke of genius to make you my advisor!"

"It was my stroke of genius that made you make me your advisor," Desmond pointed out.

"And my genius to see the genius in you," Pravus compromised.

"If you say so, my liege."

"Everything is," Pravus agreed. "Now, how do you suppose we should go about following our dastardly devil Mr. Merrick?"

"I have just the thing," Desmond replied.

Chapter 34

Chauncy faced The Dark One's horrid gaze, hand-in-hand with Valtora. Her regular hand, thank goodness. But even still, it clutched his so tightly that he worried his fingers might break. Nettie and Harry stood beside them, and Skibbard a bit behind, facing the personification of evil himself.

"Could've sworn I killed you," Nettie accused, putting a hand on her Wetstone.

"**I am immortal,**" The Dark One replied in that awful voice, one that sent fresh shivers down Chauncy's spine. "**For me, death is a brief interlude between forms.**"

"Awesome," Chauncy muttered.

"How brief we talkin'?" Harry inquired.

"**Depressingly,**" The Dark One answered.

"You got that right," Nettie grumbled. "Well go back in your stupid temple and leave us alone, or I'll depress you again!"

"**Unlikely,**" The Dark One retorted calmly. To which Nettie squeezed the Wetstone, summoning water and forming it into a long spike. One she shot out at The Dark One much as she had the first time, striking him in the belly.

Or at least, that's what *should* have happened.

Instead, The Dark One intercepted with his gigantic shadowy blade. And when its glowing red edge struck the icicle-spear, the spear exploded, sending steaming fragments flying out at them. They pelted Chauncy and his fellow Chosen Ones, small hunks of ice biting into their flesh…and leaving deep gashes in their skin, all the way down to the fat below.

Blood poured from Chauncy's face and neck, from a half-dozen wounds. It went right into his eyes, blurring his vision. He gasped at the pain, swinging his staff blindly at The Dark One. A blast of wind tore at the man, blasting some of the fog away, but the fog merely re-coalesced, forming his fog armor and sword once again.

"**Your magic is weak,**" The Dark One stated. "**You are unworthy of the destiny bestowed upon you.**"

"We'll see about that," Nettie retorted.

"**I was talking to him,**" The Dark One corrected, pointing at Chauncy. Who grimaced, gripping his staff tightly.

"I know I'm unworthy," Chauncy retorted, wiping blood from his eyes.

"**Yet here you are,**" The Dark One mused.

"I'm here for her," Chauncy replied, gesturing at Valtora. "Not you."

"**She comes with me,**" The Dark One replied.

"Not in three years I haven't," Valtora retorted. "Now let us go. I don't want you anymore."

"**So naturally I want you even more,**" The Dark One countered. "**It is human nature to attribute great value to things difficult to acquire.**"

"Well I'm impossible for you to 'acquire,'" Valtora proclaimed. "And besides, you're not human."

"**I am the personification of a part of human nature,**" he pointed out. "**And the desire for nonconsensual acquisition is a particularly evil trait.**"

"Well that's true," Harry conceded.

"Shut up Harry!" Nettie snapped. "You're right," she added. "It is evil."

"Then why'd ya tell me to shut up?" Harry inquired.

"Force of habit."

"**Enough procrastination,**" The Dark One interjected, gripping his huge sword tightly. His eyes – and it's glowing edge – flashed even brighter. "**Time to die.**"

"Not much for monologuing," Harry noted.

And then The Dark One attacked!

He swung his huge sword at Chauncy, who lifted his Staff of Wind to block. But a pillar of rock appeared between them in the nick of time, shielding him from the blow. The Dark One's sword cut through the rock with terrible ease, but his attack was slowed just enough for Chauncy to back out of range. Still, he felt the terrible heat of The Dark One's blade on his face as it swept inches from him.

Crap!

The Dark One wound up to swing again, and Chauncy slammed the butt of his staff on the ground, shooting upward into the air just as The Dark One's sword slashed inches below his feet. He watched as Nettie and Harry combined to form their earth-water elemental, bringing Valtora and Skibbard into it with them. They towered over The Dark One, the combined elemental over forty feet tall.

So The Dark One swung his sword at its legs, chopping them both off with a single slash.

Chauncy fell back toward the mountain, thrusting his staff again to land gently behind the elemental. Nettie froze the outer watery skin of the elemental around its severed legs, forming a kind of cast around them. When these melted, the rock had healed, apparently by Harry's magic.

Chauncy shook his head in amazement at the sheer creativity of it. Then he looked at his staff. It was, he realized, nothing even close to what Nettie and Harry could do.

The Dark One's right, Chauncy told himself. *I am unworthy.*

It was merely a confirmation of something he'd always suspected about himself. That he was somehow insufficient, and that nothing he could do would ever change that. Everyone in his life had tried to convince him otherwise, of course. But most of the people in his life were rather nice, and not particularly authoritative. Now he had it on the highest authority that he was unworthy, and could fool himself no more.

He was insufficient, and there was nothing he could do about it.

"Don't just stand there idiot!" Nettie shouted from way up in the elemental's chest cavity. "Do something, Chauncy!"

The Dark One attacked again, executing a triple-slash at the elemental's legs. But again, Nettie casted them with ice while Harry healed.

"**Clever**," The Dark One said, inclining his head at Nettie and Harry. "**Not all of you are useless.**"

"I think he's hitting on you," Harry said. Nettie rolled her eyes.

"Would ya shut up and kill him already?" she shot back.

"That'll just give him a brief interlude between his forms," Harry pointed out.

"Fine," Nettie replied. And then she pointed one big elemental-hand at The Dark One, sending a massive jet of water at him.

The Dark One lifted his sword to intercept, and its glowing edge turned the water instantly to steam. That steam billowed around him harmlessly, but soon obscured him completely, mixing with the falling ash to make it impossible to see ahead.

"For cripe's sake Chauncy, get off yer ass and *do* something!" Nettie barked.

"Yeah!" Valtora agreed, but in a more supportive sort of way. "Kick his ass, baby!"

Chauncy grimaced, peering through the elemental's legs at the wall of steam beyond. Two glowing red eyes appeared from within it, seeming to stare right at him…sending a fresh spike of fear into his guts.

They believe in you, he told himself, gripping his staff tightly in both hands. *They're counting on you!*

He *should* be doing something.

Chauncy took a deep breath, then squared his shoulders.

"Fine," he decided. "I'll do something."

He thrust the butt of his staff down then, flying high into the air…and over the elemental's head. He spotted The Dark One facing the elemental beyond, and lifted his staff high above his head as he fell toward the guy.

"Wind chop!" he cried, chopping downward.

A blast of wind struck The Dark One, splitting his fog-armor in twine. But it merely started flowing back together.

"Ah ha! Twisty tornado!" he bellowed triumphantly, spinning his staff like a top. It fell toward The Dark One, twisting around to form a tornado, as advertised. One that sucked all of the fog armor and even the fog-sword away…and carried that fog with it down the mountainside.

Chauncy smirked at the rather surprised The Dark One. Until he realized that he was still falling, and that his staff was quite a ways away. And that, since he'd been falling for quite some time now, that he was doing so at fatal speed.

"Oh," was all he could manage before he struck the mountainside.

But instead of dying right then and there – in lieu of a sudden fade to black, or awful agony, or transport to an afterlife good or bad – Chauncy found himself sinking into the rock. Or rather, he found that the rock was sinking *with* him, at nearly the rate he'd been falling. Such that he landed quite gently upon it, and came to a gradual stop. In a pit in the ground that'd formed quite suddenly.

Chauncy blinked in confusion, then broke out into a smile.

Harry!

For it could have been no one else than the kindhearted old man who'd saved him. Soon Chauncy found himself rising, the floor of the pit moving upward. A few seconds later it was level with the ground, bringing him right beside the elemental's big foot. The watery skin surrounding that foot bulged outward, grabbing him and sucking him in and upward. Within moments, he'd joined everyone else within the elemental.

"Heya Chauncy," Harry greeted with a grin.

"Thanks Harry," Chauncy replied. "You really do rock."

"Sure do," Harry agreed.

"Don't let it get to your head," Nettie warned Harry.

"She keeps me grounded," Harry told Chauncy with a wink.

"Incoming!" Valtora blurted out.

Everyone turned, seeing The Dark One levitating upward until he was level with the ice-windshield protecting the elemental's chest-cavity. His armor was gone, leaving him in his black suit. He floated there, smirking at Chauncy.

"**You nearly killed yourself,**" he chided. Then he turned to Nettie and Harry. "**He reminds me of your previous apprentice...Steve, was it?**"

"That's Greg!" Nettie shot back hotly. "And he didn't kill himself. Your dragon did!"

"**He dodged into a lava blast,**" The Dark One reminded her.

"He didn't blast himself with lava, now did he," Nettie retorted. "Your dragon shot the lava that killed him. He just zigged when he should'a zagged."

"**Perhaps if you'd trained him properly, he would have zagged.**"

"You son-of-a…"

"**But it appears you've trained both of your apprentices inadequately,**" The Dark One interjected. "**Imperius chose poorly.**"

"Imperius didn't choose them," Nettie argued. "Destiny did!"

"Destiny chose *all* of us," Valtora agreed. "And we're gonna kick your ass!"

"**Destiny doesn't exist,**" The Dark One retorted. "**And soon, neither shall you.**"

"Pretty good line," Harry conceded. Nettie splashed him in the face.

"Shut up Harry!"

"Can we *please* concentrate on not dying?" Skibbard interjected.

"Haven't seen *you* do anything," Nettie grumbled. "You're even worse than Chauncy!"

"Um, wow," Chauncy replied. "Bitch."

"You're the bitch," Nettie retorted. "A Little bitch," she added hurtfully. "And you're about to be The Dark One's little bitch if you don't hurry up and be a real goddamn wizard already!"

"But how?" Chauncy protested. Nettie threw up her hands.

"You're a wizard!" she replied. "Use magic!"

The Dark One watched all of this with his arms crossed over his chest, clearly amused.

"**I must say, you're the most pathetic group of Chosen Ones I've ever encountered,**" he told them. "**Entertaining, however.**"

"Isn't that what Zarzibar said?" Valtora asked.

"He said we were idiots, not pathetic," Chauncy corrected.

"So we're the best at being the worst," Valtora reasoned. "At least we're the best at something."

"I'm not with them," Skibbard informed The Dark One. "I'd like to leave now."

"**You die too,**" The Dark One replied.

Skibbard cursed, using a word that was quite appropriately inappropriate. A verb that, without Rooter's aid, he would continue to be incapable of.

"**I should have my dragon roast you alive,**" The Dark One mused. Valtora scoffed.

"Maggie won't hurt us," she shot back. "In fact, she'll probably hurt *you*, after all the times you've abused her!"

"He'd have to beat his own dragon then," Harry mused.

"He'll be doing a lot of that from now on," Valtora agreed.

"**Enough,**" The Dark One proclaimed…and his fog-armor returned with a vengeance, wrapping around his body. His fog-sword returned as well…and he hefted it over his head, preparing to chop right through the ice-windshield and destroy them all. "**Meet your doom, Chosen Ones!**"

The sword came slicing downward, cutting into the water-skin surrounding the elemental with a loud *hiss*. It cleaved right through the giant's stony flesh, sinking into the watery cavity where everyone floated. Chauncy saw that horrible blade descending right at Valtora, and he shoved her out of the way with his right hand in the nick of time.

Right as the blade sliced through the water within the cavity, boiling it on contact.

Steam filled the cavity instantly, and Chauncy cried out, squeezing his eyes shut and shielding his face with one arm. Then his stomach lurched, and he felt himself falling.

Then the world disappeared, not into blackness, not with a white light, but with nothing. And at the same time, Chauncy's inner world did the same. He felt no fear, because without *him*, there was no fear. No pain. Without Chauncy, there was nothing. Nothing to be, nothing to do, nothing at all.

So, at the hands of The Dark One, Chauncy met his doom.

Chapter 35

Meeting one's doom, it turned out, was a bit anticlimactic.

Rather than the momentous occasion one might expect from The End, it was merely the end. The end of everything good and bad, happy and sad. The end of pain and pleasure. Indeed, it was the end of any distinction between opposites, because without someone to make that distinction, opposites didn't exist. Beginnings and endings didn't exist.

So, this being so, distinction itself was a bit surprised when it resumed. In a flash of white light, which, in suddenly being brought into being, made black come into being around it. They came from the void, each created by the presence of the other.

And with the creation of these opposites, more opposites appeared.

Distinction itself observed these, or rather created these, *then* observed them, as if they existed outside of itself. And then "itself" remembered that it *was* a self, and furthermore, that it had a name.

Chauncy.

Odd, that it had a name, this thing that split the world into opposites. And that it'd accepted that name so readily.

But Chauncy didn't have much time to ponder this. For the full experience of his world returned to him with a vengeance, suddenly and without warning. And unfortunately, that experience was, at this particular moment, horribly unpleasant. For he found himself lying on his back on hard stone, soaked with hot water, every inch of his skin badly burned.

"Fuck," he gasped.

He moaned, lifting his head up from the ground to look at his body. His eyes were blurry with water, and he wiped them away with his hand. Or at least, that's what *should* have happened. Instead, nothing did.

Chauncy blinked, trying again. But again, nothing happened.

He turned to look at his right hand, and instead, found nothing. And nothing for a forearm. No elbow. No shoulder. Just blood pumping in rapid spurts from a stump where his shoulder had been. Chauncy stared at it, hardly believing his eyes. Then he turned his head away and puked.

"Chauncy!" he heard a voice cry. He moaned, staring off into the direction it'd come from. But he only saw black ground and white ash. Black and white, the two opposites he now knew *he* created.

But then, to his surprise, he saw color. It was faint at first, bobbing through the white ash. Then it grew more vibrant. A kaleidoscope of all the colors of the rainbow. He realized that it was in fact Valtora's left hand...and that she was running through the ash toward him.

"Poopy...dooz!" he gasped.

"Chauncy!" she gasped, spotting him lying on the ground. Her eyes widened with horror as she skid to a stop before him, and knelt down beside him. Her skin was beet-red, and blistering a bit, but she was otherwise intact, to his relief. Her eyes went right to his spurting stump, and she gasped in horror. "Chauncy!" she cried, pressing her diamond hand against the wound to staunch the bleeding. "Oh god, oh god!"

"Heard...that...before," he said with a pained smirk. She glared at him.

"Not the time for jokes, baby," she retorted. "Nettie! Harry!" she cried out. "Help!"

Another figure came rushing out of the black and white. It was Nettie, hobbling toward them. Her skin was less burned than Valtora's, but she was bleeding from the side of her head...and looking awfully pale.

"What in the..." Nettie began, then spotted Chauncy. It was her turn to gasp, and she turned even *more* pale, rushing up to Chauncy as quickly as she could. "Let go!" she told Valtora.

"He'll bleed to death!" Valtora shot back, her voice rising in panic. Tears streamed down her burnt cheeks, and she shook her head at Chauncy. "Don't leave me baby," she pleaded. "I don't want a life without you."

Nettie put a hand on Valtora's shoulder.

"Trust me," she insisted gently. Valtora glanced at her, swallowing visibly. Then she nodded.

"Okay," she agreed...and let go of his stump. Blood pumped from it in rapid jets, and Chauncy felt an awful wooziness come over him, threatening to pull him back into oblivion. Nettie gripped her Wetstone, guiding water to the stump…and then freezing it solid. The bleeding stopped instantly, and the pain worsened for a bit, then began to fade as his flesh went numb.

"Oh," Valtora murmured, putting a hand to her mouth. Nettie patted her shoulder.

"Help me up kid," she told her. Valtora did so, helping Nettie to her feet.

"Where's Harry?" Valtora asked.

"Keeping The Dark One preoccupied," Nettie answered.

"We have to help him!" Valtora pressed. But Nettie shook her head.

"Chauncy needs our help first," she countered. "We gotta get him to Rooter and heal him up."

"Then what?" Valtora pressed.

"Then we get the hell outta here," Nettie answered. "And never come back."

"But…The Dark One," Valtora said. "We have to kill him!"

"We can't," Nettie retorted. "We're not good enough."

"But…"

"Let's go," Nettie interrupted. She used her water magic to make a waterbed under Chauncy, then morphed it into an ice chair, forcing him to sit up. Then she and Valtora pulled him to his feet. Doing so, he felt so lightheaded that he nearly fainted, slumping against them. "He's lost a lot of blood," Nettie warned. "Gonna have to carry him."

She created a kind of ice bobsled then, and everyone got inside. That done, Nettie made a bobsled track of sorts, also out of ice, one that led down the mountainside. The sled began sliding down it, and Chauncy groaned as they picked up speed, feeling another wave of nausea. He grit his teeth against it, watching as Nettie created the ice-track ahead…and melted it behind them…so that the sled went down the mountainside as smoothly as could be. It was wonderfully creative – and quite effective – carrying them down the mountain faster than any carriage could have.

"Wow," Chauncy mumbled. He felt strangely giddy, witnessing this bit of magic. They were bobsledding down an active volcano, over pools of lava no less, escaping from evil itself to get to a little stone golem that could heal them with its magical plant-hat. It was at first glance an utterly inappropriate solution. Absolutely ridiculous, in fact.

But as it turned out, ridiculously inappropriate magic was precisely what they'd needed.

"There's Rocky 'n Rooter!" Valtora prompted, pointing down the slope of the mountain and to the right. She was right; the two were sitting by a small pool of lava, warming their feet by it. Nettie curved the track toward them, and at the same time, she made the track ahead far rougher. Such that the friction slowed them down gradually, until they came to a stop right before Rocky and Rooter. The sled melted, easing Chauncy and Valtora to the ground.

"Rootie!" Valtora cried, rushing up to Rocky and Rooter. "Chauncy's hurt bad!"

That was all Rooter needed to hear, of course. Rocky stood, scooping Rooter up in one hand and walking him to Chauncy to set him down between him and Valtora. Rooter's plant-head glowed like a miniature sun, bathing Chauncy and Valtora – and even Nettie – with its light. And to Chauncy's delight, not only did his burnt skin mend, but his right arm grew back before his very eyes, until it was whole once again.

"Well I'll be," Nettie murmured.

"Wow," Valtora breathed.

"That's some magic you got there, Rooter," Nettie admitted. Rooter shook his little head, his plant-hat bobbing adorably. He pointed a tiny finger at Chauncy, and Nettie smiled. "You're right," she conceded. "It's Chauncy's magic." She sighed then, helping Chauncy up. "Too bad our magic wasn't enough to get the job done," she lamented.

"Yeah," Valtora agreed.

"We did everything we could," Nettie reassured them. "Threw the damn book at that unholy bastard. Ah well."

Chauncy blinked.

The damn book.

He put a hand on his left thigh, feeling the familiar contours of his book within his robe pocket. The Magic of Magic, a magical book from the Cave of Wonder. His lesson – and his gift – from that most mystical place. A place where he'd gone first to be reborn, to discover the magic within himself…and that he was the source of it. And the second time, he'd learned that…

"The solution to the problem is the problem itself," he blurted out.

Everyone blinked, taken aback.

"Huh?" Valtora asked.

"What?" Nettie added.

"He's not the problem," Chauncy declared, breaking out into a smile. "*We* are!"

"Gonna hafta explain that," Nettie grumbled.

"Well, you see," Chauncy began, but Nettie cut him off.

"Tell us on the way back," she ordered. "Rocky, can you carry us up the mountain? Harry needs us."

"Okkkkaaahhh," Rocky agreed.

He assumed the position, getting on all fours and allowing everyone to mount him.

"Hey, where's Peter?" Chauncy asked.

"Huuunggrreeee," Rocky said. "Eeeet graaassss"

"Must've gone back down the mountain," Valtora said, clearly sad that the unicorn wasn't around. "Aww," she added, confirming this.

And with that, Rocky charged up the slope of the mountain, making his way toward Harry…and The Dark One.

* * *

When The Dark One's sword cut into the elemental's chest cavity, Harry's first thought was not for himself, but for his angel.

He pressed a bare foot down on the floor of the chamber, absorbing its rockiness into himself. At the same time, he wrapped his arms around his wife, holding her tight…just as the water within the chamber burst into steam, boiling instantly. The sword continued downward, The Dark One plummeting to the ground far below, slicing all the way down to cut the elemental completely in half. Something Harry couldn't see, what with the steam and all, but he could feel.

The two sides of the elemental separated, falling apart.

Harry held on tight as they fell with it, Nettie screaming in his ear. Not for the first time, Harry was glad he was a bit hard of hearing. Not stone-deaf, but getting there. He landed on his back on the obsidian slope of the volcano with a *whump*, but he barely felt the impact.

Boiling water fell toward them, and he rolled over to lay on top of Nettie, shielding her from it as best he could.

"Ow!" Nettie gasped. "God that burns!"

"It's all right angel," he reassured her as the deluge ended. "I got you."

"You always do, you old coot," she replied with a smile. "Now get off me already. This is no time for hanky-panky."

"Well shoot," he replied with a grin. He got up, pulling her to her feet. She was burned – in some places pretty good – but otherwise intact. "You all right angel?"

"Thanks to you," she replied.

They both looked at the damage around them. Their elementals were destroyed, the half they'd been in lying in shambles, and the other half hidden in dense falling ash. Chauncy was nowhere to be seen, but Valtora was a few yards away, rising to her feet. And beside her, an arm.

One that wasn't attached to the rest of a body like it should be.

"That yours?" Harry asked Valtora, who stumbled toward them. "Nope," he added, seeing that she had two.

"Well shit," Nettie swore. "Valtora, go find Chauncy."

"You go with her," Harry prompted. "I'll handle this guy," he added, nodding at a shadowy figure coming toward them from beyond the haze of ash.

"You sure?" Nettie asked.

"I'll be alright," he reassured her.

"Don't go dying on me," she warned.

"Well that's how I'd like to die, actually," he quipped. She rolled her eyes at him. "Huh," he added. "Thought you'd tell me to shut up with that one."

"I'll tell you after I come back," she promised. "'Cause you better still be talkin' when I do."

She leaned in for a kiss then, and he kissed her just as passionately as he could. It was exactly like the first time they'd kissed, so many decades ago. Every time the same, because *real* magic never got old.

"I love you, you idiot," Nettie declared, her eyes growing moist. And with that, she turned and left him, before he could say he loved her back. And Harry knew that was because she wanted to hear it *after* she came back.

Harry smiled, watching her go, then turning to face The Dark One, who emerged from the ashy haze, staring at him with those glowing red eyes. He reached into his pocket then, pulling out a small vial of silver liquid. He popped the cap, then drank it down in one gulp. It tasted like nothing at all. He felt it settle in his stomach, and burped.

"Hey there," Harry greeted, wiping his mouth, then inclining his head. The Dark One eyed him, holding his huge sword over one shoulder.

"**Surrender and I'll let you live,**" he proclaimed.

"Funny, I was just about to say that," Harry replied.

"**You cannot kill me.**"

"Sure I can," Harry countered with a grin.

"**Even if you do, I will simply rematerialize.**"

"Well that's true," Harry admitted. "But at least I'll have fun doing it."

"**Until you die.**"

"That's the idea," Harry replied. "We're all gonna die at the end. Least we can do is have a little fun getting there." He paused. "Ain't'cha ever had fun?"

"**I've had pleasure,**" The Dark One replied.

"Well that's different," Harry said. "Had that too. But fun is play."

"**Evil doesn't waste time on such trivial things,**" The Dark One stated.

"Then you're missing out on what's important," Harry replied. And with that, he dug a toe into the ground, requesting a bit of the volcano. And the volcano, delighted to have something to do, complied.

A fist-sized rock shot up from between The Dark One's legs, striking him in the family jewels.

The Dark One grunted, his eyes narrowing a bit. Then he gripped his sword, getting ready to slash at Harry. Right as a boulder – ten times as big as the rock before it – shot up from the ground, hitting The Dark One in the stones again.

This time, the guy doubled over, his sword falling to the ground.

"Well that worked," Harry noted. "And see? I had a ball doin' it."

The Dark One recovered quickly, his sword flying back into his hand.

"**Your attacks merely delay the inevitable,**" he growled.

"So does breathing," Harry pointed out. "But I still like doing it."

He shifted his weight onto his left foot, feeling the warm, rough rock there. It was rhyolite, quite naturally. The caldera at the top of the mountain gave that away. The fact that a cone volcano had formed around the caldera indicated a high gas content in the magma, and the incredible amount of obsidian pointed to the sheer amount of quickly cooling flows the volcano had produced.

Rhyolite was quite hard, not as hard as sapphire or diamond, but still pretty good.

The Dark One swung his sword at Harry, who gave himself to the rhyolite at his feet. And, it being quite fond of him all of a sudden, formed a column under his feet that shot upward a good ten feet, making The Dark One cut the column instead of him. The blade melted the cleaved ends of the column, which promptly fused together.

"Too high," Harry called out with a grin.

The Dark One flew up at him, winding his sword back to slash again. Harry dropped the column down suddenly, and the attack whizzed over his head, ruffling his hair a bit.

"Too low," Harry quipped.

The Dark One's red eyes flashed, and he shot down at Harry, chopping downward at him rather viciously. Harry gave more of himself to the rock, and a huge rhyolite hand shot up from under The Dark One, grabbing him out of the air and holding him tight in its giant fingers. The guy's sword fell from his hands, landing on the ground with a clatter.

"Too slow," Harry finished with a grin.

The Dark One struggled against his earthy prison, glaring down at Harry.

"**This is pointless. You cannot win,**" he growled.

"Only pointless if winning is the point," Harry countered. "Assuming I don't."

"**For what other reason would you fight me?**"

"For the adventure," Harry replied with a grin. And it was true. For to life a life avoiding danger was to avoid adventure, and as a consequence, to barely live at all. That was only living in a literal sense, in that one's heart was beating and mouth was eating. Harry figured it was better to live figuratively.

The Dark One's fog-armor dissipated, revealing his humanoid form. He eyed Harry with a curious look.

"**You're different,**" he stated.

"Thank heaven," Harry agreed.

"**You have the aura of Destiny about you,**" The Dark One continued. His eyes widened, and he took a sharp breath in. "**You're a Magus like me!**"

"Probably right," Harry replied. He'd figured that bit out a few decades ago, though he'd kept it to himself.

"**You were destined to ascend half a century ago,**" The Dark One protested.

"I found a different destiny," Harry replied with a smile. "A sweet little angel."

The Dark One stared at Harry for a moment, then reached out with one hand. His sword shot back into it, and he did something rather unexpected.

He cut his own head off.

Black fog spilled out of the wound, cascading over the rocky fist and settling on the ground.

"Clever," Harry said. And watched as the fog coalesced, re-forming The Dark One.

"**You chose a woman over greatness?**" the man asked incredulously.

"I chose great over greatness," Harry corrected.

"**You could have been a god!**"

"Too much responsibility," Harry replied. "Didn't seem like much fun neither."

He willed the rocky hand to reached for The Dark One, grabbing him from behind once again. But The Dark One whipped around, slashing with his sword and taking all the fingers off in one swipe. The stumps glowed faint red, then went dark as they cooled…and before they even had a chance to, The Dark One slashed at Harry's belly.

The blade went right through Harry's midsection, cutting him in half.

Harry stood there, grinning at The Dark One, who stared at Harry's wound. A wound that bled silver instead of blood.

"**What…?**" was all The Dark One could blurt out.

"Mercury," Harry explained, even as he turned the metal back into flesh. "Only metal that's a liquid at room temperature, don't'cha know."

The Dark One eyed Harry for a long moment, then lowered his sword.

"**I will not fight you,**" he stated.

"Well why not?" Harry asked.

"**My battle is not with you,**" The Dark One explained. "**I cannot serve you in that way.**"

"Spoilsport," Harry replied.

And then he heard a *thump-a-thump, thump-a-thump* approaching from behind, and quick too. He turned around, seeing Nettie, Chauncy, Valtora, and Rooter riding Rocky's back as the giant charged toward him and The Dark One. He smiled, then turned to face The Dark One.

"How 'bout them?" he inquired. "Can they kick yer ass?"

"**They can try,**" The Dark One replied.

Chapter 36

It was all Chauncy could do to not fall off of Rocky's broad back as the giant charged up the steep slope of Mount Thrall. The falling ash made it nearly impossible for them to see what was ahead, which added to the terror of it all. Struck with a sudden idea, Chauncy extended a hand, willing for something to happen. And him being a wizard and all, something did.

His staff whizzed back into his hand from wherever it'd fallen, striking his palm with a satisfying *thwap*.

Chauncy swung his staff then, blasting the ash ahead of them away. This made it quite a bit easier to see, and what he saw made his heart leap in his throat. It was Harry, facing The Dark One in mortal combat!

"Harry!" Valtora gasped.

"I've got this," Chauncy declared. And to his surprise, he meant it.

"But…" Valtora protested, gripping his shoulder.

"What?" he asked.

"You might die," she pointed out.

"True," he conceded. But he'd met his doom once already, and it wasn't nearly as bad as he'd thought. In fact, he had no fear whatsoever of meeting it again. "But I'd rather live a bit before I do."

Valtora's eyes widened.

"You rhymed," she breathed.

"Shit's getting *serious*," Chauncy agreed. Then struck with the most badass feeling he'd ever felt, he gazed down at her valiantly. "Daddy's gonna save the world," he declared. "Try to keep up."

And with that, he thrust his staff downward, flying backward and upward off Rocky's back and soaring through the air toward Harry and The Dark One. Without even frickin' looking where he was going first.

"Fucking *badass*," Valtora moaned.

As it turned out, Chauncy's aim was perfect, as he discovered when he twisted around to face The Dark One.

"Give me a baby!" Valtora screamed from behind.

"You'll have to take it!" he shouted back in mid-flight. Then he focused on The Dark One. And, instead of gripping his staff tightly, or gritting his teeth or executing a good jawline-ripple, he relaxed.

Play, he told himself. And by golly, he did.

"Ba-BOOM!" he cried in his scariest voice, chopping down with his staff. A blast of air struck Harry and The Dark One, blasting The Dark One backward. It also struck Harry, but the old man just rippled away like a piece of cloth...just as Chauncy had hoped. This separated the two nicely for the ass-whoopin' that was about to come.

Chauncy landed gently on the ground before The Dark One, holding his Staff of Wind lightly in one hand and posing heroically. Behind him, he heard Rocky's *thump-a-thump*-ing as the giant caught up with him, skidding to a stop behind him. Valtora and Nettie hopped off, and Rocky stood, putting Rooter on his broad, blocky shoulder.

"We got your back, Chauncy," Nettie said.

"Hey there The Dark One," Chauncy greeted. "You missed."

The Dark One gazed at him with those demonic eyes, sending something that had once felt like terror through Chauncy. But while it was the same feeling, Chauncy felt differently about it. Terror, it turned out, was only terrible if he turned away from it.

By leaning *into* it...why, it felt frickin' incredible.

His heart pounded in his chest, vigor coursing through him. He broke out into a mad grin, arching an eyebrow at his enemy.

"Shall we play?" he inquired.

"**We shall**," The Dark One replied.

"Ka-BAM!" Chauncy shouted...while reaching inside his right robe pocket and pulling out his Sunstone. It lit up like a miniature sun, forcing Chauncy to squeeze his eyes shut. He heard crying out from behind him, and thrust his staff down, shooting up into the air. He felt hot air on his feet, and knew that The Dark One had slashed at him, barely missing him. Chauncy cackled, reversing the effect of the Sunstone with a thought, plunging himself – and everything around him – into darkness.

Then he threw the stone down at The Dark One, seeing its orb of utter blackness envelop the man. Which of course, blinded him completely.

"Rooter, suck the life out of him!" Chauncy commanded, landing just before the sphere of blackness. "Nettie, give me my Wetstone!" Rocky stomped up to Chauncy's side, setting Rooter down. Chauncy backed up quickly, and Rooter scrunched up his cute little face. But nothing seemed to happen...even as the black sphere shot backward, the Sunstone tumbling away as The Dark One threw it aside. The Dark One's eyes narrowed, and he glared at Rooter.

"**What is this?**" he demanded.

"Guess he doesn't have a life," Nettie noted. Valtora smirked.

"That's for sure," she agreed.

"Back!" Chauncy ordered Rocky and Rooter. He faced The Dark One, shaking his legs out one-by-one.

"**What are you doing?**" The Dark One demanded.

"Loosening up," Chauncy answered, shaking out his arms. He executed a few squats, holding his staff horizontally above his head.

The Dark One just stared at him.

"Pound his ass, Chauncy!" Valtora shouted.

"Oh I'm going to," Chauncy reassured, swinging his hips in tight circles. "And I'm going to *like* it."

Nettie sighed behind him, burying her face in her hands. Then she remembered to hand him the Wetstone.

"**Are you done?**" The Dark One inquired.

"On the contrary," Chauncy countered. "Chauncy's just getting *started*."

With that, he tossed the Wetstone into the air, then swung his staff at it like a bat. It connected with the blue stone with a *thwack*, water bursting out from the stone with the impact. The Wetstone flew at The Dark One, smacking him right in the forehead, a powerful wind blowing him backward at the same time.

The Wetstone *exploded* with a shockwave of pure water.

It struck Chauncy full in the chest, blasting their air from his lungs. But upon hitting Nettie behind him, it froze in mid-air, then redirected in a huge, watery fist. One that flew after The Dark One as he sailed through the air away from them, turning to solid ice right before it punched him.

Hard.

The Dark One flew backward even faster, until he disappeared over the lip of the volcano's crater.

"Forward, Chosen Ones!" Chauncy commanded, wrapping an arm around Valtora's waist, then using his staff to fly up after the enemy. She clung to him as a fair maiden should, clearly delighting in doing so, and he guided them over the lip of the crater. The great lake of lava was below…and The Dark One landed right in it.

He burst into flames instantly, his flesh burning as it sank slowly into the molten rock.

"Nettie, Wetstone!" Chauncy cried, landing at the lip of the crater with Valtora at his side. He let her go, turning around to see Nettie extending some water – which she'd held on to from the shockwave earlier – to something on the ground between them. It was the Wetstone, of course; with her magic, she could sense water easily…and the Wetstone had a *ton* of water in it. She tossed it to him, and by golly he caught it.

"What're ya…" Nettie began…and then Chauncy threw the Wetstone just as far as he could over the lava lake. The Wetstone struck the surface of the lava, turning rapidly red-hot. Then it cracked.

Spectacularly.

For when it broke, the Wetstone's entire supply of stored water was released. Instantly. Completely. A volume of water that was beyond huge. It shot outward from the stone in all directions, superheating instantly with the lava, and blasting upward and outward in an eruption of steam and hot water. Some of which came right for them.

"Harry!" Nettie cried.

But it wasn't Harry that saved them from being struck by the blast…it was Chauncy. He swung the Staff of Wind, blasting the blast of water away from them. Then he kept swinging, even as the lake of lava filled with boiling, steaming water, until at last the lava cooled, forming a jet-black obsidian bottom to the lake. The water within the crater rose quickly, until its surface was mere feet below the lip of the crater.

"The personification of evil deserves a cool place to die," Chauncy proclaimed. "Freeze it."

Nettie complied, kneeling down and putting a hand in the water. It froze outward from her hand, the ice spreading until it was a good hundred yards away. Then it stopped.

"Well?" Chauncy asked. "Why'd you stop?"

"I got limits ya know," Nettie grumbled. "Can't freeze a whole damn lake in one go, for cripe's sake."

"It's okay," Valtora piped in. "The Dark One's iced over."

"That he is," Chauncy agreed. "Thanks Nettie."

"Thank you, Chauncy," Nettie countered, giving him a rare smile. "That was some pretty good fightin' you did there."

"Best I ever saw him do," Harry agreed.

"Finally got outta yer own way, eh kid?" Nettie asked. Chauncy nodded.

"I guess I was so afraid of dying that I wasn't fully living," he replied. "Who would've known that meeting my doom was exactly what I needed?"

"Imperius Fanning," Harry answered. Nettie shot him a glare.

"Shut up, Harry," she scolded. "Can't you see he's having a moment?"

"That's alright," Chauncy replied with a smile. He *was* having a moment. A pretty damn good one. For he'd journeyed through the Great Wood to the Cave of Wonder, then defeated The Dark One at the summit of Mount Thrall. And, thanks to him, instead of all hope being lost, hope had been found.

"So about that baby," Valtora prompted, turning to Chauncy. But she didn't get to finish the thought, because a dark fog came spilling out of the entrance to The Dark One's temple across the lake, flying over the lake's still-churning surface toward them.

"Well crap," Nettie blurted out.

"Looks more like a fart," Harry countered.

"Shut up Harry!"

"We don't need to fight him anymore," Valtora said. "I don't care if he's dead. We're divorced, and even if we weren't, that's good enough for me."

"Me too," Chauncy agreed.

"Yeah, well it ain't good enough for him," Nettie warned as the fog rapidly approached. It morphed into The Dark One, without his fog armor, levitating toward them.

The man had the gall to smirk as he stopped, floating level with them, a few feet above the ice below.

"**Congratulations,**" he congratulated. "**You've done much.**"

"Thanks," Chauncy replied.

"**And accomplished nothing,**" the man added.

"Right," Chauncy grumbled. "Well, I did make you a pool, so there's that."

"And an ice-skating rink," Harry pointed out.

"**You cannot defeat me,**" The Dark One stated. "**And wherever you go, I will hunt you down and find you.**"

"Just try it," Valtora replied. "We'll keep beating you off until you stop coming!"

Chauncy grimaced, lowering his gaze and scratching his head. The Dark One smirked.

"Is that a deal?" he inquired.

"Shut up asshole," Valtora grumbled. "You know, you really *do* need to get a life," she added, crossing her arms over her chest. "I mean, don't you have anything better to do?"

"You."

"Yeah, not gonna happen," she retorted.

"If I can't have you, no one will," he declared.

"Wow, that really *is* evil," Nettie said. "Only an utter, stank, festering asshole would say something like that."

"He doesn't have anything else," Chauncy realized. He frowned then, remembering the vision he'd had after getting his arm lopped off. How there'd been nothing, and then darkness and the light. Each arising from the void because in existing, he'd created them. But then there'd been something more. Not black or white, or alive or dead. Not opposites, but *color*.

And that, he realized with a start, was magic.

"You don't have any magic," he realized, lifting his gaze to The Dark One.

"I *am* magical," The Dark One retorted.

"Yes, but you can't *feel* magic," Chauncy argued. "You're literally evil incarnate…you said it the first time we met, six months ago!"

The Dark One's eyes narrowed.

"What're you talkin' about, kid?" Nettie asked.

"The day we met him," Chauncy explained. "He said he was evil incarnate…that Man's existence created him, and that he in turn created the Chosen Ones. By being an evil that good had to triumph over."

"So?" Nettie pressed.

"So Man created him," Chauncy continued, eyeing The Dark One with wonder.

"And?" Nettie snapped, clearly getting irritated now.

"It's what I learned in the Cave of Wonder," Chauncy replied. "The solution to the problem is the problem itself."

"I don't follow," Harry admitted, scratching his head.

"Well see, I thought The Dark One was the problem," Chauncy explained. "We all did. But he's not. *We* are."

Everyone blinked…even Rooter.

"Pardon?" Harry asked.

"Humanity," Chauncy clarified. "We're the ones who create evil, like we create good. Like we create everything, just by being us. He's just the personification of that part of us. Pulled out of us, and now in front of us."

"So…?" Nettie asked.

"Well, my magic is to put things inside things," Chauncy stated. Valtora smiled, eyeing him rather proudly.

"Sure is," she agreed.

"So I'm going to put him," he proclaimed, pointing at The Dark One, "…back where he belongs."

The Dark One's eyes widened.

"**Wait…**" he blurted out, bursting backward.

"Get him Nettie!" Chauncy cried. Nettie leapt over the rim of the crater, cannon-balling into the water with a big splash. And, thus connected with what she loved, she became one with it. A huge watery hand emerged from the water, lunging at The Dark One and grabbing him…then flash-freezing instantly. The Dark One gasped, struggling to free himself.

"I am Chauncy Little," Chauncy declared, thrusting his staff before him. The movement created a gust of wind around him, making his purple robes flutter magnificently. "Wizard of Southwick, savior of the Great Wood, and of magic itself!"

"**Wait…!**" The Dark One insisted.

"By my hand, with the magic in me, I will put you back where you belong…and fulfill my destiny!"

With that, Chauncy thrust the butt of his staff backward, shooting himself forward at The Dark One. As he neared the personification of evil, the being that – a quarter of a century ago – it'd become his destiny to defeat, Chauncy extended his left hand to the man, reaching him at last…and touching him.

And in touching The Dark One, Chauncy connected with the ancient being. With the darkness within himself and everyone else. Time seemed to slow to a crawl, and Chauncy smiled at The Dark One. For in connecting with evil, he accepted it as part of himself…and of everyone else. Evil was natural, a part of being human. And for humans, it was a part, never the whole.

"I see myself in you," he said. "And you see yourself in me. You don't belong in you," he added. "You belong in *every*body."

The Dark One vanished.

Chauncy kicked off the ice-hand, flying back to the shore of the lake beside the others. They, in turn, gazed at him in utter amazement...and bewilderment. For not a single one of them understood what had just happened. Except for perhaps Harry, who merely inclined his head a bit, his blue eyes twinkling from behind silver glasses.

"What the hell just happened?" Nettie demanded. "What'd you do?"

"The Dark One is evil personified," Chauncy replied. "So I made him nothing personal."

She just stared at him blankly.

"Huh?" she blurted out.

"My magic is to put things in things," he reminded her. "So I used it to put him back where he came from."

"So you put him in...people?" Nettie pressed. Chauncy nodded.

"That's right," he confirmed. "I put him in everyone. Everyone alive, that is. Because that's who creates him, just by being human."

"I don't get it," Valtora confessed.

"Well, remember how The Dark One said that we humans love to put things in neat little categories? Psychic boxes that we divide what belongs inside from what doesn't?"

"Yeah," she replied, rolling her eyes. "He droned on and on about that shit. Like *all* the time."

"Well, we create good and evil the same way," Chauncy told her. "By seeing a difference between the two, we create that difference."

"So...good and evil wouldn't exist without us?" Valtora pressed.

"Right," he agreed with a smile. "It'd just be what was."

"Huh," Valtora mumbled, staring at the ice-hand jutting out of the lake ahead of them. Chauncy knew that she was staring at the space The Dark One had occupied, before being cast away. They all were, he realized. For, having vanquished their enemy, they were confronting another kind of space. An emptiness of purpose.

"Well what're we gonna do now?" Nettie asked. Harry shrugged.

"Same as we always do," he answered. "Whatever we want."

"Sounds good to me," Nettie agreed with a smile. She wrapped an arm around Harry's waist, giving him a squeeze. He put a long arm around her shoulders, leaning to kiss the top of her head. Then he chuckled.

"Well this was fun, wasn't it?" he mused.

"Speak for yourself," Skibbard replied. Everyone turned to look at the dour little wizard, who eyed Rooter with terrible intensity. "You gonna heal me now or what?"

"How much life energy is it gonna take?" Valtora inquired, arching an eyebrow whilst eyeing his undercarriage. Skibbard scowled at her, but didn't justify her question with an answer. Instead, he faced Rooter.

"Can you do it?" he asked. Rooter smiled cutely, nodding in the affirmative. The magical plant atop his head cast its healing light on Skibbard for a moment, then faded. Skibbard blinked, then turned his back to everyone, looking downward and doing something with his pants. There was a great sob, cut off almost as quickly as it'd burst out, followed by a shuddering sigh of relief. "Thank you," Skibbard said, turning around and patting Rooter's plant-hat. Then he did a double-take, staring at his hand. "It even healed my finger," he proclaimed in wonder. "Had to chop the tip off years ago when it got infected."

"Careful," Chauncy warned, eyeing Skibbard's hand atop Rooter's plant-hat. "That plant is fragile." Skibbard gave him a funny look.

"Fragile?" the man exclaimed. "This plant's a survivor," he declared. "One of the toughest plants I've met. Frankly, it doesn't give a fuck."

Chauncy smiled reluctantly, remembering that this was precisely what he'd thought of the plant the first time he'd seen it.

"Speaking of which," Valtora interjected, grabbing Chauncy's hand and gripping it rather tightly. "I believe *you* owe me a baby."

"Um...now?" Chauncy replied, glancing nervously at everyone else.

"Now," she confirmed.

And with that, she yanked Chauncy down the slope of the mountain a bit, reaching a relatively flat shelf of rock. And promptly shoved him so hard he landed on his back on it.

"Hey...!" Chauncy blurted out, scrambling to get to his feet. Valtora shoved him down with her diamond hand, looming over him...and staring at him with crazy eyes. A look he knew quite well. A look that meant that whatever she wanted to happen was about to happen, whether he liked it or not.

"Gimmee that baby!" she commanded, lifting the hem of his robe. And exposing the underwear Valtora had forced him to wear.

"Oh," Nettie blurted out, turning her back to him just as quickly as she could.

"Is that a...?" Skibbard asked, his eyes widening.

"Sure is sparkly," Harry noted. "Matches the robe."

"But doesn't it ride up his..."

"Butt out," Nettie scolded. "Turn around idiots, before you see something you can't unsee!"

"There's people watching!" Chauncy protested, trying to pull his robe back down. But it was far too late, and Valtora hardly seemed to care. To his relief, four stone walls rose up around them to shield them from any gaze that grew too curious, thanks to Harry's magic.

And thanks to Valtora's magic, despite the public nature of it all, Chauncy soon found himself rising to obey her command.

So, having vanquished The Dark One and saved humanity, Valtora got to work adding another member to it. And despite Chauncy's protestations, he proceeded to give her precisely what she'd asked for, in a symphony of sounds that mere walls could not contain. Chauncy's magic was in putting things into things, and having done so, he was able to so in what he hoped would be a far more monumental way.

Thusly spent, his magic cast, Chauncy closed his eyes at last.

So it was that, though destiny had at first had a case of initiation interruptus, followed by quite literally catching Chauncy with his pants down, it was, at long last, no longer deferred. And Chauncy was quite a bit wiser, for he'd found his power in the present, and in play. And while ignorance could indeed be bliss, for Chauncy, it turned out that wisdom could be too.

And that could've been it, dear reader. The end of this peculiar story. But as it was, it wasn't. A fact that was soon to become all too clear.

"Thank you baby-cakes," Valtora cooed, nuzzling Chauncy's nose with her own. He opened his eyes, staring into hers and smiling with an enormous sense of contentment.

"No problem, poopy-dooz," he replied.

Her eyes widened, and she bolted to a sitting position.

"Poopy-dooz!" she gasped. I almost forgot!"

"Huh?"

"My hellcat ZoMonsterz," she explained, standing up...and pulling him up with her. He pulled his robe down, in a futile attempt at hiding the evidence of his recent activities. "I'm *totally* taking her home with me."

"I thought you wanted a dog," he countered. She gave him a look.

"You're the one who said I'd have to walk it every day," she reminded him. "No *thanks*. I'll take my cuddly widdle pussy wussy cat *any* day." She broke out into a gorgeous smile, tossing her hair a bit. Which in retrospect, should have alarmed him. "That okay hon?"

"Uh, sure," he replied with a shrug. She leaned in to kiss him, melting into his arms.

"My *hero*," she murmured. Then she pulled away. "Wanna use your staff and fly us out of here?"

Chauncy reached out with one hand, and his staff flew up from the ground and into it.

"Anything for you, Val," he replied. And that was most certainly true. He'd proven his love and devotion beyond a reasonable doubt, and even an unreasonable one. "Hold on tight," he told her, gripping his wizardly staff while she wrapped her arms around his waist. And with that, he sent them skyward, over the edge of the impromptu rock enclosure, and toward whatever adventure came next.

Chapter 37

Having exited the gate leading out of Cumulus, Gavin Merrick used his magical ring to let what remained of his army go back to Borrin to recover. And to summon forth his Shadowsteed, whose shadow was pinned to a location mere yards from where the ring's portal led to. The powerful black stallion stepped through the ring, pulling its carriage behind it.

"Stay here," he ordered it. "I'll be back."

Gavin stepped through the portal his magical ring had created, and was instantly transported back to the campus of Evermore's corporate headquarters in Southwick. The headquarters were a U-shaped brick building ten stories high, with windows at regular intervals. It looked for all the world like a prison, save for the fact that there were no bars on the windows. He made his way through the entrance and across plain, gray hallways and stairwells to his office on the eighth floor. His secretary Gretchen was seated at a desk in front of his office, a mousey woman with glasses and short brown hair.

"I want to find someone," he told her. "Chauncy, a Chosen One. He should be in Pravus."

"Yes sir," Gretchen replied. She needed no further instruction, of course. If she had, he would have fired her. Gretchen knew that Gavin had access to artifacts with magic that could find just about anyone, anywhere they happened to be. "I'll have the Rod of Reclamation primed for you in a few hours."

Gavin nodded, then strode past her and into his office. He sat down at his desk, ignoring the growing pile of paperwork sitting atop it. The Rod of Reclamation would point him in the direction of whomever it was primed to seek. And it would glow brighter the closer he got to his target.

Gavin stared past the paperwork, resting his elbows on his desk and steepling his fingers. It wouldn't be long now before vengeance would be his...and Marie's murderer would be brought to something far worse than justice.

The thought should have given him some measure of satisfaction. Or at least some element of impending closure. But he couldn't stop thinking about what would happen *after* he'd gotten his revenge.

Then what?

For Gavin knew beyond a shadow of a doubt that he'd be right back to where he was now. Where he'd been ever since Marie had died. Alone, despondent, living in a world without color or magic of any kind. A world of paperwork and office hours and meetings and such, all to accumulate more market share, more products, more money.

A dead world.

More, more, more. And never enough. That'd been his life up until now. But now he'd had quite enough of never enough, knowing too late that he'd had enough when he'd had Marie. His pursuit of more – refusing to stop after he won the game – had made him lose everything.

Sick from symbols, he thought, staring at the symbols on the top page of the stack on his desk. And true enough, just looking at them made him feel nauseous. Exhausted. They were repulsive, those endless symbols, in that they repelled him.

Gavin stood abruptly, pushing his chair back with a *screech*.

He began to pace before his desk, chin in hand. Back and forth, back and forth. Skibbard's words came to him then.

My life didn't feel real, so I didn't feel real.

He continued pacing, thinking of the bank the little man had owned. The largest in Grissam, it was remarkably successful. And yet Skibbard had grown to hate it…so much so that he'd decided he'd rather die than go on living.

I went into the woods to kill myself, Skibbard had confessed. *And found me waiting for me there instead.*

Gavin imagined himself going off into the forest with just the clothes on his back. Wandering amongst the trees. It was ridiculous, of course. Stupid nonsense. He couldn't very well abandon his family's empire, or bring shame to his grandfather's great name. Gavin had no children, and no successor picked. If he just up and left, the Evermore Trading Company would fall into shambles, unless a competent board member took the reins. Which was possible, of course. There were talented people in his organization that would carry on the legacy of the company, if not the family legacy.

He imagined letting it all go. Leaving it all behind.

The thought terrified him.

Not the loss, which was considerable. But the fact that, if he let it all go – just tossed it aside – he'd have no idea what to do. His purpose in life had been determined from birth, after all. His father and grandfather had groomed him from the beginning for this role. It was all he'd ever known. All he'd ever known how to be. Without the identity he'd been given, who would he be? *Nothing.*

Gavin stopped pacing, his gaze drawn once again to his desk. The center of his universe, the place upon which contracts had been signed, assets and liabilities accounted for, and so on. Every important act in his life had been made here, or at least had started here. Every one of them, except for the act of choosing Marie.

This is my life, he realized. Right here in this office, sitting at his desk. Forty years from now, it would be the same. Eighty. A hundred. As long as magic allowed him to live, his life would be this. There would be little difference from year to year, decade to decade. Minor changes. But ultimately, he would have a long life of not living.

In that moment, in his office, staring at that damn desk, he understood Skibbard. For his greatest asset – his life – had become a liability, and despite his endless cycle of profits, he was at a loss.

Okay," he muttered.

Gavin took off his green suit jacket, walking it to his chair and draping it neatly over the chair back. Then he untied his golden tie, draping it over the chair so it seemed to be wearing it. He gazed at it for one final moment, then turned away, leaving his office and walking up to his secretary. Who looked up, surprised to see him without his suit jacket and tie.

"Let my men rest until we get Chauncy's location," he told her. "Then have them wait by the ring-portal. I'll go to the target's location and teleport them in."

"Yes sir," she replied.

And with that, Gavin made his way back down to the first floor of the building, exiting to reach the ring-portal he'd come from. He stopped before it, staring at the landscape of Pravus beyond it. He felt a little sick to his stomach, and suddenly wanted nothing to do with what he was about to do. He just wanted to get it over with now, so he could leave everything behind. So he could close this chapter of his life forever. But he couldn't very well let Marie's murderer get away with it, out of respect for Marie's memory.

Just one last thing, he promised himself. And then he would leave his past where it belonged, and search for a future where *he* belonged.

Thus Gavin Merrick would leave Evermore looking for something less than more. For the mysterious thing that Skibbard claimed to have found, a thing more magical than any artifact in Gavin's possession:

Enough.

Chapter 38

Having defeated The Dark One, the Chosen Ones set forth on the long journey home. With a stop to retrieve ZoMonsterz, Valtora's hellcat. Fortunately, they didn't have to go far to get the cat. U*n*fortunately, ZoMonsterz happened to live deep within the maze-like goblin caves on the opposite slope of the mountain.

"I can just go alone if you're nervous," Valtora told Chauncy as they hiked down the mountainside toward the caves.

"That's *why* I want to go with you," Chauncy countered. "What if the goblins attack you? They might be mad, seeing as how we defeated their master."

"I can just beat them off," Valtora reassured. "I've done it before."

"Kinda wanna see that," Harry piped in.

"Anyway, the incubi live there too, and they'd *totally* protect me," Valtora continued. "We're very close."

"So we heard," Nettie grumbled.

Chauncy slowed, then stopped.

"Wait," he said. "We're going to meet the guys you…?"

"Huh?" Valtora asked, adopting a familiar blank expression.

"The five hundred guys you had orgies for a week with," Nettie said, saying what Chauncy couldn't.

"Huh?"

"I'll stay behind," Chauncy decided, crossing his arms over his chest. For while he applauded Valtora's liberated self – in theory, anyway – having it become a reality was too much. "I don't think I can handle meeting all of them."

"Probably what she thought," Harry mused.

"Shut up Harry," Nettie grumbled. But then she cackled.

"You're coming," Valtora decided for Chauncy, grabbing his arm with her diamond hand and hauling him forward.

"But…" Chauncy protested.

"Meeting them will make you feel better, trust me," she promised. "They're super nice. Totally not intimidating."

"Um…" Chauncy began, then thought the better of it. For Valtora gave him a warning look as she hauled him forward, and one of her patented jawline ripples. Which meant that she meant business. When Valtora's jawline rippled, Chauncy knew, there could be no debate. "Yes dear," he mumbled.

Down they went, until they reached over a dozen cave entrances pockmarking the slope of the volcano. *Huge* caves, a few dozen of them, pockmarking the side of the mountain. Valtora led them to the largest of them, which made Chauncy even more uneasy than he already was. For there were an absolutely *obscene* number of black goblins swarming in and out of the tunnel entrance, like so many ants on an anthill. Except ants were relatively harmless, while goblins were possessed of deadly claws and sharp, pointy teeth.

"You look nervous," Skibbard noted.

"There's a lot of them," Chauncy argued.

"No tree branches to hit your head on though."

"Granted," Chauncy conceded with a rueful smile.

"You do have a lich, you know," Skibbard reminded him. Chauncy blinked, then realized the little wizard was quite correct. He *did* have a lich.

And that changed everything.

He willed Zarzibar to pull out of his body, and the lich did so readily, floating ahead of them.

"All right Zar," he stated. "Any of these goblins tries anything, do your thing." Which was to murder them instantly and steal their life force. But that was a bit grotesque, so saying "do your thing" was far more palatable for a heroic type such as himself. Still, it felt a little super-villainy to use a lich to murder one's enemy. He turned to Valtora, his eye naturally drawn to her glittering, crystalline hand.

Crystalline.

An idea came to him then.

"Hey poopy-dooz," he told Valtora. "Um, how do you feel about having a lich inside of you?"

"I mean, I've never tried it," she answered. "But I'm not opposed to it, if you're okay with experimenting a little. We just have to keep the lines of communication open, so we can manage any feelings of jealousy you might have."

"I meant in your hand," he corrected, blushing furiously.

"We can start there," Valtora agreed. "That'll be the least intimate interaction. If you're okay with that, we can move on to more interesting things."

"I meant using your diamond hand as the storage crystal for Zarzibar's soul!" Chauncy blurted out, his cheeks burning furiously. He stole a glance at Nettie, who was busy burying her face in her hands. Harry seemed rather amused, in an intrigued and somewhat jealous sort of way.

"You got a good woman there Chauncy," the old man said.

"Like hell he does!" Nettie retorted.

"Well a bad good woman," Harry corrected. "Best kind if you ask me."

"Oh," Valtora replied. "Well, that's fine too I guess." Her eyes lit up. "That's even better than that stupid fog-armor. A frickin' diamond hand of frickin' death!"

"Right," Chauncy agreed. Which was why he'd mentioned it. Villainy, after all, came to Valtora with disturbing ease. Through no fault of her own, of course. Living with pure evil for most of her formative years had made a lasting impression on her psyche, for better and for worse. Mostly for the better, for though she was a villain, Valtora was the most cheerily heroic villain he'd ever met.

"How do we, you know, do it?" she inquired.

"Um…" Chauncy began. And then Zarzibar flew into her diamond hand, vanishing from sight, and Chauncy felt his connection with the lich vanish instantly. "Oh," he mumbled. "Guess that was it."

"He didn't have a crystal anymore," Valtora told him. "So he put his life force into this one. Otherwise he would've had to do some really high-level necromancer shit to make the exchange."

"Good to know," Chauncy mumbled.

"Ooo, this guy's *fun*," Valtora exclaimed, clearly able to sense Zarzibar's thoughts in much the same way that Chauncy had. "Dark though. Real dark." She paused. "*Nasty* dark."

"Can we get your damn cat already?" Nettie interjected.

"Right," Valtora agreed. With that, she made her way to the entrance to the goblin caves, approaching the lines of goblins going in and out without a care in the world. Chauncy and the others followed behind, ready to massacre some goblins if they made any attempt to attack. Which they didn't. "Hey guys," Valtora greeted, waving at the nearest goblins cheerily.

"Eh," one of them replied, and got back to work doing whatever it was that goblins did.

So, without any fanfare – or warfare, for that matter – the Chosen Ones plunged deep into the caves of Thrall. Goblins worked all around them, wielding pickaxes and chopping away at various veins of ore. The only one who was at all interested in their work was Harry, who watched with bright blue eyes.

"That's kimberlite," he said, pointing to one of the veins. "And that's peridotite," he added, pointing to another.

"No one cares about your damn rocks," Nettie grumbled.

"Well they do," Harry countered, gesturing at the goblins.

"And they're nobodies," Nettie replied.

"Shhh," Chauncy scolded. "They might hear you!"

But the clanging of pickaxes was far too loud – and the goblins far too hyper – and hyperfocused – to pay them any attention. So they made their way through the tunnels, weaving this way and that, Valtora leading them through various forks in the proverbial road. Until, at long last, they reached a small, but very tall, chamber. Valtora's eyes lit up as she reached it, and she looked up, cupping her hands around her mouth.

"Oh poopy-dooz!" she yelled.

Chauncy looked up, seeing the chamber vanish into darkness above. It was so high that he couldn't see the ceiling, even with the torchlight from torches bolted to the walls.

"Keekee booboo kitty buck bow, buddy buck bow!" Valtora called out.

Two deep purple-pink eyes opened, peering down at them from somewhere beyond the darkness above.

"Come here ZoMonsterz," Valtora cooed. "Mama's home, widdle cootie kitty pie!"

The eyes blinked slowly. Cat-eyes, for sure, but glowing with their own eerie light.

"This is Chauncy," Valtora said, gesturing at him. "I love him and I'm gonna marry him. So *no* murdering him, okay?"

The cat eyes closed. And didn't open.

"Huh," Chauncy said. "Must not want to come with us. Should we go…?"

Then he realized that everyone's eyes were on him. Or rather, not precisely *him*, but on his left hand, resting at his side. Looking down, he realized that they weren't looking at his hand, but something his hand was inexplicably resting on…and even more inexplicably, petting without even realizing it.

The head of a cat.

* * *

Chauncy *shrieked*.

He jerked his hand away from the cat's head, stumbling back from it, then thrust his staff before him to defend himself. Which was unnecessary, seeing as how the cat just stared at him serenely.

ZoMonsterz, it turned out, was a cat three times the size of a normal one. She had long-ish gold and black hair, a fluffy tail, and those strange purple-pink eyes he'd noticed earlier.

"Meow," she meowed. While staring at Chauncy. With sexy eyes.

"How did she…" Chauncy sputtered, looking up at the darkness where the cat had been a moment ago.

"ZoMonsterz is a magical widdle pussy, isn't she?" Valtora cooed, kneeling down and opening her arms to the cat. ZoMonsterz trotted right up to her, purring loudly and nudging against her hands.

"Huh," Harry said, adjusting his glasses. "Woulda thought a hellcat'd be black."

"Or on fire," Nettie added.

"Or something," Harry agreed.

"Come on ZoMonsterz," Valtora urged. "I'm gonna take you home with me."

With that, Valtora turned and strode back the way they'd come, ZoMonsterz trotting agreeably at her side. Harry glanced at Nettie, who shrugged, and Chauncy and Skibbard took up the rear. Chauncy felt rather silly that he'd shrieked. And in such a high-pitched, not at all heroic manner. So he stayed quiet as they walked, making their way out of the goblin tunnels with Valtora's expert guidance.

He glanced at Skibbard as they walked, eyeing the strange man curiously.

"So…you used to live in Pravus?" he asked. "Before Marie…um…felled your forest?"

"Yes," Skibbard replied.

"And you got imprisoned after that, by the Evermore Trading Company?" Chauncy pressed.

"Yes."

"Oh," Chauncy replied. Then he frowned. "How'd you escape?"

"I didn't," Skibbard answered. "They let me go."

Chauncy blinked.

"They did? Why?" he asked. For letting wizards go was not Evermore's standard operating procedure.

"The president let me go so he could get back through the gate into Pravus," Skibbard explained. "He needed a wizard to open the gate."

"Oh," Chauncy replied. This, of course, aroused some suspicion. The last time Gavin Merrick had gone into Pravus, it'd been to destroy the source of magic. "What for?"

Skibbard shrugged. Which didn't make Chauncy feel any better. He picked up his pace to catch up with Harry and Nettie, leaving the little wizard behind. Chauncy relayed what Skibbard had told him to the old couple, and everyone stopped, turning to face each other near the entrance to the goblin tunnel.

"Wait, so you're saying Gavin's back in Pravus?" Nettie asked Skibbard, who nodded. "Well crap," Nettie declared. "Now why'n hell would he come back here?"

"Who knows?" Chauncy replied. "But whatever the reason is, it can't be good."

"Darn tootin'," Nettie agreed. "That bastard tried to con King Pravus into giving away all his magic. If Gavin came through the gate uninvited, it can only mean trouble."

"Or revenge," Valtora piped in. Everyone turned to look at her. "If I were an evil bastard, and my armies got demolished by the guy I was trying to screw, I'd like *totally* want vengeance."

"*If* you were an evil bastard?" Nettie inquired, arching an eyebrow at her.

"I'm an evil bitch," Valtora pointed out. "Chauncy's a bastard."

Chauncy blushed, grimacing at the comment. For he *was* technically a bastard, having been born out of wedlock. He'd never met his father, and didn't even know who the guy was, or if he was even still alive. Or how his mom had died, for that matter. He suspected he'd never know, now that Grandma Little was gone.

"She's right," Skibbard stated. Chauncy frowned at him.

"That I'm a bastard?" he asked.

"That Gavin would want revenge," Skibbard corrected. "He's a businessman. Business is war. Pravus is competition, and Gavin won't stop until he's dominated his competition."

"How would you know?" Nettie countered.

"I was a businessman," Skibbard reminded her. "No amount of success is ever enough. When the only thing that makes you happy is more, what you have can never be enough."

Everyone considered this solemnly. It was true, Chauncy knew all too well. The entire country of Borrin was based on this principle.

Always wanting more was a good way to make people ever faster and more productive, but at the cost of taking the time and space to enjoy what they produced. It was success at the cost of joy, productivity at the cost of peace of mind.

A Borrin life, at least to him, was no life at all.

"We have to do something," Chauncy stated. "If Gavin's in Pravus, he could try to destroy The Wilds again. We have to stop him!"

"I don't know," Nettie countered. "King Pravus should be able to handle that guy."

"We can't bank on that," Chauncy insisted. "The fate of magic hangs in the balance!"

"Little dramatic, don't'cha think?" Nettie grumbled.

"No, he's right," Skibbard countered. "There are no wizards among Borrin's citizens – and over most of the world now – because of Borrin's way of life. If we allow The Wilds – and Pravus – to fall, magic may fall with it. Once people live a life purely for profit, everything will be lost."

"What he said," Chauncy agreed.

"This from the guy who dragged his feet all the way here," Nettie complained. "I was hopin' to get back to the Order and relax."

"I dragged my feet because I didn't want to kill The Dark One," Chauncy explained. "That's why I lost my magic. Because only doing what I want to do is magical…and by golly, I want to do this."

Nettie eyed him for a long moment, then glanced up at Harry, who beamed at Chauncy.

"Well what'd'ya know," the old man said. "Chauncy found his balls."

"You found them first during our sparring matches," Chauncy replied with a rueful smile.

"I was trying to help you find 'em," Harry explained.

"It was a smashing success," Chauncy quipped.

"All right," Nettie decided. "Guess we're gonna save the world again."

"Twice in one week?" Valtora replied. "Sounds exhausting."

"You're telling me," Nettie agreed. "Come on toots, let's get this over with."

With that, the Chosen Ones – and their companions, save for Peter, wherever the heck he was – started off on their journey to Cumulus, capitol city of Pravus. And with each step they took toward their destination, Chauncy felt the power of purpose in them. For, having lived in a world without magic, it was his greatest desire to bring magic back into the lives of others. Not just to make magical trinkets for people, he realized suddenly, but to *teach* them magic, like Nettie and Harry had. To show other people how to become wizards in their own rights.

"I feel marvelous," Chauncy declared, breaking out into a big smile. And not just because they'd managed to avoid meeting up with the incubi. Valtora smiled back at him, holding his hand in hers and resting her head on his shoulder as they hiked down the slope of the mountain.

"Me too," she told him.

"Because you get to save the world?" he asked.

"Because I'm spending my time with you," she replied.

Chapter 39

Chauncy and his ever-growing group of friends reached the bottom of Mount Thrall, making their way over the dead, ashen land that marked The Dark One's lands to the living world beyond. It was an enormous relief to emerge from darkness and devastation into light and life, the charred ground giving way to grasses and wildflowers. And while the sky beyond the ashen atmosphere was a bit overcast, a light mist in the air as if it'd just rained, it was a grand improvement over what they were leaving. Chauncy took a deep breath in as they left The Dark One's domain, feeling positively...well, positive. For, hand-in-hand with the love of his life, he was finally doing what he wanted to do. Spending time with the people he cared about, and saving magic.

"There's the carriage," Valtora noted after they'd walked nearly another a mile. It was standing at the end of the road they'd taken to get here, just where they'd left it. "But where's Peter?"

They reached the carriage, stopping before it and looking around. But Peter was nowhere to be found.

"Oh well," Chauncy said, shrugging his shoulders. "Guess we'll ride Rocky then."

"Ooo," Valtora blurted out, pointing to their right. "Pretty rainbow!"

"Never grew up, did she?" Harry mused.

"Air's thin on top of a mountain," Nettie noted.

"Lotta fumes too," Harry agreed.

Chauncy ignored the two, following Valtora's finger. There was indeed a rainbow, and it was rather pretty. And while it wasn't nearly as exciting for him as it was for Valtora, Chauncy was happy that she was the type of person for whom beautiful things were still noteworthy.

"It is pretty," he told her, wrapping an arm around her shoulders. "But not as pretty as you," he added. She gave him a look.

"You're just trying to get in my pants," she accused.

"Yep," he agreed with a smile.

"It's working," she admitted with a smile of her own. She arched an eyebrow, getting a rather mischievous expression...and putting a hand on his lower belly. "How about I try to find peter a little later?"

"I certainly won't mind you riding him if he pops up," Chauncy replied with a wink and an eyebrow waggle. Which was a bit much, and not at all sexy, but for Valtora, it worked. Which was just as well, because Chauncy couldn't be anyone else but his often-awkward self.

"Deal," Valtora agreed.

"Ugh," Nettie muttered, pretending to gag.

But then, to Chauncy's dismay, Peter did pop up.

The rainbow before them grew brighter, each band of color condensing into countless bright sparkles. And *these* coalesced into a rainbow silhouette of a unicorn...one standing mere yards away from them. The lights faded, revealing Peter in all of his oversized glory, his rainbow-colored mane whipping about rather dramatically in a slight breeze.

The stallion looked Valtora right in the eye, lifting his chin up a bit and snorting. Sexily.

"Peter!" Valtora gushed, tearing free from Chauncy and rushing up to the unicorn. She gave the handsome beast a huge hug, burying her face in Peter's pure white chest. And snuggling it in a way that, to Chauncy, was a bit dismaying. He found his gaze dropping to Peter's most impressive attribute, and found with further dismay that Peter was as happy to see Valtora as she was to see him.

"Yay, he's back," Chauncy grumbled.

"Hell of an entrance," Nettie said.

"Rainbows only come when its wet," Harry noted.

"I have a feeling I know what'll be at the end of it," Nettie muttered with a smirk, eyeing Peter's bedazzlements.

"Come, Peter," Valtora urged, ending their one-sided embrace and vaulting expertly onto the unicorn's back. "We need to save magic!"

"Wait a second," Chauncy protested, crossing his arms over his chest. "How the hell did Peter do that?"

"Do what?" Valtora asked.

"The whole rainbow-appearing thingy," he clarified.

"He's a unicorn," Valtora explained, as if that explained anything.

"No he's not, he's a horse," Chauncy countered. "He's just bedazzled to look like a unicorn."

Valtora gave him a funny look.

"Nuh uh," she shot back. "I bedazzled him and now he's a unicorn. And unicorns can travel by rainbows."

"Can they though?"

"They can if I say they can," Valtora replied haughtily. And gestured at Peter. Which was, Chauncy realized, evidence enough that she was right.

"I thought bedazzling things just made them...um...pretty," Chauncy admitted. Everyone else but Valtora nodded, for that's precisely what everyone had thought.

"What? No," Valtora retorted. "That'd be like, a *super* lame power."

Everyone glanced at each other, then back at Valtora. And to everyone's credit, they said nothing, ending the conversation. Chauncy sighed, for now that Valtora was riding Peter again, she wasn't next to him. Rocky pulled the carriage up to Peter, and Chauncy helped Harry hitch the vehicle to Peter. Then they all went to their usual positions, Chauncy, Nettie, and Skibbard in the carriage, Rooter on Rocky's shoulder, Valtora bouncing happily on Peter.

"Hey," Chauncy said with a frown. "Where's ZoMonsterz?"

Nettie gave him a funny look, and it was only then that he realized that his hands were resting on something soft and furry. And that he was petting said soft and furry something.

He shrieked, jerking his hands away.

For there, sitting on his lap, was ZoMonsterz, purring quite contentedly.

"How in the hell?" Chauncy blurted out. "Did you see her get in?"

"Nope," Nettie answered.

"The carriage doors are closed!" Chauncy protested, staring at the cat with a mixture of fear and awe. ZoMonsterz just stared back at him. With eyes that said "pet me Chauncy. Pretty please."

Sexy eyes.

Chauncy hesitated, then did pet her. Because she was soft and warm and furry, and she really *really* seemed to enjoy it. In return, she began licking his other hand contentedly. But unlike a normal cat's tongue, ZoMonsterz's wasn't rough at all.

"Anyone know where Gavin might be?" Chauncy asked, trying his best to make peace with the cat's inexplicable presence.

"If I were a betting woman, I'd say Cumulus," Nettie replied. Chauncy just stared at her blankly. "The capitol of the kingdom, where King Pravus lives," she clarified.

"Oh," he replied. "Where's that?"

"We know the way," Nettie assured him.

Harry gave a shrill whistle, and Peter set forth, pulling the carriage down the road toward their destination. Chauncy sat back in his seat, gazing out of the window. But instead of feeling like the carriage was rolling over the land, he had the curious sensation that the carriage was standing still, its wheels moving the world instead. To his point of view, it was true enough. And it gave him a sense of power and purpose that they could do such a thing, to move the world.

I matter, he realized.

Which was undeniably true. He'd not so much defeated The Dark One as put the guy back where he belonged, but it was perhaps a sweeter victory than mere defeat. For within humanity, evil existed in proportion to good, and was therefore subject to constraint. Perhaps The Dark One had married Valtora because of her effervescent goodness, in an attempt to mimic what happened in the human soul. In that way of thinking, Chauncy could hardly blame The Dark One for marrying her…or Valtora for being so attracted to darkness. The darkness within her was attractive to Chauncy, after all, balanced as it was by her considerable good. And that she was so accepting of both sides of herself.

A bump in the road broke Chauncy from this rather random reverie, and he blinked, seeing scenery once more. The sensation of moving the world faded, replaced by the strangely standard view of being moved by it. Both were true simultaneously, of course, because the world and Chauncy were the same.

"Hey, who's that guy?" he asked, pointing out of his window. For he'd spotted a man standing beside the road as it curved to the left ahead. An old man with long white hair and a long white beard, wearing a blue wizard's robe and a pointy blue wizard's hat. With blue eyes. And carrying a large staff topped with a blue crystal, one far more formidable than Chauncy's staff. The old man had seemed to simply appear out of thin air, but then again, Chauncy had been woolgathering.

"What guy?" Nettie asked, leaning over him to look out the window. Her eyes widened. "Holy crap!"

"What?" he pressed.

"That's Imperius Fanning!" Nettie exclaimed.

* * *

Nearly a quarter century ago, a great wizard had come to Chauncy Little's doorstep to reveal to him his destiny. A powerful wizard of the Order of Mundus, who would have taught Chauncy to become a great wizard himself at the tender age of ten. But alas, in a fit of misguided love, Grandma Little had answered the door for Chauncy, and in trying to protect him from the dangers of the world, had protected him from its magic as well. And without magic, Chauncy had found life not worth living.

But here and now, Imperius Fanning stood. Beside the stopped carriage, staring Chauncy right in the eye through the carriage window. He stared right back, feeling a chill run through him. As if he were ten again, and meeting a wizard – a real *wizard!* – for the first time.

"Wow*ee*," he breathed.

"Open your damn door already," Nettie grumbled, following her own advice. She got out of the carriage with some help from Harry, and Chauncy, feeling quite awkward, slid across the seat and got out of Nettie's door instead. And then walked all the way around the carriage – awkwardly – to face Imperius. Valtora, Chauncy noted, stayed mounted atop Peter, eyeing Imperius with an optimistically pessimistic expression.

Chauncy stopped a few yards from Imperius, feeling the vast chasm of time that the last twenty-five years represented. And at the same time, feeling as if time were of no consequence, and that from being ten till now had occurred in the blink of an eye.

"Chauncy Little," Imperius stated in a booming, bone-chillingly authoritative voice. "I've had to wait a long time to meet you."

"Wow*ee*," Chauncy repeated, quite unable to say anything else.

"I am Imperius Fanning," Imperius Fanning introduced, leaning on his staff and eyeing Chauncy with those glacier-blue eyes. "Our world was in grave danger," he stated, his tone darkening dramatically. "The Dark One resurrected, and was gathering his hordes. They spread across the land like a great plague, and threatened to destroy everything you know and love!"

Then he broke out into a smile, putting an old, wizened hand on Chauncy's shoulder.

"And the only one who could stop him was you, Chauncy," he declared, his eyes twinkling. "And so you did."

Chauncy just stared at him for a long moment.

Then he broke down and cried.

It wasn't a good cry. No, it was a particularly ugly one, and had Chauncy been possessed of a mirror, he would have been justifiably mortified. But it wouldn't stop, and the harder he tried to stop it, the worse it got. He barely registered Nettie coming to his side and putting a hand on his shoulder, or Valtora dismounting Peter and rubbing his back from behind. Despite these efforts, Chauncy continued to weep for an embarrassingly long time, until at last he could weep no more.

Then, thoroughly ashamed, but feeling inexplicably *much* better, he lifted his gaze to Imperius.

"Nice to meet you," he replied. "Guess I needed that."

"I suspect you did," Imperius agreed. "Or it wouldn't have happened."

"Sorry," Chauncy offered. Imperius arched an eyebrow.

"For what?" he inquired. "Feeling what you felt…or being honest about it?"

"Um…"

"If you're sorry for being you, you'll never be the *you* you want to be," Imperius instructed. "Better to be you unabashedly."

"He rhymed," Valtora hissed in Chauncy's ear.

"I've kind of been sorry for being me my whole life," Chauncy confessed, scratching his head.

"Because who you were wasn't what others wanted you to be," Imperius agreed. "So you ended up wanting to be what they wanted you to be…something you could *never* be. And therein began your tragedy."

"*Another* rhyme," Valtora hissed, seeming quite impressed.

"So…that's the secret?" Chauncy asked. "To want to be who I want to be?"

"To want to be who you already *are*," Imperius corrected. "And I believe you've gotten there," he added. "Or rather, that you've come quite far."

Imperious removed his hand from Chauncy's shoulder, turning his formidable gaze on Valtora. Who smiled sheepishly, waving unnecessarily.

"Hi Impy," she greeted. "Missed you!"

"And I you," Imperius confessed. "Though that was a bit rude, to slam the door on me. But such rudeness was fated to be."

"See?" Valtora said, prodding Chauncy with an elbow. "He rhymes all the frickin' time." Then her eyes widened. "I just rhymed!" And then she was immediately disappointed, for that last bit hadn't.

"Hey boss," Nettie greeted. "Why're you here, anyway?"

"To tell you to return to the Great Wood," Imperius answered. Nettie blinked in surprise, then frowned.

"Why?" she pressed. For she'd clearly been eager to go home.

"I don't know," Imperius answered irritably. "My gut told me, of course."

"Well shit," Nettie grumbled.

"Bet his gut tells him to do that too," Harry piped in. Nettie elbowed him, then yelped, rubbing her elbow. Then they both chuckled.

"Knucklehead," she grumbled.

"Head is always hard for you," he countered with a grin and a twinkle in his eye. And it suddenly seemed quite impossible to Chauncy that – with so many twinkles in Harry's eye – that none of them had been transferred to Nettie and been born. For as randy as the old couple was, he would've expected them to have produced a small city's worth of children by now.

"You'd better get going," Imperius warned.

"But we have to get to Cumulus to…" Valtora began.

"No," Imperius interjected. "You don't."

"But…" she insisted.

"I'm not going to argue with you Valtora," he told her. She crossed her arms over her chest, glaring at him.

"I'm not arguing with you," she retorted. To which he ignored her. She lowered her arms to her sides, looking quite dejected. "Aww," she pouted.

"Go," Imperius urged. He turned back to Chauncy. "I'm proud of you Chauncy," he declared. "Perhaps we'll meet again."

"But…" Chauncy blurted out. "I need to talk to you," he said. "I need you to teach me how to be a better wizard!"

"The first step to being a better wizard is to stop trying to be a better wizard," Imperius replied. "Magic is joy, Chauncy, and joy only exists in the here and now. If you want to be a wizard, feeling joy is the how."

And with that, he turned away from them…and promptly vanished.

"Wow*ee*," Chauncy breathed. For blue sparkles were falling to the ground from where the great wizard had been.

"Alright, let's go," Nettie prompted. "Guess we gotta rush back to the Great Wood before something bad happens."

"Worked so hard to keep it up the first time," Harry agreed. "Hate for it to fall."

"Shut up Harry!" Nettie shot back.

And so off to the Great Wood they went. And Chauncy felt quite happy to go on this newest journey. For he'd finally met the great Imperius Fanning, and the man had not disappointed Chauncy. Having been given a mission by legendary wizard – in person, at last! – Chauncy had no intention of disappointing him.

Chapter 40

There were few things in King Pravus's life that were more exhilarating than mounting and riding a magnificent dragon. With a ginormous serpent between his legs, he felt marvelously alive, as if he were flying high. Which, incidentally, he was. For he was riding the same great red fire dragon he'd ridden the last time his kingdom was in danger, thousands of feet above his sprawling kingdom. This time, he was using the dragon's services to track down that dastardly villain Mr. Merrick, who was almost certainly traveling to Mount Thrall, if not already there.

"Do you feel it, Templeton?" he inquired. For his cousin was seated right behind him, that gorgeous, toned body all smooshed against his. Templeton had even wrapped his arms around Pravus's ridiculously narrow waist, hot little hands on his belly below his bellybutton. Which certainly contributed to a feeling he was quite sure Templeton *wasn't* feeling. And if Pravus continued to feel this feeling, Templeton would soon be feeling more than his belly with those hands.

"Exhilarating, isn't it?" Templeton replied, while Pravus desperately focused on distracting himself from his growing problem.

"Brings back memories, eh?" Pravus mused.

"Fond ones," Templeton agreed. "Though I daresay all of my memories with you in it are," he added cheerily. And oh! How it warmed Pravus's heart to hear it.

"I daresay the same," Pravus replied, smiling contentedly.

The wind blew in his hair, ruffling it gently, what with the crown on his head. For all forces could only be gentle to him whilst wearing it, such was its magic. Being king was anything but gentle to the soul, however. Only the love of his friends – and engaging in what felt magical, which for him was the gym – had powerful enough to protect it.

"Ah, our destination awaits!" Templeton declared, pointing ahead. A great volcano sprouted from an awful, blackened landscape a few miles away, its huge crater filled rather curiously with water instead of lava. And while Pravus had heard countless stories of the endless ash shot into the sky by The Dark One's temple, not so much as a puff of smoke issued forth from the temple's many chimneys presently. Which was quite odd, for legends said that the ash had spewed without pause for millennia.

"How strange," Pravus said. "Tell me dear cousin, have you ever heard of clear skies over Mount Thrall?"

"Only as a figure of speech," Templeton replied. And it was true. When something seemed impossible to happen, the citizens in Pravus often said "pfft, yeah right. That'll happen when there's clear skies over Mount Thrall."

"Hmm," Pravus hmmmed. "I say we circle around the rim a bit before plunging in. What say you, Templeton?"

"Your wish is our command!" Templeton declared at once.

And it was true, but only for those wishes that *were* commands. For even a king could not have everything he wanted. Still Pravus had enough, for his friendship with Templeton was wondrous indeed. To ask for more would be understandable, but to demand it would be greedy. And there was no magic in greed. Far better to not have everything than to lose everything in trying to. Lifting too heavy a weight would result in catastrophe; a weight just heavy enough led to hypertrophy.

"See the goblins," Pravus said, eyeing swarms of black-fleshed creatures coming in and out of the volcano two-thirds of the way up the mountain or so.

"Industrious, aren't they?" Templeton mused.

"T'would be an admirable quality, if their industry wasn't evil," Pravus replied.

"Indeed."

They traced the rim of the gaping crater for a bit longer, on the lookout for the second-deadliest creature on Mount Thrall: Magmara, The Dark One's personal lava dragon. Pravus assumed the dragon would reside somewhere close to the crater, but alas, even this creature was nowhere to be seen. Which was odd, given that it was rumored to be quite huge…and that it was supposed to be the ever-present guardian of The Dark One's temple.

"Now where's that dragon gone?" Pravus wondered.

"Perhaps it hid in a cave?"

"Perhaps so," Pravus said. "Dragons do love caves, don't they?"

"Favorite place to hide," Templeton agreed.

"I haven't spotted Gavin," Pravus noted.

"I was thinking the same."

Pravus paused, eyeing the volcano.

"Right," he stated. "Shall we land?"

"It could prove dangerous," Templeton warned.

"So could we," Pravus countered. "But if it proves too much a weight to manage, we'll turn and flee."

"Very well then," Templeton decided. "Down we go!"

And so they went, aiming their dragon not for the rim of the crater, but for the black temple standing on a small island in the center of the lake there. For Pravus felt suddenly that he would very much like to face his true enemy head-on. Enough dilly-dallying and hemming and hawing. Enough with tossing and turning and – above all – with worrying.

The Dark One threatened not only Pravus's kingdom, but his peace of mind. And by the power vested in him, why, he was going to do something about it.

Something oh-so very *violent*.

"Into the belly of the beast, eh cousin?" Templeton inquired. But not with a single trace of worry or question, Pravus noted. His sweet, dear cousin's utter confidence in him was touching, and made Pravus vow to continue to be worthy of it.

"Better to die bravely than live fearfully!" Pravus proclaimed.

"Indeed!" Templeton agreed.

And with that, they touched down on the island before the black temple of The Dark One, ready to face evil not with their backs, but with their fronts. Head on, they would face their enemy…together, united as one!

Chapter 41

Gavin stared out of the window of his carriage as his Shadowsteed pulled it across the untamed wilderness that dominated the kingdom of Pravus. The Rod of Reclamation had led Gavin to the Great Wood. So Gavin had taken his Shadowsteed through the ring-portal back to the kingdom of Pravus, and had made his way to that destination. Rolling grassy hills greeted his gaze, followed by a small forest, which led to rockier terrain beyond, littered with bushes and tall grasses. It was mind-boggling, how much land was wasted in this strange country. To think of what they could accomplish with all of this land, and all of its untapped resources!

It was beyond perplexing.

Even more perplexing to Gavin was that King Pravus was quite aware of how the rest of the world worked. He knew of the benefits of developing land and mining resources, of developing industries and growing his kingdom's economy. And he knew that, by *not* doing these things, the rest of the world would rapidly outpace and outpopulate his kingdom, developing and perfecting advanced technologies that could give them a vital advantage in business and in war.

Pravus knew this, just as his father and grandfather before them had known it. And yet they'd steadfastly defied the world's conventions, choosing to stay primitive.

It was only by way of their superior magic that Pravus continued to be a formidable contender on the world stage. And if King Pravus was to be believed, the very wildness of his country was somehow the key to that magic. It was common knowledge that untamed wilderness tended to produce magic, but despite intense and thorough investigations as to how, the precise mechanism was still unclear.

Skibbard had known, that much was certain. Perhaps all wizards did. But none – including the Order of Mundus – had ever given up their secret. Sure, they'd issued platitudes like "it's a feeling" and "you'll know it when you experience it." But those were information-poor. Vague, flimsy, artsy nonsense. When pressed for a rubric – for cold, hard facts, and a sure-fire method for learning magic – the wizards Evermore had questioned had all looked at Evermore's researchers as if there'd been something wrong with them. A pitying look that'd suggested that the concept was simple, and that the researchers' failure to grasp it was somehow…congenital.

It'd been profoundly irritating for Gavin to watch those interrogations, back when he'd still been interested in doing so.

Gavin realized he was woolgathering, and forced himself to snap out of it. Mostly due to habit, for it was his habit to never woolgather. Aimless thoughts accomplished nothing, after all, and he prided himself on his ability to focus long after weaker-willed men and women needed to rest. It was the key to his remarkable productivity, and why he'd grown Evermore into a worldwide success.

But that was over now, for after finding these Chosen Ones, he would be done with his obligations. So his brain, with nothing to do, was doing whatever it wanted to do. Thinking about nonsense, thoughts that led nowhere and did nothing.

It was *irritating*.

He found himself fidgeting, and was irritated by this as well. It betrayed impatience. Nervousness.

Weakness.

"What does it matter?" he asked himself. No one was here to witness him fidgeting. No one would judge him. And there was no more need to cultivate an aura of invulnerability. Marie's death had proven that he was more vulnerable than he'd ever imagined. It'd broken him apart.

Gavin felt a sudden twinge of fear, and stuffed it down automatically. But his heart began to race, *thumping* madly in his chest, panic rising within him.

He closed his eyes, gritting his teeth. Willing himself to calm down.

You're fine, he chided himself. *You're overreacting. Stop being weak.*

Still, his heart hammered in his chest, his breath coming in short gasps.

You're better than this, he reminded himself, repeating the mantra his father had taught him, and the mantra his grandfather had taught his father.

You're better than THEM!

But it didn't help. It didn't work. And in the end, he knew that it was because he wasn't. He'd made himself vulnerable when he'd let Marie into his heart, and the hole she'd gotten in through was still open. She'd made him *not* better than everyone else. She'd ruined the perfect man he used to be.

No, he told himself. *She made you better.*

He grabbed the handle of the door to his right, gripped by the sudden, mad urge to open it. To throw himself out of the carriage. He couldn't stand sitting in it for a moment longer, in this awful box, breathing stale air.

"Stop!" he commanded the Shadowsteed.

The stallion obeyed, the carriage rolling to a gentle stop. Gavin lurched out of the carriage, stumbling on the road below. He bent over then, his hands on his knees, feeling his heart pounding in his chest.

It isn't stopping, he realized. *Oh god oh god…*

And in that moment, he felt with absolute certainty that he was going to die.

Gavin stumbled to the Shadowsteed's side, resting against its flank. It tolerated this, allowing him to press his chest against it. He felt its warmth, and took a strange comfort in it. And in its steady breathing, in and out. In and out.

In and out, he told himself, matching the horse's breathing. *In…and out.*

He buried his head in the horse's rough coat, smelling its unique scent. Gradually, he melted into it, relaxing into the stallion. He let go of holding himself up, letting the horse do it for him. The Shadowsteed could have stepped to the side or bolted, and let Gavin tumble to the ground. But it didn't. It held him up, reaffirming the trust he'd put in it. That it would carry his burden for a while.

His heart slowed, his breathing doing so as well. Eventually he recovered enough to pull away from the horse's flank. But he didn't, choosing to rest there instead. Just because.

At length, he stood up straight, taking a deep breath in, then letting it out slowly. He gazed at the stallion, standing there peacefully. A powerful beast, nearly as intelligent as a human. Just standing there, perfectly content.

"Can I ride you?" he asked.

It snorted, nodding its head.

Gavin mounted the Shadowsteed, riding the powerful animal bareback. There were no reins for him to grab, so he leaned over, grabbing the horse's mane and twisting it around into a kind of rope to hold on to.

"This okay?" he asked it. Once again, the nod. "All right," he told it. "Let's follow the road."

The Shadowsteed started again, pulling the carriage behind them. But atop the stallion, the journey was entirely different. Gavin could feel the horse's muscles moving under him, and he had to use his thighs to hold on. A breeze ruffled his hair, bringing the scent of grass and flowers, and the sun felt warm on his skin and scalp. It was as if while in the carriage, the world couldn't touch him. That the constructs of man were like armor, protecting him from the world of non-humans. But now that world exerted itself on him, making him acutely aware of its presence.

Without his magical suit to protect him, Gavin felt profoundly vulnerable atop the horse. A fall could kill him, whereas before it wouldn't have hurt him at all. The threat of injury or even death was terrifying...and at the same time, gave a poignancy and exhilaration to this moment unlike any he'd ever felt.

Safety, Gavin realized with startling clarity, was perhaps the most dangerous thing of all.

He gazed ahead, feeling more alive than he had since Marie had died. A huge forest of tall trees stood ahead, far in the distance, kilometers away. The Great Wood, where Marie had left this world. And where Gavin hoped to enter it.

I'm coming, he said silently, speaking more to Marie's spirit than himself. *I'll be there soon.*

And yet, even as he said it, for the first time in a long time, he felt that he was already *here*.

* * *

On paper, the Great Wood had been just another forest. An array of trees so-and-so square miles, at such-and-such elevation. Packed with a certain density of magical creatures and artifacts whose value Gavin's army of assessors had taken great pains to estimate. On paper, it was flat, factual, calculable, measurable. Neatly situated within the rectangular box of a page, in black and white. Recorded...and in the act of recording it, *reduced* it to that recording.

But as Gavin rode the Shadowsteed – no longer attached to the carriage he'd left behind – through the forest, weaving carefully around the massive trees, he discovered that, in reducing the Great Wood to symbols on a page, he'd left most of it out.

For the Great Wood was magnificent, beyond any forest he'd ever seen. Trees taller than any building, each tree itself home to countless vines, mosses, lichens, bugs, birds, and mammals. Having come from Borrin, where all trees were relatively young because, like most things useful to man, they were regularly killed. The Great Wood, in contrast, was useful precisely because it *wasn't* used. Its greatness was in man's non-interference. For Pravus had neither attempted to harvest nor save the Great Wood, either of which would have reduced its majesty. It had been left alone, and – allowed to do unto itself as it pleased – it accomplished more than any would-be-savior could have dreamed.

It was immediately apparent to Gavin that this could be the secret to magic. A not-doing rather than a doing. A trusting that the world would be quite alright without any effort whatsoever. For everything around him seemed effortless. Nothing in this forest had been planned, or designed, or built. It had merely grown, quite by itself, without anyone telling it what to do.

This, of course, was the exact opposite of everything Gavin had ever been taught. For in Borrin – and in business – great things were only accomplished by virtue of enormous effort. Workers wouldn't do their work without managers to force them to…and managers to force the managers to manage the workers. After all, most people were inherently lazy, which was why most people were relatively poor. They led sad, unaccomplished little lives, never reaching their potential. Dragging their feet until they retired or death retired them.

The Great Wood did its thing without management. Without laws or records or spreadsheets or contracts. Life was the only work, for nature didn't need to make a living. It just went about living.

"Stop," he told the Shadowsteed. "Please," he added, for it'd seemed harsh to order the stallion around, especially in a place like this, where orders were foreign things. The Shadowsteed agreed to do so, and Gavin dismounted, his shoes striking the forest floor with a muffled *whump*. He stepped away from the horse, continuing through the forest. And was surprised when the stallion followed him. Gavin accepted this, wandering at a stroll's pace. A pace that felt strange to him. For perhaps the first time in his life – or at least as far as he could remember – he had nothing planned. No meetings.

No to-do list. No goals to accomplish before day's end. His schedule wasn't just open…he *had* no schedule. There was no structure to his day at all. No structure to *him*.

And without the structure of Gavin Merrick, president of the Evermore Trading Company, his persona melted away. And he didn't quite know who to be, because he'd never been anything else but who he'd been told he should be.

So he just strolled, and experienced. And perhaps an experience was what he was. What he *really* was, deep down.

Onward he went, not really knowing where he was going. Or caring, for that matter. He'd left the Rod of Reclamation behind in the carriage. The Shadowsteed continued to follow him for whatever reason, and he was glad for its company. No, *his* company. For the horse of course wasn't an "it" at all. It wasn't merely a means of conveyance, or a means to an end. It was a thinking thing, like Gavin.

Which meant that Gavin wasn't a means to an end either.

"My father used me," Gavin told the horse as they walked. "The same way my grandfather used my father. A means to an end, and that end was Evermore."

The horse snorted.

"I think I've spent my whole life doing the same thing," Gavin confessed. He lowered his gaze to his feet. "I don't think I really enjoyed any of it, except Marie. But then again, she was the only thing in my life that *wasn't* a means to an end," he added.

She *was* the end. An end in and of herself.

Maybe everything was.

Gavin spotted the shimmering surface of a lake ahead, and strode toward it, feeling the air grow a little cooler as he approached. But as he came closer to the shore, he noticed that he was not alone. For there was a small group of people standing near the water, by what looked to be a crude shelter and a dead campfire.

There was a tall, elderly man dressed in brown, wearing a strange vest made of interlocking pebbles. And a short, robust woman in a blue shirt and white pants, with short, curly white hair. And a young woman who was absolutely stunning, with gorgeous brown hair that rippled hypnotically in the breeze. She stood hand-in-hand with a much less attractive man wearing what looked like a glittering purple dress and carrying a large stick, who looked to be in his forties. Rounding this out was a twenty-foot-tall giant with his flesh partly turned to stone, a small rock-creature resting on its broad shoulder. And, inexplicably, a unicorn. A...gifted unicorn.

And last, and certainly least expected, none other than Skibbard. It was Skibbard who spotted Gavin first, freezing in place, his eyes widening in recognition. Gavin thought about stopping and pretending not to notice the man, but it was too late.

"Skibbard," Gavin greeted coolly, walking until he was a few yards from the odd group. He stopped, inclining his head at Skibbard. "We meet again."

"What the hell are *you* doing here?" Skibbard demanded.

Chapter 42

Chauncy eyed the man standing before them, his heart leaping in his throat. For while he'd never met Gavin Merrick – president of Evermore Trading Company, grandson of the founder of Southwick, and the richest man in the world – he'd seen paintings and statues of the guy. Artistic representations Chauncy had assumed had been embellished to make Gavin look as roguishly handsome and profoundly masculine as possible. To Chauncy's dismay, there had been no embellishment required, for Gavin was every bit as remarkable as the art he'd inspired. In fact, he was so astonishingly handsome that it made Chauncy feel terribly insecure. He found himself clutching Valtora's hand more tightly, as if she might lunge at the man quite involuntarily and make *his* baby instead.

"Who the hell are you?" Nettie asked. The man stopped a few yards away, eyeing them all calmly.

"He's Gavin Merrick," Skibbard answered. "President of the Evermore Trading Company."

"Oh," Nettie replied.

"Uh oh," Chauncy corrected. For Gavin Merrick was not just the richest, most powerful person in Borrin – and perhaps the world – but also the man who nearly succeeded in destroying magic.

"Are these your friends?" Gavin asked Skibbard.

"Ish," Skibbard answered.

"Bullshit ish," Valtora retorted, while clearly admiring Gavin's exterior. "We're tight. We just beat The Dark One."

"Not that Skibbard did anything to help," Nettie pointed out.

"I'm not a Chosen One," Skibbard countered. "Not my job."

Gavin's eyebrows went up, and he eyed the group.

"You're...the Chosen Ones?" he inquired.

"Damn right," Valtora agreed, executing a flawless hair-toss. To Chauncy's dismay, it clearly impressed Gavin.

"*Damn*," Skibbard breathed.

"Just killed The Dark One," Valtora continued proudly. "Saved magic too, oh, about six months ago or so. Right about here, in fact."

"Oh really," Gavin replied, his expression unreadable.

"Yeah," Valtora confirmed, putting a hand on her hip. And striking a pose, Chauncy noted with dismay. "Saved it from that bitch and her little army. What was her name?"

"Um, darling..." Chauncy began, squeezing her hand. Hard. But it was her diamond hand, which was far harder.

"Marie," Gavin offered.

"Right," Valtora agreed.

"Which one of you killed Marie?" Gavin inquired.

"Baby..." Chauncy tried to interject.

"Oh, that was *totally* me," Valtora answered, flashing Gavin a proud smile. "Chauncy was all like, 'no, don't kill her, we're heroes, heroes don't murder people, just let her go.' So I cracked her in the head with this," she added, holding up her diamond fist. "Knocked her right off her feet. Then I called her a bitch and spat on her," she continued, demonstrating by spitting, "...and she was dead."

"Valtora!" Chauncy blurted out frantically.

"Chauncy tried to get Rooter to revive her, but nope, she was dead," Valtora concluded, crossing her arms over her chest. "Good riddance, I say."

Gavin stared at her, swallowing visibly. And Chauncy, standing at Valtora's side, died a little inside.

"Honey," he stated. "Marie was Gavin's wife."

Valtora blinked, lowering her arms to her sides, then clutching her hands behind her back.

"Really?" she asked. "Oh. I mean, she was gorgeous, but geez, *such* a bitch."

"Rest her soul," Harry offered politely, putting a hand over his heart.

"So it was you who killed her?" Gavin pressed, ignoring him.

"Yup," she confirmed. "All me."

Gavin stared at her for a long, silent moment, then reached into his pants pocket, fiddling with something inside of it. Then he pulled it out: a golden coin. He stared at it as it glittered in the sunlight.

"Sorry for your loss," Chauncy offered lamely.

"She *did* try to destroy magic," Nettie pointed out. "And so did you, by the way. We didn't want to fight her, but she attacked us first ya know."

Gavin said nothing, staring at the golden coin.

"She had a lich," Harry piped in. "Told it to kill us the minute she met us."

Gavin gripped his coin tightly, balling his hand into a fist. So hard that his knuckles turned white. He looked up at them – at Valtora – his eyes moist, his lips drawn in a thin line.

"You murdered my wife...and you think it's *funny*?"

"Hell yeah," Valtora answered, crossing her arms over her chest defiantly. "She tried to destroy magic and kill me and my friends, and so did you. So *totally* not guilty about it," she added. "Asshole," she also added, unhelpfully.

Gavin stared at her expressionlessly. Then he relaxed.

"You're right," he told her. "I am an asshole." He paused, opening his hand and staring down at the coin. "Consider this a token of my apology," he told her, tossing the coin to her. She caught it reflexively in the palm of her regular hand.

And turned instantly to solid gold.

"Valtora!" Chauncy gasped.

Gavin snapped his fingers, and the coin flew back into his hand. He chucked it at Chauncy, who dodged in the nick of time. But the coin hit Rocky, who was standing behind Chauncy...and turned the giant to gold too. And Rooter, perched on Rocky's shoulder, was similarly transformed.

Chauncy was about to reach for Valtora when he froze, realizing the awful truth. If Rooter was turned, that meant that touching Valtora might change *him*.

"Harry!" Nettie cried. She reached for her Wetstone, but of course it wasn't there, having been destroyed by the lava at the summit of Mount Thrall. Gavin chucked the coin at her, and she too turned to gold.

Gavin snapped his fingers, and the coin zipped back to his hand.

"Hey," Skibbard interjected, taking a step toward Gavin.

"Don't intervene," Gavin warned. "My fight isn't with you Skibbard."

"Your fight is with yourself," Skibbard retorted. "Even if you win, you lose."

Gavin paused, staring at the little man.

"Now see here," Harry stated. "You'd better turn my wife back."

Gavin's eyes flicked to Harry.

"Or what?" Gavin countered.

And then a pebble shot up from the ground, smacking him right between the legs. The pebble bounced off the man's green pants, seeming to hurt Gavin not at all.

"His pants are magic!" Chauncy warned...just as Gavin flung his coin at Harry. Another pebble shot up from the ground to intercept the coin in mid-flight, knocking it up into the air with a *ping*. Gavin snapped his fingers, returning it to himself, then flung it at Harry again.

Or rather, he pretended to. For he'd faked Harry out. Harry popped another rock out of the ground to intercept the nonexistent toss, and Gavin took the opportunity to fling the coin again, smacking Harry right in the forehead.

The old man turned to gold, as frozen in place as a statue.

Skibbard cursed, tossing a seed on the ground at his own feet and shoving it into the dirt with his big toe. A vine grew up from the earth with shocking speed, one with thorns all along its length. It grew rapidly toward Gavin, snaking over the ground. It soon surrounded him, growing upward to form a kind of loosely woven basket around him.

"That's a Pricklevine," Skibbard warned. "One prick from its thorns and you'll have to cut off the flesh around the wound or suffer horrible infection!"

"Nope," Gavin replied, touching part of the vine with his coin. The whole plant turned to gold around him, and he lifted the whole vine-basket up over his head, getting out from it. With the thorns turned to gold, their prickly poison was neutralized.

"Uh oh," Skibbard blurted out. Right as Gavin tossed the coin at *him*, turning the little wizard to gold as well. And leaving Chauncy and Peter alone to face Gavin. For everyone else was turned to gold, and ZoMonsterz was still in the carriage, parked at the edge of the Great Wood miles away.

"Crap," Chauncy blurted out.

Peter neighed, rearing up on his hind legs, then charging at Gavin, his rainbow-colored horn aiming right for the man's heart. Gavin didn't even bother sidestepping, tossing his coin at the unicorn and turning him instantly to gold. A golden statue that slid across the ground, falling onto its side on the forest floor. Gavin snapped his fingers, returning the coin to his hand. Then he turned his steely gaze to Chauncy.

"Crap," Chauncy repeated, taking a step backward. "Look, now hold on a second..."

But it was too late. Gavin chucked the cursed coin at Chauncy's head!

Chauncy jerked his staff forward reflexively to intercept the coin, and a blast of wind struck the thing, making it fly right back at Gavin's head. It struck the man smack in the forehead, making his head snap backward. But to Chauncy's surprise, the man didn't turn to gold. Instead, he stumbled, then recovered, rubbing a rising welt on his forehead.

"Now see here," Chauncy began. But Gavin snapped his fingers, returning his coin to his hand. Chauncy cursed, thrusting the butt of his staff downward as the man wound up to throw, and flew up into the sky, the coin sailing below him. He realized that there would be no reasoning with Gavin.

That he was the enemy, and the battle was on.

"Facial blast!" he cried, thrusting the butt of his staff down at the man's head. A bolt of wind shot down at Gavin, snapping his head back a second time. "Taste my staff!" he added zestily, thrusting again and again. Each thrust send him backward and upward, and struck Gavin in the face over and over again. The man tripped and fell, landing on his back on the forest floor.

But he recovered quickly, scrambling to his feet and glaring up at Chauncy, even as Chauncy reached the peak of his flight, falling back down to earth. Chauncy thrust downward with his staff at the last minute, landing gently on the ground a dozen yards away. And posed valiantly.

"Beware, Gavin Merrick," he warned imperiously. "For you face a great wizard!"

"Won't be the first time," Gavin retorted.

"Turn my friends back to life," Chauncy warned, "...and return to life my...wife," he added, wincing at the rather terrible rhyme.

"Your friends will turn in a few hours," Gavin replied. "As will the woman who murdered my wife. But she'll be in a prison in Borrin by then, facing justice for her crimes."

"In Borrin?" Chauncy countered. "That's days away!"

"Not for a Shadowsteed," Gavin countered. "And not with this," he added, reaching into his pants pocket and pulling out a ring. He tossed it onto the ground between them.

Chauncy eyed the ring, then glanced up at Gavin.

"Ooooo," he said, widening his eyes and wiggling his fingers spookily. "Scary!"

Then the ring rotated so it was standing up, expanded rapidly, and a veritable army of men swarmed through it...all wearing the green suits and golden ties of Evermore.

"Oh," Chauncy mumbled. "That *is* scary."

"Distract the wizard while I bring this woman through the portal and imprison her," Gavin told the men, gesturing at Valtora's statuesque form.

The men turned to look at Chauncy…and charged, weapons drawn!

"Skyward shot!" Chauncy cried, slamming the butt of his staff onto the ground. He shot skyward, soaring high above the men's heads. "Toppling tempest!" he added, swinging his staff in a wide arc down at them. And indeed they were toppled, blasted off their feet and slammed into the ground so hard they bounced. Chauncy landed gently near Valtora's golden statue, his robe swirling epically in the wind.

In that moment, standing alone before an army without a trace of fear, Chauncy smirked. Because *damn* it felt good to be a wizard!

"Blown away?" he asked Gavin, who'd recovered quicker than the others. The man glared at him.

"Hardly," he retorted.

"Surrender or I'll blow you again," Chauncy warned. "All of you."

Gavin just stared at him, and Chauncy grimaced, regretting his Valtora-esque word choice. Still, he powered through.

"Leave now," he insisted. "And never come back."

"I'll leave when I've gotten justice for my wife," Gavin shot back.

"Justice?" Chauncy scoffed. "You came into Pravus to destroy The Wilds," he argued. "We were just trying to stop your wife from illegally destroying this forest. She's the one who tried to kill us!"

"You defeated her," Gavin retorted. "But Valtora murdered her when she didn't have to."

"She knew Marie would never stop," Chauncy said. "Evermore can't stop. Borrin can't stop. We have to keep growing and profiting and extracting…and Pravus is the last place our way of life hasn't destroyed!"

Gavin frowned.

"*Our* way of life?" he inquired, raising an eyebrow. Chauncy grimaced.

"*Your* way of life," Chauncy corrected. But Gavin crossed his arms over his chest, eyeing Chauncy suspiciously.

"You're from Borrin?" he pressed.

"Yes," Chauncy admitted. "But I'm better now."

"How did you become a wizard?" Gavin demanded. "Borrin doesn't produce wizards."

"I...um, well, I figured it out I guess," Chauncy replied. "Nettie and Harry taught me," he added, in direct contradiction to the first statement. Gavin stared at him with a funny expression, and Chauncy squirmed a bit. "What?"

"I thought magic was something you were born with," Gavin stated.

"It is," Chauncy agreed. "Everyone is born with it. We just lose it along the way, because we're taught that we're not."

"Everyone?" Gavin pressed. Chauncy nodded.

"Even you," he wagered.

"You're wrong about that," Gavin countered.

"That's what I used to think," Chauncy replied. "But I learned the truth after the Borrin way of life nearly made me kill myself."

Gavin considered this.

"Like Skibbard?" he ventured.

"Like Skibbard," Chauncy agreed. Gavin paused, then his jawline rippled.

"It doesn't matter," he stated. "Stand aside and let me finish my mission. Then I promise you'll never hear from me again."

"I won't let you hurt my girlfriend," Chauncy warned. "You try to take her, you'll have to take *me* on first."

"So be it," Gavin growled. "Attack!" he commanded. "Surround him!"

The army spread outward before Chauncy, rapidly forming a ring around him. He stood with Valtora's statue, and with the statues of the rest of his friends, the last man standing among them. The last of the Chosen Ones.

It was up to him now. There was no one else.

"Spiral storm!" he exclaimed, spinning in a circle while swinging his staff...and blasting the men away. They flew backward, slamming into tree trunks or falling onto their backs on the ground. Only Gavin managed to keep upright...and the man flung his golden coin at Chauncy as Chauncy finished his twirl. It struck Chauncy's staff...and Chauncy let go of the staff just as it turned to gold.

It fell toward him, and he sidestepped frantically, the now-golden staff falling to the ground with a *thunk*.

The surviving men of Gavin's army got up, brushing off their suits and brandishing their weapons once again. And Gavin snapped his fingers, returning his coin to his hand.

"You can't win," Gavin told Chauncy. "If you insist on fighting me, you'll die."

"I've already lived a life where I was dead inside," Chauncy retorted. "But then I found magic, in myself anyhow. So I've already died, and already won...because I live in the here and now."

Chauncy felt a familiar weight on his hip then, a weight that felt right. And *fell* right, for it was the Magic of Magic. He pulled the book out of his pocket, gazing down at the ridiculous cover. Then he eyed the troops surrounding him, a smile growing on his lips.

"Time to throw the book at you," he stated. And did just that, chucking it at Gavin.

The book flew rightward instead of striking the man, flying into one of the soldiers instead and smacking into his chest. A blow which did no damage at all. But it managed to spill quite a few words from the book's pages on the ground. And as the soldier shoved the book away from him, it flew rightward again, parallel to the line of troops, spilling words everywhere it went.

"Attack!" Gavin ordered.

The men charged, but promptly tripped over Chauncy's words, landing face-first on the hard forest floor.

"You'd better book it out of here," Chauncy warned, thrusting a hand out at the book. To his delight, it zoomed back into his hand, striking his palm with a satisfying *thump*. He spun in a circle, words spilling out all around him, forming a ring on the forest floor. Such that the soldiers who managed to reach him tripped over these words, toppling over before ever putting a finger on Chauncy.

"Just chuck a sword at him or something!" Gavin barked.

One of the soldiers did just that, hurling a battle-axe at Chauncy's head. Chauncy shrieked, but before he could act, a stone popped out of the earth, smacking the axe in mid-flight and sending it flying upward and away.

Chauncy blinked, then turned, seeing the golden statue of Harry standing before him, smiling down at him.

"Go get 'em Chauncy," the old man said, in a somewhat hollow and metallic voice.

"Harry!" Chauncy exclaimed. "You're...okay?"

"Enjoying my golden years," Harry replied.

"But why...?"

"Just wanted to see what you'd do," Harry said.

And with that, a ring of sheer rock walls shot up from the earth all around them, blocking most of the soldiers from getting near...while trapping Gavin within. The few soldiers that remained, Harry tossed over the edge of the wall, sending them screaming, then landing with a *thump* beyond.

Harry and Chauncy turned to Gavin then.

"Hey there guy," Harry greeted, his golden flesh fading back to...well, fleshy flesh. "Nice coin ya got there."

Chapter 43

Gavin stared at the two wizards standing before him, the one called Chauncy, and the taller old man called Harry. More specifically, he stared at Harry, hardly believing his eyes. For no one had ever been turned to gold by his magical coin and simply kept moving, or had been able to transform themselves back to flesh so quickly.

"How?" he blurted out.

"How what?" Harry asked.

"How did you resist my coin's magic?" Gavin clarified. Harry gave him a funny look.

"I didn't resist nothing, ya see," the old man replied. "I love metal, and it loves me."

Gavin just stared at him.

"What'cha love is magic," Harry explained. "Like my angel here," he added, smiling at the statue of the short old woman. He turned to Gavin. "Ain'tcha ever loved someone?"

"My wife," Gavin replied. "And you people killed her. So now nothing is magic to me."

"I see," Harry murmured, pushing his glasses up his nose.

"We're sorry about your wife," Chauncy stated. "But she was trying to destroy magic."

"I have to avenge her," Gavin insisted.

"How ya gonna do that?" Harry inquired, eyeing the rock wall all around them.

"I'll die trying," Gavin answered. He swallowed past a sudden lump in his throat. "Dying would be a kindness, believe me."

"Don't got nothin' else, eh?" Harry mused.

"It doesn't have to be like this," Chauncy insisted. "We can just go our separate ways. Live and let live."

"I can't do that," Gavin replied. "I have to do this."

"Why?" Chauncy pressed.

"Because Marie would want it," Gavin answered. "I can't let her murderer go unpunished."

"We could say the same," Chauncy argued. "You were the ones who tried to destroy magic, and attacked us six months ago, and today. We should kill you to make sure magic stays safe. But I don't want to, so I won't." He paused. "Do you want to kill me?"

"No," Gavin admitted. "I don't even want to kill her," he added, gesturing at Valtora. "But it's what I *should* do."

"Should shmood," Chauncy retorted. "Nobody ever did anything good on should."

Gavin frowned.

"What?" he asked.

"Forget 'should,'" Chauncy told him. "If you don't want to do something, you'll hate doing it. And there's no magic in that. Believe me," he added. "I just spent the last week or two figuring this out."

Gavin lowered his gaze to his feet, feeling his eyes moisten. He blinked rapidly, shoving down the rising feeling, not wanting these people to see him weak. Vulnerable. But he couldn't deny Chauncy's words. He pictured his desk back at Evermore, with its ever-growing pile of paperwork. He hadn't wanted to do any of it anymore, and in forcing himself to do it, he'd hated it. Hated his life. There'd been no magic in it...just in Marie. In his *relationship* with Marie. Because being with Marie hadn't been for any goal at all. There'd been no purpose in it, other than enjoying each other's company. He'd enjoyed *her* company far more than he'd enjoyed running his.

"Nothing feels magical anymore," he confessed. "Not without Marie."

"Ironic isn't it," Harry mused. "Spent your whole life taking magic from others, and now it's been taken from you."

"I'm sorry she's dead," Chauncy said. "But you have to understand, The Wilds is like Marie. It's magical, wild and free. If she'd destroyed it, she would've destroyed magic for so many other people...the way that magic was destroyed for you."

"It's not the same," Gavin said. "These are just woods. They don't do anything."

"Not for you or me," Chauncy agreed. "But magic isn't what something can do for you. It's your relationship with the world. And The Wilds remind us that there's a world without a point. Without a purpose or a goal, except for the here and now. So it puts us there. And that's where magic is, waiting for us."

Then Chauncy smiled, opening the purple book he was carrying and reciting a poem:

"To Before and After it
Will never bow,
For The Magic of Magic is
Here and Now."

Gavin felt a chill run through him, and shivered despite himself.
"That's what Marie did for me," he realized.
"That's what you're trying to destroy," Chauncy explained. "Borrin uses everything for something, even its people. And if you treat people like things to be used, they become things instead of people. They spend the rest of their life waiting for a time when they can be free, and finally fulfill their destiny. But by then, it's too late."
"There's no other way," Gavin retorted. "People need jobs. Economies need workers. We can't live like savages."
"But you *do* live like savages," Chauncy countered. "Only a savage country would treat people and magic like you do."
"So what'cha gonna do?" Harry interjected, putting his hands on his hips. "Fight or what?"
"What else can I do?" Gavin countered.
"Well, anything you want," Harry answered. "Just gotta figure out what that is."
"So…you'd just let me go?"
"Well sure," Harry replied. "Right Chauncy?"
"Right," Chauncy agreed with a smile.
Gavin shook his head at them.
"I don't get it," he confessed. "You could kill me right now. You could win, and never have to worry about me again."
"I'm not interested in winning," Chauncy declared. "I'm interested in being interested. That's winning to me."
Gavin stared at them both, feeling…unmoored. It was strange, talking with these wizards, much like it'd been watching other wizards captured in Borrin be interrogated. They spoke oddly, in a way that was profoundly confusing. He'd never understood them. At least, not until now. For he recalled the feelings he'd had riding his Shadowsteed toward the Great Wood, and his feelings when wandering through the forest. His revelation about how nature did its thing without management.
Nature didn't need to make a living. It just went about living. And perhaps that was what Chauncy was trying to tell him.
There's no point in making a living if I'm not living, he realized.
"So…what do I do?" Gavin inquired.

Chauncy glanced at Harry, smiling at the old man with a sudden mischievous twinkle in his eye. Then he turned that twinkling on Gavin.

"You want to learn magic?" he inquired.

Gavin blinked.

"You mean...how to use it?" he asked.

"Magic isn't something you use," Chauncy countered. "It's something you feel. It's not control, it's a letting go of control."

"But..."

"And in letting go of control," Chauncy concluded, "...you'll have it."

"I...don't understand," Gavin confessed.

"You will," Chauncy promised. "If you let yourself."

Gavin lowered his gaze, feeling a sudden wave of emotion. He couldn't tell what it was, just that it was good, but also terrifying.

Maybe it was hope.

His mind rebelled against it, even as his heart yearned for it.

"No, I can't," he muttered bitterly. "I'm too broken."

"Broken apart?" Chauncy inquired. "Or broken open?"

Gavin lifted his gaze to Chauncy's, feeling another chill run through him.

Broken open.

Suddenly he saw it. The vast expanse of the life he'd led before this moment, day after day of the same. Always working, save for his moments with Marie. Endless lists of tasks to complete, and when completed, more tasks. With Evermore, there had been ever more work to do. Ever more money to make. Ever more of the world to dominate.

And for what?

Because in that moment, Gavin realized that he'd been used by Evermore as much as he'd used it. He'd been used by his father and grandfather, who'd demanded that he continue their legacy, whether he wanted to or not. And by money, symbols that were useful, but at the same time, had used him.

Without the armor of being used and useful, Gavin had nothing more to do but *feel*. And it felt terrifying to feel, and at the same time, absolutely necessary.

"You mean...I could be a wizard?" Gavin asked, his voice cracking. His eyes welled up with moisture, and this time, he didn't think to brush them or blink them away.

"If you wanted to be," Chauncy replied.

"I could try," Gavin offered. Chauncy smiled, walking up to the man and putting a hand on his shoulder.

"With magic," he said, "…it won't feel like trying. It'll feel like playing."

Gavin smiled, then inclined his head slightly.

"Very well," he decided. "I accept your offer."

"All righty," Harry interjected. "Better wake everyone up then."

The old man put a hand on Nettie's golden shoulder, drawing the goldness out of her. She blinked rapidly, then frowned as she took in the scene around her.

"What the…!" she blurted out. "What happened?"

"Battle's over," Harry replied.

"Well, we're still alive, so we must've won," Nettie reasoned, eyeing Gavin. "What're we gonna do with this idiot?"

Chauncy smiled, holding up his book.

"I've got it covered," he replied.

"What the hell's that supposed to mean?" Nettie pressed.

"I'm taking a page out of your book," Chauncy said. "Gavin's from Borrin, and I'm going to do to him what you did to me."

"Kidnap him?"

"No, I'm going to do what I was supposed to do after we saved the world the first time," Chauncy replied. "I'm going to teach magic, not just make it."

Nettie's eyes widened incredulously.

"You're gonna teach *that* asshole magic?" she blurted out.

"Yep," Chauncy confirmed.

"Why in hell would you do that?" she demanded.

"Because once he feels magic, he won't ever need to win again," Chauncy replied. Nettie just stared at him, as if he were an idiot.

"You're an idiot," she stated.

"But…" Chauncy began.

"You're seconds away from killing your worst enemy, and you're gonna go make him *more* powerful instead?" Nettie accused.

"Well I…"

"Idiot!" she interjected.

"I'll go get the others," Harry offered. He touched Rocky, Peter, and Valtora, absorbing their metal and turning them back to flesh. Then he closed his now-golden eyes, no doubt to meditate for a bit and clear the metal from his system. Valtora blinked, focusing on Gavin and glaring at him.

"I don't want your stupid money," she began...and then frowned. "Hey, where'd these rock walls come from?" she asked.

"You were turned to gold by Gavin's magical coin," Chauncy explained.

"And now your idiot boyfriend is going to teach him to be a damn wizard!" Nettie piped in, putting her hands on her hips. Valtora turned to Chauncy, putting a hand on her own hip, along with one of her patented jawline ripples. The sight of which made his family jewels rise up a bit to hide within the relative safety of his body.

"I can explain," he explained.

"No," Valtora stated. Or rather, commanded.

"Valtora," Chauncy began.

"Don't Valtora me," she argued. "He wants to kill us, just because I murdered his wife!"

"In self-defense," Harry offered.

"Sort of," Valtora sort of agreed.

"I don't want to kill you," Gavin countered. "I just want to leave the mess I've made behind me."

"Uh huh," Nettie grumbled, crossing her arms over her chest. "Right."

"So where exactly are you planning on teaching him?" Valtora inquired. "Not anywhere near me, I'll tell you that."

"Agreed," Gavin concurred.

"Oh," Chauncy stated, looking taken aback. "Well, I was planning on going back to Southwick, but I guess you're right." He frowned, rubbing his chin. Then he looked down at the book in his other hand, and his eyes lit up. "Of course!" he exclaimed.

"I can't believe you were going to teach him anywhere near where we lived," Valtora complained. But Chauncy ignored her.

"I don't need to teach you at all," he told Gavin. "Take down these walls, Harry," he requested. "I'm going to take Gavin somewhere where he can learn magic for himself."

"Oh yeah?" Nettie replied. "Where's that?"

"The same place my destiny took me," Chauncy answered with a smile. "You've made it to the Great Wood," he told Gavin. "Now it's time to brave the Cave of Wonder!"

Chapter 44

After Harry had lowered the rock walls around them – and Gavin had ordered his men to stand down and return to Borrin where they belonged – Gavin did indeed venture to the Cave of Wonder, finding the entrance only with Chauncy's help. And then it was just Chauncy and his friends by the old lean-to, standing around not knowing quite what to do.

"Well, guess that's it," Nettie said. "Better get going I suppose."

"Where to?" Chauncy inquired.

"Isle of Mundus," Nettie answered. "Order'll want us back for more training."

"Training?" Chauncy asked. For Nettie and Harry were seasoned wizards, and training seemed to be the last thing they'd need.

"Well sure," Nettie replied. "Ya never stop learning, kid. We got a whole eternity ahead of us. Gotta be prepared ya know."

"Better than being pared," Harry mused.

"Shut up, Harry," Nettie grumbled. "No one wants to hear your damn jokes!"

"Well I do," Harry countered, winking at Chauncy.

"That's 'cause you're a nobody," Nettie shot back, shooting him a glare as well. Then they both burst out laughing, as per the usual.

"So very strange," Skibbard muttered, shaking his head at them.

"What are you going to do, Skibbard?" Chauncy asked.

"Go back to my forest," Skibbard answered. And with that, the man began the long trek back to his forest. But not before stopping and turning his head to gaze at them. "Thanks," he said. "For everything."

"You're welcome," Chauncy replied.

Skibbard continued his journey, eventually vanishing into the forest. Chauncy watched him until he couldn't see him anymore, then turned back to Valtora.

"Well, guess we'd better get home," he said.

They all began the long walk back to the carriage at the edge of the Great Wood, Valtora mounting Peter as usual, and Rooter riding

Rocky. Everyone else went on foot. But they didn't rush, all of them satisfied to stroll. For this journey wasn't an intermission between events, an unfortunate necessity to be tolerated. No, it was *the* event itself. Walking in the most gorgeous of forests, surrounded by good friends, and enjoying it all immensely.

In this marvelous way – the way of wizards – they made it to the edge of the forest. Chauncy spotted the carriage ahead, and led everyone toward it. But then he noticed something in the deep blue sky.

Something *huge*.

"What the hell is that?" Nettie blurted out. But she didn't have to wait long to find out. For it was clearly a huge dragon, silhouetted against the sky, flying right toward them.

"Magmara!" Chauncy warned, gripping his staff.

"No, it's not," Valtora countered. "Too big, and not glowing."

She was right, Chauncy discovered. The dragon didn't look anything like Magmara. But it *was* familiar. For he'd seen it once before. It was a great red dragon – a fire dragon – and mounted upon its back were two men. The dragon landed a good hundred yards away, the *whump* of its impact with the earth taking a second to reach them. One of the men on its back leapt off, gliding downward through the air to the ground, then sprinting toward them. The other unrolled a ladder down the side of the dragon, and began climbing down it.

"Here we go again," Nettie grumbled. For it was none other than King Pravus himself sprinting toward them, dressed in his tight-fitting black and gold robes, with a crown on his head.

The monarch reached them in record time, skidding to a stop before them. And not at all out of breath. Once again, Chauncy regarded the man – tall, distressingly handsome, and simply bursting with muscle – with dismay, feeling like a spindly little boy in comparison.

"Ah!" King Pravus said, eyeing the ensembled friends with his hands on his hips. "If it isn't the errant Chosen Ones. Been looking for you all for some time, you know."

"Looking for us?" Chauncy inquired.

"Kneel first, ask questions later," Pravus ordered. Everyone knelt, Harry and Nettie having a bit more trouble than the others. Then they rose. "What was the question again?" Pravus inquired.

"You were looking for us?" Chauncy repeated.

"Naturally," Pravus confirmed. "You were supposed to defeat The Dark One," he accused, choosing to cross his arms over his huge chest instead. He gave them an imperial glare. "You promised you would," he reminded them.

"We did," Chauncy replied. "I did," he added rather proudly, crossing his arms over his considerably less developed chest.

"So I deduced," Pravus stated. "Templeton and I scoured that damn volcano for hours looking for The Dark One, so I could give him a good thrusting," he added, pantomiming a devastatingly heroic-looking sword thrust into his imaginary enemy. "When we couldn't find him, we suspected the very opposite of foul play."

"Heroic play?" Harry guessed.

"Indeed," Pravus agreed. "And I thought to my royal self, now where would Chosen Ones go after beating The Dark One?"

"The Great Wood," Valtora guessed.

"Right-o!" Pravus confirmed. "They always do, you know. Every time. Why, I honestly couldn't say. But there it is, and here you are."

Chauncy just kind of stood there.

"I suppose I should thank you for helping me defeat The Dark One," Pravus continued rather reluctantly. "Although you were a bit late."

"Helping?" Nettie inquired, her eyebrows shooting up.

"A lot of people died you know," Pravus said, ignoring her. "Innocent townspeople and such. Terribly sad. And preventable."

"Sorry," Chauncy offered.

"Pfft," Valtora retorted with a hand on her hip. "Our destiny was to save magic, not beat The Dark One. That's what Imperius told me. I mean, until he told me that we *should've* beaten The Dark One. But that was like, a couple weeks ago. And we totally went right away to defeat him and shit. So don't even *try* to put that on us," she told him. "Asshole," she added, disrespectfully.

"Honey!" Chauncy protested.

"He's trying to guilt us," Valtora insisted. "Only thing we're guilty of is misinformation."

"She's right," Nettie agreed. "Imperius's gut didn't tell him that we needed to defeat The Dark One until recently."

"So it was a dick move to pin it on us," Valtora concluded rather smugly.

"Yes, well," Pravus stated. "I *am* known for my dick moves. In any case, what's done is done, and I suppose I'll pardon you for your crimes."

"Crimes?!" Valtora blurted out.

"Thank you for your consideration," Chauncy interjected. "And your kindness."

"You're most welcome," the king replied. "Now, I must warn you, a most dastardly villain is hunting you down at this very moment. Perhaps the most dangerous man in the world, other than myself of course. A man obsessed with revenge, who'll stop at nothing until he…"

"You mean Gavin?" Nettie interrupted.

"Um…yes," Pravus confirmed, appearing rather miffed that his monarchal monologue had been disrupted.

"We took care of him already," Nettie told Pravus, with a satisfied smirk. "You're welcome," she added.

"Oh," Pravus replied, taken aback. "Thank you for helping me defeat him then, I suppose."

"Helping?!" Nettie mouthed to Harry, who just stood there, content to take it all in. At that point, the other gentleman who'd come with Pravus on the dragon – the man called Templeton, if Chauncy remembered correctly – had caught up with them, stopping beside King Pravus. And not at all short of breath. Or even sweating, despite having sprinted there.

"Hello all," he greeted. "Ah, the Chosen Ones!" he declared. "We've been looking all over for you."

"So we've been told," Nettie replied.

"What'd I miss?" Templeton inquired, glancing at Pravus.

"It appears they've helped us defeat The Dark One, as I predicted," Pravus replied. "And they've taken care of that devil Gavin Merrick as well."

"Ah," Templeton replied. "Most fortunate indeed!"

"A bit of good fortune after all of our misfortunes is a bittersweet finish, don't you agree?" Pravus inquired.

"Indeed," Templeton agreed. "But it's better to finish sweetly and leave the bitterness behind."

"Just so, sweet cousin," Pravus replied. "Which is why I've chosen to pardon them for their crimes."

"Without temperance, justice is tyranny," Templeton mused.

"And temperance fits my temperament," Pravus agreed. "Now then, shall we all return to Cumulus for a celebratory feast in our honors?"

"Delightful idea, my liege," Templeton stated with gusto. Which, Chauncy noticed, he said everything with. The man was perhaps the cheeriest he'd ever met. He glanced at Valtora, who glanced back at him.

"Um, I mean we *would*," she told Pravus. "But gosh, after beating…"

"Helping to beat," Pravus corrected.

"…helping to beat The Dark One and Gavin, we're just *pooped*, aren't we honey?"

"Spent," Chauncy agreed.

"I mean, we…uh…helped to save the world twice in one week," Valtora continued, finding her stride. "That's like, *three* times in one year. Honestly, we've been kicking so much ass I think we need a break from all this excitement."

"A feast would be a marvelous break," Pravus pointed out.

"Yeah, but there'll be speeches and parades and toasts and polite applause and tiny forks and shit," Valtora countered. "Honestly, just thinking about it is exhausting."

"Well, I can't argue with that," Pravus admitted, giving Templeton a rueful smile. "How many times have I told you how much I hate pomp and ceremony, dearest cousin?"

"The world's largest abacus couldn't begin to count them," Templeton replied at once.

"Very well then," Pravus decided. "Perhaps some other time? Some disappointingly distant moment in the future, after you stand me up again?"

"Probably," Valtora confessed. "We're not good people."

"Well that's true," Harry agreed. Nettie elbowed him, then yelped, rubbing her elbow.

"Anyway, nice seeing you," Chauncy interjected. He faked a yawn, stretching his arms up and to the side. "Golly, it's been a long day. Ready to go home poopy-dooz?"

"You betcha," Valtora replied with a gorgeous smile.

"Then safe journey to you," Templeton declared. "The Kingdom of Pravus thanks you!"

"Except for all the dead villagers," King Pravus countered. "And their grieving families."

"Right," Chauncy mumbled. He grabbed Valtora's hand as she began to open her mouth, no doubt to start an argument. For while arguing with the commonfolk was fun enough, arguing with royalty had to be her dream come true. "Let's go hon," he prompted.

"Aww," she said with a pout.

"Goodbye," Chauncy told Pravus and Templeton. "Thanks for everything."

"More like thanks for nothing," Nettie muttered under her breath. This time Harry elbowed her, and she yelped, shooting him a glare. Then they both chuckled.

"Farewell," King Pravus stated. Then he turned to Templeton. "Fancy a run back to the old dragon?"

"A spirited race would do us good," Templeton agreed.

"And no matter who is ahead and who behind, the race itself will be the prize!" Pravus declared zestily.

"I suspect I'll be right behind you, my liege," Templeton said.

"Behind me or before me, I'll enjoy you wherever you happen to be!" Pravus proclaimed. And with that, the two men dashed back to the dragon in the distance, sprinting at jealousy-inducing speed. Pravus took the lead as Templeton had predicted, but not by too far. Everyone watched them go, then turned to face each other.

"Huh," Harry said, adjusting his glasses.

"I know, right?" Valtora replied. "God, I wish they'd just break down and *do* it already, you know? What I wouldn't give to see that!"

"What I wouldn't give to *not* see that," Chauncy countered.

"Oh come on," Valtora scolded. "Two men going at it can be *so* hot. Believe me."

"You've seen it?"

"Hell yeah," she replied. "Like I said, incubi are my favorite minions. And half of them are gay."

"Right," Chauncy grumbled. "The incubi."

"Hot as hell," Valtora stated.

"Well you would know," Nettie piped in. "Seeing as how you…interacted with all of them."

"Not *all* of them," Valtora retorted. "Just half of them."

"How many are there again?" Nettie inquired, arching an eyebrow.

"Anyway, I'm going now," Chauncy interrupted. "See you around Nettie and Harry?"

"Oh sure," Nettie replied. "We'll be around forever."

"Literally," Harry added with a wink. Chauncy smiled, then gave the old man a hug. And then turned to hug Nettie. She gave him a big squeeze, then separated from him, wiping her eyes.

"And now you've made me cry," she accused.

"I'm going to miss you guys," Chauncy admitted. "You'll visit soon?"

"Oh don't you worry," Nettie answered. "We'll be bugging you an awful lot, believe you me."

"You could visit us too," Harry pointed out. "At the Isle of Mundus."

"Order won't let them into the castle though," Nettie countered.

"Beach is nice enough," Harry replied.

"Good enough for me," Chauncy stated. And that it most certainly was. For no matter where they went to meet each other, the fact that they were all there would be all that mattered. Magic was about one's relationship with others and oneself, after all. And if his relationships were wonderful, they would be wonderful anywhere…and his "self" would be happy indeed.

"Bye bye Harry-kins," Valtora said, giving the old man a hug. Harry hugged her back, holding on to her a bit longer than Nettie found reasonable.

"Do I need to get you two a room?" she inquired testily. Harry turned to her, giving her a hopeful look.

"Could we?" he asked.

"Go soak yourself!" Nettie snapped, prying them apart. Harry chuckled.

"Guess I'm gonna have to," he replied.

With that, Chauncy and Valtora turned away from the old couple, to make their way back to Southwick with Rocky and Rooter.

"Now wait just a damn second," Nettie called out after them. They both turned around, seeing her standing there with her hands on her hips. "You didn't give me a hug," she accused Valtora.

"Oh," Valtora replied. "I thought you hated me."

"Well you know what they say," Nettie told her. "Keep your friends close and your enemies closer."

"Aww," Valtora replied, clutching at her chest. "I'd be honored to be your enemy!"

"Then give 'er here," Nettie demanded, waddling up to Valtora and giving her a hug. Valtora leaned down to reciprocate, and they held each other for a moment longer than enemies would find reasonable.

"I love you Nettie," Valtora confessed. "Even if you don't love me."

"Keep treating Chauncy good and maybe one day I won't hate you as much as I do now," Nettie replied, separating from her. Valtora smiled.

"I'll treat him *so* good, you'll see," she promised.

"I'd rather not," Nettie retorted.

"Well you'll see him smiling anyway," Valtora offered. "And a whole *village* full of babies!"

"Well that'd be…" Nettie began.

"I'm gonna pop 'em out like a frickin' baby factory," Valtora interrupted, pantomiming this very act with disturbing accuracy…and ferocity. "*So* many babies. Like a frickin'…"

"Okay," Nettie interjected. "I get it!"

"You better be ready Chauncy," Valtora warned. "I'm gonna put you to work."

"Well, you know what I always say," Chauncy said with a smile.

"Make sure your work is play," Valtora recited.

"You rhymed," Chauncy pointed out.

"Sure did," Valtora agreed. "I'm a goddamn wizard, and don't forget it."

"She bedazzles shit," Harry reminded Nettie.

"I don't bedazzle my shit!" Valtora snapped. Then they all shared a laugh, wiping moisture from their eyes. For while they'd all only known each other for a half year or so, somehow it seemed like they'd always been meant to be. A feeling quite appropriate, Chauncy supposed, given their shared destiny.

Nettie and Harry waved one last goodbye, then got into the carriage in their usual places.

"Peter!" Valtora gasped, rushing up to the unicorn and giving him a hug. "I'll miss you," she told him. Peter whinnied, nuzzling her with his white nose. "I'll see you soon?" she asked. He nodded. "Come any time you want," she told him. And judging by Peter's response, he was happy to oblige.

So, having said their goodbyes, the Chosen Ones chose to go their separate ways. But Chauncy didn't shed a tear. For the magic of magic was in the now, and wherever he was, it was here. So he vowed to enjoy each moment as it passed instead of yearning for a future like the past. And if destiny perchance ordained that they should see each other again, then this meeting wouldn't be their last.

Chapter 45

King Pravus the Eighth always felt absolutely marvelous after a good workout at the gym. Which was why it was so perplexing that he'd deprived himself of its particular perks for as long as he had. The dreadful duties of state had dragged him down into the depths of despair, and had nearly shattered his very soul. But now that he was back at the gym – with Templeton at his side! – his soul was safely whole.

"Isn't this marvelous?" he inquired as he waddled in leg-day fashion to the seated calf-raise machine. A contraption he'd invented himself, based on his extensive review of human anatomy. For the calf was actually two muscles, one atop the other. And whilst standing, calf-raises predominantly exercised the outermost muscle, while seated raises stressed the innermost. Neglecting one's insides was a sure path to folly, he knew all-too-well. So to the seated calf raise machine Pravus went, to balance himself out.

"I even like the smell," Templeton mused, taking a big whiff of the gymnasium's particular musk. Most of which was Pravus's musk, given that it was ridiculously early, and as a result, there were few others in the gym other than the guards.

"The scent of sweat," Pravus agreed, falling into the seat of the machine, then getting his knees under the padded bar ahead of him. "The odor of excellence!"

"A perfume to be treasured," Templeton declared. "For it is the very evidence of our exertions!"

"Quite so," Pravus agreed. "Now load me up, dearest Templeton."

"Four-fifty?" Templeton inquired.

"Nice and slow," Pravus confirmed. Templeton did indeed load him up, and Pravus got to work, letting the weight push his knees down until his calves were at maximum stretch, then slowly bringing them up. For the inner calf muscle reacted better to slower repetitions, while the outer layer responded to rapidity.

"Perfect technique as usual," Templeton observed.

"As perfect...as I...can be!" Pravus grunted. It wasn't long before his calves began to burn. And as any avid gym-goer knew – at least those wise enough to never skip leg day – the calves burned the worst of any muscle, a pain that threatened to overwhelm, even after the exercise was done. But for those who possessed the courage to push through the agony of this fire, a precious reward would be claimed. Meaty, bulging calves that looked for all the world like upside-down hearts, that no boots could hope to contain.

He bellowed as he finished the last repetition, his calves feeling like they would explode. Then he stood up, stumbling a bit and nearly falling. Templeton – sweet Templeton! – caught him from behind, holding him by his shoulders.

"Are you alright cousin?" Templeton inquired.

"I am now," Pravus replied. To his dismay, Templeton let go of him, sitting down on the seat to take his turn. "Three-sixty?" he guessed.

"I think I'll give four-fifty a go," Templeton ventured. To which Pravus arched a perfectly-plucked eyebrow.

"Are you sure?" he said. For it was more than Templeton had ever attempted.

"I've been at the same weight for too long," Templeton confessed. "It's comfortable now."

Pravus nodded, knowing full well that comfortable rarely led to growth. For it was only in abandoning comfort for the unknown that one would develop their full potential. A frightening journey to consider indeed, which was why most never took it. But for those brave enough to not take a path, but to create one for themselves, a glorious, magical future awaited.

"To discomfort!" Pravus declared. And in lieu of the *cling* of champagne glasses to mark the toast, the *clang* of weights would have to do. So Templeton faced his fear, and with Pravus's watchful presence, he did what he had never dared do before. One, two, three repetitions, then a struggling, shuddering fourth, veins all popping out everywhere under Templeton's gloriously thin skin. His cousin's face turned red on the last rep, but he brought it to its conclusion with success, gasping as he finished. He moaned then, leaning back in his seat with sweat slicking his skin, utterly spent.

"Spectacular finish, dearest cousin!" Pravus congratulated.

"Ow," Templeton replied, his calves twitching madly with the memory of their struggle. He breathed through the pain, relaxing into it. Experiencing it. And Pravus dared not interrupt this meditation, for it was sacred indeed.

At length Templeton recovered, opening his eyes and focusing on Pravus as if seeing him anew.

"I did it," he proclaimed with an exuberant smile. "Well done, me," he added, patting himself on the back. "You're up," he prompted, rising up from the machine shakily. This time it was Pravus who stood behind him. The leering rascal in him hoped that Templeton fell back into him, but it wasn't to be. So instead, he took his cousin's place on the calf raise machine.

"Hmm," he murmured, eyeing the plates.

"More?" Templeton inquired.

"I daresay you've inspired me," Pravus confessed.

"Five hundred?" Templeton proposed.

"Make it so," Pravus agreed. And so Templeton made it, adding two twenty-five-pound plates. He set his knees under the padded bar, then focused, preparing himself for the battle ahead. A battle not with the weight, but with himself. For whether he succeeded in lifting it was, first and foremost, dependent on whether or not he believed he could. Success was a habit, after all. And to be successful, one had to be habitual not necessarily about succeeding, but in attempting to.

"I'll spot you," Templeton reassured. Pravus smiled, secure in knowing that his cousin was there to help him should he fail. As he'd done when Pravus *had* nearly failed in his duties as king. When the weight of his crown had grown too heavy for him to carry, Templeton – and Desmond, bless his wrinkly, liver-spotted heart – had been *his* spotters. And while Templeton would never carry the load Pravus dreamed he would, his cousin had helped carry the weight of Pravus's duties.

It was, he realized as he started the first repetition, lowering the marvelously heavy weight until his muscles were stretched to their very limit, the same lesson he'd learned before, but in reverse. For after the Great Wood had been attacked by Marie Merrick, he'd discovered his role as king. Not to micromanage every aspect of his kingdom, nor plunder it for his own gain. No, his role was the spotter, the one who would forever stand behind the people of Pravus, allowing them to do what they needed to do. And if they should falter, if the weight they carried on their shoulders should prove too much for them to bear, he would be right there, waiting to help them lift it. To bear the weight with them, even if that weight would not have challenged him.

This time 'round, Pravus had learned that he too could falter. That the weight he carried on *his* shoulders could sometimes prove too much for him to bear. And that it was quite alright – indeed, necessary! – for him to trust in his people to be right there for him, waiting to help him lift it.

That was the lesson being a monarch had given Pravus. That he'd started somewhere less than his future best. The same trials could be borne easily by some, and only with the greatest of effort by others. Regardless, it was not the ability that mattered, but the effort. And as long as he did what he could, he would have to trust that his people would be right behind him, and that their capable shoulders would carry what he could not.

With that, Pravus set to test his mettle, lifting a weight he'd never before attempted. And his delight was not in lifting it, nor reaching a number of reps. No, it was in the attempt. In the trial itself, pushing through resistance. Succeed or fail, win or lose, the result was sometimes beyond one's control. But the effort was not.

With that in mind, Pravus *did* succeed, and afterward, went shakily to the next set, then the next. He knew that he had a whole day of drudgery ahead of him, and that his body would be weak and sore. But though he would feel drained, he would be positively giddy. For as he'd often found, a good workout was like a vaccination against the evils of the world.

As long as he attended to what was magical to him before attending to everything else, everything else would be just fine.

Chapter 46

After returning to Southwick, Chauncy Little felt right at home. For he *was* at home, in Grandma Little's house about a mile from the center of the city. He and Valtora quickly fell into their comfortable routine, waking up each morning to go to the shop, then coming home to enjoy each other. And after all the heroics Valtora had seen Chauncy perform, there was quite a bit of enjoyment to be had. So much so that he found himself barely able to stay up to the task, both literally and figuratively. But when he woke up one fine morning, a mere three days after they'd returned home, he found Valtora eager as ever. And despite his protestations – or perhaps *because* of them – Valtora saw fit to sizzle his sausage and devil his eggs anyway, evil wizard that she was. Though his capabilities were sorely tested – and afterwards, a bit sore – Chauncy's magic was to put things into things. And despite everything, putting himself in her was magical indeed.

"Still creeps me out that Zarzibar's always watching," he admitted as they lay side-by-side on their very pink bed. "Bet this is the first time you've had two men inside of you at the same time," he joked.

Valtora's face went blank.

"Huh?" she asked.

"Never mind," he grumbled.

Thusly disturbed, Chauncy got up to prepare breakfast, sizzling and deviling some eggs of his own. They sat down to eat at Grandma Little's little kitchen table, digging in to the admittedly delicious meal. He was getting pretty good at cooking, he had to admit. Not near the chef that Grandma Little had been, but getting there.

"You're humming again," Valtora noted. Chauncy realized she was right, and smiled, scooping another bit of eggs into his mouth. And humming anyway. Because the food was good, and he wasn't at all ashamed to enjoy it in the way that he did.

He ate quickly – far more quickly than Grandma Little would've liked – then took their plates and put them in the sink. With that, they got ready for what most people called work, but Chauncy called play.

"Ready?" he inquired as he grabbed his cane, having already changed into his purple wizard's robe. He felt the weight of the Magic of Magic on his left hip, falling right where it should.

"I'll grab your staff," she told him, grabbing his Staff of Wind. She offered it to him, and he gave her a smile, opening the door for her.

"After you, poopy-dooz," he prompted.

"My *hero*," she gushed, giving him a peck on the cheek.

They stepped outside, locking the door behind them. Down the front steps they went, turning right onto the sidewalk leading to the city center. And with his destiny fulfilled at last, Chauncy was free to not walk, but stroll. For with nothing to do but what he wanted to do, what he wanted to do was to enjoy what he was doing. Whatever that was. And at this particular here and now, he enjoyed the sunlight warming his skin, and the warm breeze ruffling his hair, carrying the sweet scent of flowers and grass. Yes, everything was perfectly perfect.

Or rather, it was supposed to be.

"Ugh," Valtora groaned, putting a hand on her belly and making a face. Chauncy frowned.

"Are you alright?" he inquired.

"Huh?"

"Are you alright," he repeated. She gave him a rather pained smile.

"I've been called more than…" she began, then stopped, covering her mouth with her hand.

"What's wrong?" he pressed, stopping alongside her.

"Nothing," she answered immediately, which usually meant that she was lying.

"Valtora…"

"I'm *fine*," she insisted irritably.

Chauncy's mouth snapped shut, and he resisted the urge to continue his interrogation. For Valtora was rarely irritable, but when she was, it could only mean one thing. That it was that time of the month again. Which was about bloody time, he supposed.

"Shall we?" he inquired, hooking an arm in hers. She nodded, and they resumed their stroll. It took a few minutes for Chauncy to relax into the moment again, having been jarred out of it for a bit. It wasn't long before they made it to the center of Southwick, the large circular courtyard with its statue of Archibald Merrick in the center just ahead. They crossed over the well-manicured grass per their routine, passing the statue as they went. And as usual, Valtora executed her glittering, sparkly violence upon the likeness of Gavin Merrick's ancestor, punching one stony thigh particularly hard. There was a loud *crack*, one that echoed across the courtyard. A distressingly large hunk of thigh fell from the statue, landing on the grass.

"Oh," Chauncy blurted out, looking around nervously. But there wasn't anyone nearby, thank goodness. Especially not a city guard.

"Ha!" Valtora declared rather smugly. "Serves the bastard right."

"Come on," Chauncy urged, pulling her away from the scene of the crime. For while he didn't know the fine for defacing the city's beloved statue, he was sure it was prohibitively expensive. Particularly considering he was planning on spending much of his savings on his newest hobby. Or rather, a place to entertain it.

They hurried to the narrow three-story building beyond the courtyard and across the street bordering it, reaching the front door. Chauncy unlocked it, then rammed his shoulder into it, popping the door open with a *dong*.

Valtora giggled, delighted as always by dongs. Chauncy smiled, gesturing for her to go through first.

"M'Lady," he purred.

"Why thank you, m'Lord," she replied, curtseying politely. Then she pulled him into the shop after her. "Okay Chauncy," she told him, stopping at the broom closet. "What's the most important rule?"

"Make sure your work is play," Chauncy recited. With a rueful smile, for this was a role reversal. Something Valtora was quite keen on from time to time, particularly in more intriguing aspects of life. She smiled gorgeously, then retrieved his broom from the closet, handing it to him. While the door was open, he spotted a length of rope coiled on the floor. The same rope, he realized, that he'd nearly hung himself with minutes before Harry had entered this very shop. He'd almost killed himself before he'd had a chance to remember what living was really like. Before becoming an adult had ruined the perfectly perfect child he'd once been.

"Go slay me some dust bunnies," Valtora commanded. Chauncy inclined his head.

"As you wish, m'Lady," he declared gallantly.

With that, he set about with the minor heroics of preserving the aesthetics of their shop, finding and collecting every last dust bunny in the shop. It was a pleasure to do so, not a chore. For the thought of how a customer might feel entering this shop, with gleaming floors and sparkling artifacts filled with honest-to-gosh magic, was simply marvelous to consider. If a single customer that day entered the shop and had the same feeling about it that Chauncy had possessed as a ten-year-old boy, then that would be payment enough for his efforts.

"Done!" he declared valiantly, striking a pose. "Thine bunnies art vanquished!"

"Then bring me your staff so that I might bedazzle it," Valtora ordered. Chauncy smiled, walking behind the counter where she was sitting. He offered his broom, but as it turned out, it was not the staff to which she was referring. She had him sit down, then grabbed quite another thing altogether. He squeaked, being a bit sore still.

"Honey!" he blurted out. But she would not be denied.

"It's about time you let me bedazzle it," she told him.

"I don't want to be bedazzled," he protested. For up until that point, they'd agreed that Chauncy would remain himself. But true to the theme of the day, Valtora was not in the mood for consent.

"It's gonna happen," she told him. "Whether you want it to or not."

"Just stop," he grumbled, pushing her hand away. She pouted.

"Fine," she decided. "I'll get you in your sleep."

"You wouldn't," Chauncy said. She got a terribly mischievous twinkle in her eye.

"Oh I *totally* would."

"Like you did with Peter?" he inquired irritably. For he detested being pressured into doing things. Particularly after all this business with destiny.

"He was awake," she countered. "And he didn't resist."

"Oh really," he grumbled.

"Nope," she confirmed. "He liked it, actually."

Chauncy frowned, eyeing her with sudden suspicion.

"What do you mean he liked it?" he asked. She stared at him, her expression suddenly blank.

"Huh?" she asked.

"You know what I mean," he accused, crossing his arms over his chest. "What do you mean he liked it when you bedazzled his..."

Dong!

The front door opened, the first customer of the day entering the shop. It was Mr. Schmidt, as usual. The tall, creepy old man's eyes went right to Valtora, lingering there. Creepily.

"Ah, good morning Mr. Schmidt," Chauncy greeted. "Welcome to A Little Magic! What can I get for you today?"

"The usual," the old man answered. His gaze went immediately to the "Lotions & Potions" aisle, searching for his favorite product. Then he frowned. "Where's my lotion?" he asked.

"Hmm?" Chauncy replied innocently.

"My lotion," Mr. Schmidt repeated, gesturing at the aisle. There were lots of potions, but not nearly as many lotions, and the particular lotion Mr. Schmidt…enjoyed was absent.

"It's been discontinued," Chauncy informed him. Mr. Schmidt just stared at him blankly.

"Huh?"

"It's been discontinued," Chauncy repeated, with a twinge of apprehension. For he'd been both dreading and looking forward to this day. After being forced into his latest adventure, he refused to be forced into doing things he hated doing just to make others happy. Unless of course that "other" was Valtora.

"Discontinued?" Mr. Schmidt blurted out incredulously.

"Discontinued," Chauncy confirmed.

Mr. Schmidt just stood there, not certain what to do with this information. Chauncy just gave the man his best A Little Magic smile, honed to perfection after twenty-five years of Grandma Little's expert tutelage.

"When's it coming back?" Mr. Schmidt demanded.

"It isn't," Chauncy replied with inappropriate – but to be honest, brutally honest – cheer. "Anything else I can get for you?" he inquired.

Mr. Schmidt glanced at Valtora, then back at Chauncy. Then back at Valtora again.

"No," he muttered at last. And with that, he turned about, leaving the shop with a disappointed *dong*. Chauncy let out a breath he hadn't realized he'd been holding, turning to give Valtora a smile. She smiled back at him, slugging him on the shoulder. With her normal hand, thank goodness.

"See?" she told him. "I *knew* you could do it!"

"It wasn't so bad," Chauncy admitted. "Saying no."

"Well you didn't say that, but at least you didn't say yes," Valtora corrected. "Or like, 'Right away sir. Of course sir. I'll get that right to you. Sure I'll have it by tomorrow. Blah blah blah, I'm a guy, but somehow I'm also a p-'"

"I get it," Chauncy interjected. "No need to be a..."

Dong!

Another customer entered the shop. This time it was Mrs. Biggins. The crotchety old woman barely made it through the doorway with her wide hips, seeing as they were a bit wider than they'd been a few weeks before. And considerably wider than a few years ago. It was the strange property of hips and bellies that they nearly always grew and rarely shrank, except in times of illness.

"Morning Mrs. Biggins," Chauncy greeted.

"Where the heck have *you* been?" Mrs. Biggins demanded, coming up to the counter and glaring at him. With a makeshift splint still on her previously broken wrist.

"Out on a little trip," Chauncy replied.

"Little?" she stated incredulously. "It's been weeks!"

"A little trip for us Little's isn't as little as one might think," Chauncy conceded.

"Went on for a little longer than we expected," Valtora agreed.

"Did you make something to heal my wrist?" she asked, holding up her injured limb. Which, to be fair, had almost certainly completely healed by now.

"A while ago," Chauncy answered. "A golem named Rooter. I asked if he wanted to come to Southwick, but he decided to stay in Pravus."

"What?" Mrs. Biggins asked.

"I thought about bringing him here to help you, then taking him back to Pravus, then coming back here. But gosh, that would've taken days and days, and I just didn't want to do it," Chauncy confessed. Mrs. Biggins' eyes widened, for she was quite taken aback.

"Chauncy Little!" she gasped. "For shame!"

"Pardon?"

"I'm in pain," Mrs. Biggins declared, glaring at him as if he were a particularly naughty child. "I asked you to help me and you promised you would."

"I said I'd try," Chauncy corrected.

"Well you should've tried harder," Mrs. Biggins argued. "You're a wizard you know. You have responsibilities."

"I do," Chauncy agreed. "And my first responsibility is to myself."

"But…"

"If you'd like Rooter to heal you, travel to Pravus and follow the road for a day or so until you reach a stone bridge. You'll find him there."

Mrs. Biggins drew herself up indignantly, giving him the stink-eye.

"I'm an elderly woman," she protested.

"Take a carriage," Chauncy recommended.

"I don't have one."

"Rent one," he shot back.

"I can't get through the Gate," she pointed out.

"I could unlock it for you," Chauncy offered. "It's the least I could do," he added with his sweetest smile.

"On that," she retorted, "…we agree."

"Anything else we can do for you?" he inquired. She scowled at the fact that he'd ended that particular argument, but turned to the "Lotions & Potions" aisle. After which her scowl deepened.

"Where is my lotion?" she snapped.

"Discontinued," Chauncy replied serenely. And it surprised him at how serene he felt. For he'd spent much of his life afraid of what might happen if he said "no" to people. As it turned out, what might happen wasn't so scary after all.

"Discontinued?" she blurted out incredulously. "What do you mean, discontinued?!"

"Not continuing," Valtora piped in. "Continuing no longer."

"I know that!" Mrs. Biggins snapped. "How could you discontinue it?"

"Honestly, I don't like making them," Chauncy answered.

"So?"

"So I don't make them," he concluded.

"That's not a good reason to stop," she argued. "Being an adult means doing things you don't want to do, because that's what's best for others."

"If everyone does that, then everyone's doing things they don't want to do," Chauncy pointed out. "And then everyone's unhappy."

"It's called being considerate!"

"I call it being miserable," Chauncy countered. "From now on, I'm going to do what I enjoy doing. And if other people enjoy the things I do, all the better."

"What if everyone did that?" Mrs. Biggins argued, throwing up her arms. Without wincing at all, he noticed.

"Why, then we'd all be happier," Chauncy answered.

"Chaos!" Mrs. Biggins all but shouted. "That's what!"

"Is there something else you'd like to purchase?" Chauncy inquired.

"I want my lotion!" she snapped, slamming her palm on the countertop. Her injured wrist, he noted. And again, no wincing. Valtora shot up from her chair, grabbing said wrist with her diamond hand.

"Cut the crap," she warned, giving Mrs. Biggins' wrist a little squeeze. And making the old woman's eyes pop out a bit. "No lotion. Got that?" she added, squeezing a bit harder. Mrs. Biggins yelped.

"Okay!" she blurted out, trying in vain to extract her hand. Valtora gave her a sweet – and totally fake – smile.

"Good," she replied. "Now gggluuurrrbbbb!" she barfed, spewing eggs and sausage all over Mrs. Biggins' top.

Mrs. Biggins *shrieked*.

"Oh," Valtora gasped, putting a hand over her mouth. "I'm so saarrbblooorrrgg!" she vomited, giving Mrs. Biggins a second helping. Having had quite enough, Mrs. Biggins stumbled away from the counter, hurrying out of the shop. She threw the door open with a *dong*, exiting the building, but being sure to slam the door behind her with a loud *dong-bang*.

"Ugh," Valtora groaned, staring at the pool of vomit on the counter. And the vomit-waterfall that led to a lake of vomit on the floor beyond.

"Are you okay poopy-dooz?" Chauncy inquired, putting a hand on her shoulder. She gave him a weak smile, then dry-heaved, luckily keeping her insides inside this time. "Maybe it was the eggs," he ventured.

"I think it was the sausage," Valtora countered.

"I don't know," Chauncy told her. "It was pretty fresh. Addie said it was made yesterday when I bought it. And I cooked it pretty well."

"Not that sausage," she retorted. He frowned.

"What do you mean?"

She just stared at him. Then dropped her gaze to his...

Dong!

A man entered the shop then. One that, to be honest, Chauncy had never seen before. He was perhaps eighty, and dressed in a sharp-looking white suit, with a white tie and white shoes.

"Welcome to A Little Magic," Chauncy blurted out automatically, though his mind was quite elsewhere.

"Sorry about the mess," Valtora offered.

"Oh," the man in the white suit stated, spotting the vomit. He stopped well short of it, looking a bit green himself at the sight. For vomiting was as infectious as laughter, yawning and syphilis, though why was a mystery to all.

"I'm pregnant," Valtora notified the complete stranger. And at the same time, Chauncy.

"Congratulations," the man said, inclining his head. "And my condolences," he added, glancing at Chauncy. "I'm Ginny Smithers, owner of the second and third floors."

"Oh yes," Chauncy said. "Right." For he'd arranged to meet the man here immediately upon returning to Southwick. "Um…"

"You wanted to discuss buying the second-floor dance studio?" Mr. Smithers inquired.

"Um…I uh," Chauncy blathered, tearing his gaze from the man to stare at Valtora. He swallowed, gazing down at her belly. And feeling strangely numb.

Pregnant!

"Yes," Valtora answered for him. "Chauncy wants to clear it out and use it to open a school."

"A school?" Ginny Smithers inquired, raising an eyebrow. "For dance?"

"For wizards," Valtora corrected. "We'd want to kick the dance people out."

"I see," Ginny murmured, rubbing his chin thoughtfully. "A school for wizards. Hmm."

"The first in Southwick," Valtora pointed out. "And in Borrin."

"Indeed it would be," Mr. Smithers agreed. "I would have to terminate the lease for the dance instructor," he added. "She's a friend of mine."

"Oh," Chauncy mumbled, feeling a bit disappointed. He'd hoped to have the school right above the shop.

"But I suppose if I find her an alternative location, she'll be alright," Mr. Smithers reasoned. "I owe your grandmother a great deal, you know. Her magic cured me of cancer."

"So she told me," Chauncy replied, doing his best to smile convincingly. For Grandma Little had only really cured Ginny Smithers of the *idea* that he had cancer, for he'd never actually had it in the first place.

"Shall we discuss pricing?" the man inquired.

"Maybe later?" Chauncy proposed. "Valtora isn't feeling well at the moment."

"Urrgghhh," Valtora agreed, dry-heaving a bit.

"I'll have my lawyer on the third floor draft an offer," Mr. Smithers decided. "Congratulations Chauncy, and my condolences for your grandmother. She was a remarkable woman."

"That she was," Chauncy agreed. And it was true. For Grandma Little had been many things: a liar, a cheat, a swindler. A consummate salesman indeed. But she'd loved every minute of it, and everything she'd done had been with the very best of intentions. Not just for herself and Chauncy, but for her customers. She'd been devout in her belief that the people she'd swindled *needed* swindling, for without magic in their lives – real or imagined – their lives wouldn't have been worth living. With no magic of her own, she'd resorted to the illusion of it.

"I'll be in touch," Mr. Smithers promised, inclining his head. With that, he turned and left the shop, his exit marked with yet another *dong*. Chauncy turned to Valtora, having absolutely no idea how to feel.

"You're pregnant?" he asked. She gave him a look.

"Have you *seen* my boobies?" she asked.

"You mean breasts," he corrected, flushing a bit. For it was only proper. Valtora scoffed.

"They're *spectacular*, she declared. And indeed they were. "More so than usual," she added.

"I just assumed you'd bedazzled them again."

"Thought about it," she confessed. "But once I start, I have a hard time stopping."

"So I've learned," he replied, recalling the events of the morning.

"Probably why I'm in this pickle in the first place," she mused. "Because your pickle was in…"

"I get it," he interjected. "So you're pregnant," he stated, running a hand through his hair. "Wow."

"Are you okay?" she asked. "I thought you'd be happy."

"I will be," he reassured. "Just…taking it all in I guess."

"It's a super big deal, right?" she agreed.

"Sure is."

"Take your time," she told him, patting his leg and giving him a warm smile. "Urrggghhh," she added, putting her hand on her mouth and lurching forward.

"Do you want to...?"

"Yep," she answered. And got up from her chair, leaning over to kiss Chauncy goodbye, then thinking better of it. She waved instead, then rushed out of the shop to go home. Chauncy watched her go, then sighed, his gaze drawn to the very large mess on the counter. And on the floor.

"Well then," he mumbled. "Guess I'd better clean you up." And he was about to stand up when he realized that a cat was sitting on his lap. And that he'd been scratching its head for who-knows-how-long. "For the love of...!" he blurted out, nearly falling off his stool. It was ZoMonsterz, naturally. Or rather, un-naturally. For the cat had gone missing after their ordeal with Gavin back at the Great Wood.

"Reeowwrr," ZoMonsterz meowed, staring sexily up at him. While he continued to pet her, quite involuntarily.

"Sorry Zo," he apologized, standing up. ZoMonsterz hopped down from his lap, scurrying away. And promptly began what could only be described as howling to her ancestors, being ridiculously loud in the process.

Chauncy went to the broom closet, finding the mop within, and a bucket of water. He paused then, spotting the rope still sitting there, and was struck with the urge to throw it out.

Don't, he told himself. It was a reminder of a terrible, painful time in his life, it was true. But it was also a reminder that no matter how bad things got – even so bad as to want to commit suicide – that beyond seemingly infinite darkness, there was always light.

Nettie and Harry had taught him that, but so had The Dark One. For The Dark One existed in everyone, even the most wonderful of souls.

Chauncy closed the closet door, setting about to clean the mess that Valtora had made. When he was done – the floor and counter polished to a mirror-shine once again, he put the mop and bucket away.

Then he turned gazing out at the aisles of magical goodies, more marvelous than any he'd seen as a child. A Little Magic had turned into something Grandma Little would've been proud to behold. Suddenly, Chauncy wished terribly that she was here to see it.

To see *him*.

"Littles do a lot," he murmured, a tear coming to his eye. He let it roll down his cheek, smiling at the results of his destiny. For he knew without a shadow of a doubt that here, amongst artifacts and potions and tinctures and lotions, and crystals and staves and books, he was where he wanted to be.

There really was nothing more magical to him than magic, and magic made work into play. But the work of having a child, a living being that depended on him...

"You're scared you'll be a bad father," he realized, the revelation sending a chill through him. He'd never met his own father, after all, and didn't really know how fathers were supposed to be. What if he screwed it up? What if he ended up abandoning them like his father had abandoned him?

It was possible, he knew. For The Dark One lived within him as well. Whatever evil had caused Chauncy's father to leave existed in Chauncy himself.

He felt a familiar weight pressing right on his left hip, and put a hand there, feeling The Magic of Magic in his robe-pocket.

The solution to the problem is the problem itself.

The problem of course was that he didn't trust himself. Didn't trust that things would be okay in the future. And by giving in to that fear, he'd deny himself that very future, and ensure that his actual future would be bleak. But if there was one thing this journey had taught him, it was not that he should trust himself...but that he *could*. And that by doing so – by getting out of his own way – he invariably *got* his way.

"It'll be alright," he reassured himself, remembering the rope in the closet. He gazed at the aisles of artifacts, picturing an absolutely enormous quantity of children playing within it. One sweeping the floor while another polished the countertop, with still another reading one of the various hokey magic books Grandma Little had kept around. Children everywhere, and every one of them like he had been, experiencing the magic of magic for themselves. Just filled to the absolute brim with wonder and joy, with smiles all around.

He found himself smiling at the vision, his mind's eye making it seem almost real.

"You're going to be a wonderful father," he realized. And he knew without a doubt that it was true.

For he was Chauncy Little, the choicest of the Chosen Ones. He had traveled through the Gate to the Great Wood, then once again braved the Cave of Wonder. And, mounting Mount Thrall, he had faced the personification of evil itself...and put that evil back where it belonged.

Now he would build Southwick's very first school for wizards, and share the magic of magic with others. Why, when they stepped through the front door of A Little Magic – and A Little Magic School – Chauncy would find a way to make them feel just like he had as a boy, when he'd entered Grandma Little's shop. That same feeling of childlike wonder. For childlike wonder was really the best way to regard the world, as strange and spectacular as it was. And half of becoming a wizard was in rediscovering that.

"I'm going to be a father," he told himself, breaking out into a smile. And not just to one child. He was going to have an enormous quantity of children. And as Grandma Little had told him long ago, children would bring joy into his house. "This is going to be *awesome!*"

Suddenly Chauncy wanted nothing more than to rush home and throw his arms around Valtora, and share this joy with her. Instead, he went behind the counter, to the safe hidden behind a painting of Grandma Little there. He twisted the dial until he'd entered the combination, then swung it open. The ring he'd gotten Valtora was still there, of course. Waiting for him. It was still plain in that it was mundane, with no magic at all. And as he reached for it, he hesitated, struck with the thought that it really *should* be magical.

Then he frowned, reaching into his robe-pocket for The Magic of Magic. He opened it to page six, seeing the illustration of the Vile Lord Shuud sucking the life out of the people around him. He realized then and there that this was the awful power of "should," and that it'd nearly sucked the life – and magic – out of him.

And that, in making himself wait until Valtora's ring was magical, he was making the same mistake yet again, casting what he really wanted into the future instead of enjoying it where it really belonged.

In the present.

Chauncy broke out with a laugh, putting his book back in his pocket. He grabbed the ring, then rushed to the exit, turning the sign at the door from "open" to "closed." Then he left the shop, locking it up, and broke out into a run to get home.

"Where are you going?" asked a man walking toward the shop, one of Chauncy's regular customers.

"To get married!" Chauncy cried. And while the answer wasn't quite right, it was exactly true. He'd postponed proposing to Valtora for a good long while now, waiting to put a little magic into her ring. But now he knew that it wasn't necessary at all. For the mere fact of Valtora accepting it on her finger would serve as potent magic indeed.

For as a wise, wise-cracking wizard had once taught him, magic was one's relationship with the world. As a symbol of his wonderful relationship with the very best part of his world, the ring in his hand had no power at all.

But on Valtora's, through the magic of magic, it would make both of their dreams come true.

Epilogue

Imperius Fanning sighed, easing himself onto one of the many ornate park benches in the inner courtyard of the Castle Mundus. A levitating park bench, one that sank ever-so-slightly as he sat on it. There was really no need for the bench to levitate, particularly mere inches from the ground. But the Order of Mundus was an order of wizards, and wizards did not live merely for their needs. It was a place of dreams come true, designed and built over millennia by those more concerned with joy than pure function. For the truly wise knew that joy was the function of life, and that the necessities of maintaining one's life existed purely to allow that function to continue.

"Well then," he stated to himself, for there was no one else in the vicinity. Mostly due to the hour, as it was nearly midnight, moonlight casting long shadows across the courtyard. He patted his gut, pleased that it too was pleased. For he'd followed its rumblings to quiet its discontent, and in doing so, had helped Chauncy Little and his friends fulfill the destiny he'd given them.

Or rather, the destiny his gut had given *him* to give them.

Imperius gazed upward at one of the many tall, gray stone towers jutting out from the body of the castle. One of them in particular was quite crooked, its peaked blue roof identical to the color of his robes. And his eyes. And indeed, the large crystal atop his most impressive wizard's staff. It was *his* tower, one of the tallest in the Order. For he was one of its highest-ranking members.

"Now what?" he wondered, rubbing his belly absently. For the first time in quite some time, Imperius had nothing to do. Which was quite odd for a man with a gut tuned to ward off tragedy. Tragedy was forever around the corner, after all. Waiting in the shadows to strike.

He felt a sudden twinge in his gut, and frowned, his hand freezing in place atop it. Then he played back his thoughts to see what had triggered the twinge.

Tragedy, he thought. No response. *Around the corner.* Maybe a little something? *Waiting in the shadows to…*

His gut twinged again, and he blinked, realizing he was staring at his tower ahead. He followed it down to the long, dark shadow it cast, one that terminated a mere few yards from where he sat.

"Show yourself," his gut told him to command, which was why he did.

A figure seemed to slither through the shadow, or perhaps it was the shadow itself that was moving within itself, like a wave within the ocean. Then the whole shadow itself moved, extending toward him until it had engulfed him altogether.

Imperius sat there, leaning back in the bench, waiting for the mystery of what was to come to be revealed.

The faint outline of a figure seemed to step out toward him, still within the boundary of shadow. And the very faintest of twin red lights, which seemed to peer down at him.

"Imperius," it whispered, its voice as faint as a feather's touch.

"The Dark One," Imperius replied evenly. "Or should I say, One of Many?"

"Temporarily," The Dark One whispered.

"Clever boy in the end, wasn't he?" Imperius mused. For his gut told him it was precisely what to say. He didn't question it, for letting his conscious mind take over for his subconscious would be like letting a toddler take over driving one's carriage.

"Indeed," The Dark One agreed. He paused then. "May I sit?"

"For now," Imperius replied.

So The Dark One did. Imperius gazed at the personification of evil, feeling not the slightest bit threatened. For one, he was possessed of extraordinarily powerful magic, what with his staff, robe, numerous rings, the amulet hidden under his robe, and quite a few other ancient artifacts to boot. And because his gut had quieted, meaning he was doing precisely what he was supposed to be doing.

"How are you here?" Imperius inquired. "I expected that everyone you were split into would've had to die first to release you back into your personification."

"Enough have died for me to be a shadow of what I was," The Dark One explained. "I'll only become fully myself again when they all do."

"A process you won't attempt to hasten," Imperius half-stated, half-warned.

"I have no need to," The Dark One replied. "My work this generation is done."

"Yes it is," Imperius agreed, gazing off at the moon. "Chauncy's finally realized his purpose, and is building that school."

"I exist for self-actualization," The Dark One stated with a ghostly smile. Imperius smiled back.

"That you do," he agreed. "And thank goodness for that. You didn't have to kill all those people in Pravus though," he countered. "I haven't seen you do that in ages."

"I lost my temper," The Dark One confessed. "Jealousy brings out the worst in me, as does rejection."

"I daresay it brings out the worst in all of us," Imperius mused.

"Indeed," The Dark One agreed. "Took quite a lot for me not to kill Chauncy and the rest of them. Nearly did, in fact. But I stopped myself just in time."

"Be glad you did," Imperius replied. "If you hadn't, we would've had to deal with you ourselves."

With a thought, the crystal atop his staff glowed a faint blue, as did his eyes…and his robe. The Dark One shrank away from that light. Only a little, but enough to confirm that he knew what Imperius was capable of. There were far worse things Imperius – and the Order – could do to The Dark One than banish him for a generation.

Far worse.

"No need to get testy," The Dark One stated. "We're on the same side, remember?"

"Of course I do," Imperius scoffed. "I was the one who found you and taught you that you were a Magus too." He shifted his weight on the bench. "And as long as you follow our rules, you'll find no quarrel with us."

"Haven't I always?"

"You have," Imperius conceded. "Frankly, I don't know how you do it. I wouldn't want your job for all the riches in the world."

"What's magical to me is mundane to you," The Dark One replied. "And sometimes what's magical to me becomes less magical over time."

Imperius raised an eyebrow, and The Dark One sighed.

"It's human nature to want what we don't have," he mused. "And I don't have goodness within me anymore. Valtora was good, so I wanted her. And when she didn't want me, I wanted to destroy her."

"I see," Imperius replied.

"But to destroy good would be to destroy what I want," The Dark One philosophized. "And with nothing to want, I'd have no reason to be."

"So on with the game then," Imperius supposed.

"Forever wanting," The Dark One agreed with another sigh. "But while there's pleasure in pursuit, not-having is wearing me down. I'm getting tired," he confessed.

"You require a sabbatical?" Imperius inquired.

"I believe I do," The Dark One replied.

"I'll arrange it with the Order," Imperius promised. Then he paused. "Is that why you came to meet me? To ask for it?"

"Yes," The Dark One answered. "But I have another question."

"Then ask it."

"Is the Order planning on telling Chauncy about his father?" The Dark One inquired.

Imperius turned away from him, eyeing the tippity-top of his tower, silhouetted by the bright silver moon. It looked in that moment for all the world like the slit-like pupil of a snake's eye gazing down at them. He sighed, knowing that it was no coincidence that he'd turned to see this sight. That it was his gut – once again – foretelling what had to be done.

"I suppose we have to," he answered at last. "It's only right."

They sat in silence for a while, which seemed appropriate. A moment of silence was well-deserved, to honor those whose sacrifice had helped to create the world they lived in today. If Imperius's gut was to be trusted, it was a better world for it.

"The evil we do in the name of good," Imperius mused, sighing wearily.

"Indeed," The Dark One agreed.

Thus our story ends, dear reader. For after destiny had been twice deferred, Chauncy had been forced to fulfill it at last. Or at least, to self-actualize to the point where he could. He'd found his bliss, and was chasing it wherever it led him. And at least for the moment, everything was all right.

But ignorance is bliss, and bliss, like any other emotion, only lasts for so long. For when ignorance is lost and knowledge is gained, bliss can turn into pain.

So at this point, dear reader, you might have noticed that the end of the world hasn't begun. And if you feel quite cheated, perhaps even lied to, I wouldn't hold you to blame. But rest assured, the beginning of the end of the world is nigh. Patience is a virtue, and seeing as how you've come this far, a little more patience and you'll find your reward. So until our next adventure, well, I've said it before and I'll say it again:

And that, dear reader, was how the end of the world *really* began.

Made in United States
North Haven, CT
04 May 2023